Performing al-Andalus

PERFORMING AL-ANDALUS

Music
AND
Nostalgia
ACROSS THE
Mediterranean

JONATHAN HOLT SHANNON

INDIANA UNIVERSITY PRESS
Bloomington & Indianapolis

This book is a publication of

INDIANA UNIVERSITY PRESS
Office of Scholarly Publishing
Herman B Wells Library 350
1320 East 10th Street
Bloomington, Indiana 47405 USA

iupress.indiana.edu

♾ The paper used in this publication
meets the minimum requirements of
the American National Standard for
Information Sciences—Permanence of
Paper for Printed Library Materials,
ANSI Z39.48–1992.

*Manufactured in the
United States of America*

*Library of Congress
Cataloging-in-Publication Data*

ISBN 978-0-253-01756-7 (cloth)
ISBN 978-0-253-01762-8 (paperback)
ISBN 978-0-253-01774-1 (ebook)

1 2 3 4 5 20 19 18 17 16 15

In Memoriam

Pamela Kay Shannon (1959–2009)
Brian M. Stross (1940–2014)

Dedicated to the innumerable Syrian victims
of systematic brutality.
May the promise of music create peace in the world.

I know there is no
straight road.
Only a giant labyrinth
of multiple crossroads.

—FEDERICO GARCÍA LORCA

Contents

· *Prelude*   xi

· *Acknowledgments*   xiii

· *A Note on Transliteration*   xvii

· Overture: Performance, Nostalgia, and the Rhetoric of al-Andalus: Mediterranean Soundings · *1*

1 In the Shadows of Ziryab: Narratives of al-Andalus and Andalusian Music · *22*

2 The Rhetoric of al-Andalus in Modern Syria, or, There and Back Again · *52*

3 The Rhetoric of al-Andalus in Morocco: Genealogical Imagination and Authenticity · *84*

4 The Rhetoric of al-Andalus in Spain: Nostalgic Dwelling among the Children of Ziryab · *119*

· *Finalis:* The Project of al-Andalus and Nostalgic Dwelling in the Twenty-First Century · *158*

· *Glossary*   181

· *Notes*   185

· *References*   203

· *Index*   227

PRELUDE

This book investigates the rhetorical uses of medieval Spain (al-Andalus) in contemporary Syria, Morocco, and Spain. Focusing on the performance of varieties of Andalusian music in these three contexts, I explore the ways musical performance contributes to the creation of senses of place, collective memory (and often amnesia), and hopes and desires for the future. In other words, it is an examination of the role of musical practices in promoting rhetorics of belonging and forms of nostalgia in the context of the Mediterranean and beyond. In the interest of reaching a wider audience, including students, scholars, and general readers curious about cultural politics in the contemporary Middle East, North Africa, and Mediterranean, I have avoided debates and certain details more appropriate for specialist publications. *Performing al-Andalus* should be understood as an interpretive essay that aims to provoke as much as to resolve questions about belonging and collective memory in the Mediterranean. Exhaustive studies of the musical traditions of each of the locales I investigate already exist, and I direct interested readers to those fine volumes for more detail on performance practice, modes and rhythms, song forms, and lyrics.

The research for this book was conducted in fits and starts over many years, including extended stays in Aleppo and Damascus, Syria; Fez, Rabat, Tangier, and Tétouan, Morocco; and Granada, Córdoba, and Madrid, Spain. All interviews were conducted in Arabic, Spanish, French, or English, when appropriate.

Acknowledgments

This work, so long in the making, would never have seen the light were it not for the excellent staff at Indiana University Press. I especially wish to thank Rebecca Tolen for her encouragement and patience throughout the project in the hopes that the final product was well worth the wait! Funds to support research in Syria, Morocco, and Spain were generously provided by awards from Fulbright-Hays (2003–2004), the PSC-CUNY (2002, 2003), and the John Simon Guggenheim Memorial Fund (2009). A sabbatical leave from Hunter College (2008–2009) allowed me to conduct research in Spain and Morocco and to begin outlining the project. My students and colleagues at Hunter College and the Graduate Center of the City University of New York provided opportunities for me to test some of the ideas in this book. I especially wish to thank the members of the Middle East Studies Faculty Research Seminar—Anna Akasoy, Yitzhak Berger, Alex Elinson, Karen Kern, Jillian Schwedler, and Chris Stone—for their comments on a draft of chapter 2. I also thank the receptive audiences at the New York Academy of Sciences, Columbia University Ethnomusicology Center, Princeton University Department of Near Eastern Studies, Yale University Department of Anthropology, Rutgers University Center for the Study of Genocide and Human Rights, the College of New Jersey Department of Political Science, and various conferences here and there for offering suggestions and constructive criticism at various waypoints along this voyage.

I wish to thank "The al-Andalus Road Show"—Carl Davila, Jonathan Glasser, Brian Karl, and Dwight Reynolds. Their insightful and humbling scholarship and generous support over the years have sustained this project when I thought it not worth pursuing (especially after reading their works!). Thanks, guys. The late María Rosa Menocal encouraged me in the project through her inspiring and inspired writings on things Andalusian and offered kind advice on how to go forward despite the challenges of working in several languages and in several locales.

A special *shukran* to my many friends and teachers in Syria, most suffering from the aftermath of the violence that has shaken Syria for so many months beginning in March 2011: 'Abd al-Raouf 'Adwan, Ghassan 'Amouri, Muhammad Qadri Dalal, Hala al-Faisal, Muhammad Hamadiyeh, 'Abd al-Halim Hariri, Nouri Iskandar, Zuhayr Minini, the late Sabri Moudallal, 'Abd al-Fattah Qala'hji, Muhammad Qassas, Hussein Sabsaby, Fadil al-Siba'i, and the late 'Abd al-Fattah Sukkar, who early on taught me how to separate the wheat from the chaff when it comes to things musical. In Morocco I thank my many friends, teachers, and associates, including Anas al-'Attar, 'Abd al-Fattah Bennis, 'Abd al-Fattah Benmusa, Ahmed El-Khaligh, Omar Metioui, 'Abd al-Malik al-Shami, 'Abd al-Salam al-Shami, Omar al-Shami, Radouane al-Shami, Yunis al-Shami, al-Hajj Ahmad Shiki, and Ahmed Zaytouni, among others, for facilitating much of the research. Deborah Kapchan was an interlocutor at the early stages of the research in Morocco and Spain, offering me numerous insights into Moroccan culture, including valuable connections. I thank her for her generosity. In Spain, I wish to thank Slimane Baali, Dar Ziryab, the Granada International Festival of Music and Dance, the Casa-Museo Federico García Lorca, the Escuela de Estudios Árabes in Granada, and the Centro de Documentación Musical de Andalucía, as well as, once more, the indefatigable Dwight Reynolds, whose intimate knowledge of Granada allowed me to move through that charged *lieu de mémoire* more quickly than I might have otherwise, as well as to enjoy great tapas.

Above all I wish to thank the close friends and family who have supported me in many ways over the many years in which I researched and wrote this text. Some of my earliest ideas for the book were developed in conversation with the late Brian Stross of the University of Texas, a valued friend and colleague whose insights, warmth, humor, and inspiring playlists will be sorely missed. My mother, Linda Shannon-Rugel, bore the heaviness of the loss of her daughter and still managed to ask me about how "the book" was coming along. I remember my late sister, Pamela Kay Shannon, whom fate took from us too soon. She encouraged me to pursue the dream of working in three different countries and languages despite the challenges, and I wish she were here to see the result. My brother, Chris Shannon, and stepfather, Herman Rugel, have been solid sources of support over the years in more ways than they can know. Lots of love to all of them.

Last but never least, I thank my son, Nathaniel "Nadim" Kapchan Shannon, for his patience with a father who was always either doing research, writing, playing music, or riding his bicycle (though not usually at the same time). May he grow to join me in at least some of these pursuits. Patricia Winter, through her outsized patience, enduring love, generosity of spirit, and unending kindness, allowed me the physical and emotional space to write this book, the inspiration to continue when I didn't believe in myself, and enough Nespresso to finish the job. To her I give infinite thanks and all my love.

A Note on Transliteration

One difficulty in working across national and linguistic boundaries is that different transliteration systems may be in use for the same language. For example, the Arabic letter *shīn* can be transliterated in English as *sh*, in French as *ch*, and in Spanish as *x* or *š*, whereas *jīm* is usually transliterated in English as *j*, in French as *dj*, and in Spanish as *y*. In this work I have aimed for clarity and in most cases have brought the transliteration in line with standard Arabic using a transliteration system adapted from that of the *International Journal of Middle East Studies* (*IJMES*). In the text, diacritical markings in Arabic transliteration are generally left off, with the exception of ' for the 'ayn and ' for the hamza. In the endnotes and bibliography, diacritical marks do appear in the names of authors and titles of works in Arabic. Reported speech is usually translated into English or transliterated in the closest approximation to the variety used. I use non-*IJMES* transliterations when individual artists use them in their own publications or recordings (e.g., Moudallal and not Mudallal). Unless noted otherwise, all translations from Arabic, Spanish, and French are my own.

Performing al-Andalus

Overture

Performance, Nostalgia, and the Rhetoric of al-Andalus: Mediterranean Soundings

Standing on the cliffs of Cape Malabata in Morocco overlooking the Strait of Gibraltar, I see the Spanish coastline in the distance, hovering like heavy clouds along the horizon just a few kilometers away. It was here, legend has it, that in 711 CE the Muslim general Tariq Ibn Ziyad launched his armies across the narrow stretch of water that now takes his name—Gibraltar, that is, Jabal Tariq, Tariq's Mountain—a crossing that led to the occupation and colonization of the land of the Vandals, what Arabs and Muslims refer to as the "opening" (*fath*) of "al-Andalus," and the beginning of a rich and tempestuous eight centuries of Muslim involvement in lands we now call Spain and Portugal. As I stand there looking out at the Spanish coast, I imagine I see what Tariq must have gazed upon: undulating mountains, a rocky coastline, choppy waters, the odd group of seagulls making their own passage. I would be sailing that route the following morning to make my first voyage from Morocco into al-Andalus.

Arabs cast the story of al-Andalus as one of a fulfillment of destiny, of the Arab people (usually understood in the singular) arising from distant deserts, conquering and opening one new land after another in order to raise the flags of Islam and civilization in pagan lands. (It is worth recalling that Europe at the time was a relative backwater, while the Muslim lands were embarking on imperial expansion and cultural efflorescence on a scale on par with, if not exceeding, the development of the Roman Empire.) Spanish historiography has tended to see this story in a different light—one of conquest and reconquest, and a fulfillment of another destiny. For each people its history, its destiny.

But before Tariq takes his first steps we need to acknowledge that the story of al-Andalus, its cultural itineraries, its routes and roots, are not so straightforward. Tariq himself was a Berber, and his forces were already a mélange of Arab, Berber, and other peoples, some recently converted to the new faith of Islam, others perhaps more interested in military adventurism, some Jews bringing what they imagined to be relief to their people suffering under Christian Vandal barbarities. In later centuries, Spanish Christian princes would employ Muslim commanders, and Muslim rulers would rely on Jewish statesmen and emissaries, a wonderfully human confusion that clouds our simple vision of either-or, Arab or Christian or Jew or Berber or Other. . . . Today we cannot know the full story, for it remains obscured in the shadows of history. But for many Arabs around the Mediterranean, and increasingly for Spaniards too, an important turning point was marked with this initial voyage across the strait.

My own trip will take me to Granada, home of the Alhambra, the Albaicín neighborhood and its Calle Calderería Nueva—full, of course, with tourists visiting the little *artesanía* (handicraft) shops and *teterías* (teahouses), but also North African and Arab merchants, Spanish converts to Islam, and musicians. Then to Córdoba and its magnificent Mezquita mosque-cathedral, its *judería* reverberating with echoes of times past. I am in search of music, traces not only of the medieval musical past but of contemporary performances that resonate with the past and sound the complex depths of the present. How do Spanish, North African, Arab, and other artists perform al-Andalus today? What do these reverberations and echoes tell us about the Mediterranean today and the multiple crossings the music has made with various peoples from one end to the other, over many centuries of contact, influence, and expulsions?

This musical quest began much earlier in Syria, where I lived and studied the classical Arab traditions, parts of which are linked with the shifting periods of Arab-Muslim rule in Iberia known as al-Andalus.[1] Like the story of al-Andalus, this book's story also begins in Syria—in Damascus, the capital of the Umayyad Dynasty, which would stretch from China to Iberia and which for the early Umayyad princes of Iberia would be a cultural referent and a basis for departure and return; and in Aleppo, the traditional seat of Arab music in the East and the proud preserver of Andalusian musical traditions today. The story then takes us across the length of the Mediterranean to Morocco, to the ancient medina of Fez, to the hills of Tangier and Tétouan and the guardians of the Andalusian musical traditions there, young masters attempting to follow in the footsteps of their ancestors. Then across the strait to the region of Andalucía to follow the routes and circuits of these musical cultures and the itinerant musicians, our modern troubadours, who keep the spirit of the music alive while infusing it with new forms, new life. The quest will take me back time and again to Spain, Morocco, Syria, and beyond. The routes are forever redoubling, reverberating with echoes of past performances, hinting at what might yet come to pass. Harbingers of the unfulfilled promise of playing and performing together, the sounds of al-Andalus ring and sound the trajectories of peoples and their hopes and frustrations. For this reason the standard story of al-Andalus, especially when presented as a self-fulfilling narrative of conquest, reconquest, and possible reconciliation (or, indeed, redemption), has multiple departure and arrival points. The standard narratives are misleading, for instead of mapping a single set of voyages of conquest and then expulsion, we must follow the ebbs and flows of peoples and their musics across and around the varied spaces of the Mediterranean, hearing the indeterminate voices of the "openings" of al-Andalus but also the closings and reopenings of yesterday, today, and tomorrow.

And so, as I stand on the decks of the good ship *Bismillah* (In the Name of God), retracing in my own way Tariq's voyage (no doubt like others before and since who have taken these very steps), I feel some excitement at the dawn of my own "opening" of al-Andalus, the beginnings of a voyage of discovery into the complex interstices of history, imagination, and politics that musical performance sounds out and illuminates for us.

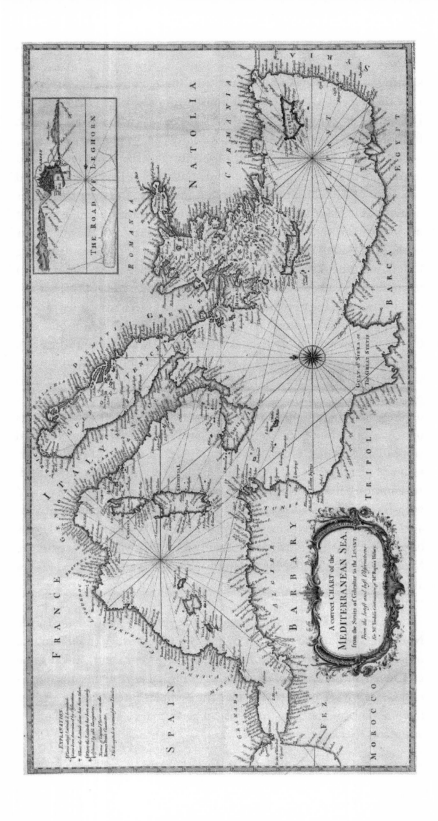

This book offers an interpretation of the dynamics of the cultural politics of the performance of musical forms around the Mediterranean that have a shared connection to medieval Iberia, known in Arabic as al-Andalus. From Damascus to Fez, from Tangier and Tétouan to Granada, I explore how artists perform not only Andalusian music but also al-Andalus itself. Drawing on the multiple manifestations of the Andalusian heritage, they weave a multicolored and sonorous tapestry across and around the Mediterranean that far exceeds in complexity the simplistic labels of "Arab," "Muslim," "Christian," and "Jew." Rather, their musical practices in all their complexity and messiness point toward more nuanced understandings of subjectivity not only for the medieval and early modern eras but for our own time as well, for al-Andalus remains today both an inspiration for cultural tolerance and a cautionary tale of the fragility of human community.

The story of al-Andalus and Andalusian music is easily told, for it is a typical narrative of the rise and fall of what María Rosa Menocal (2002a) called a "first-rate place" of genius innovators, cultural efflorescence, and modern efforts at revival and memorial. It is a tale told in countless ways in books, CD liner notes, and popular memory among musicians, scholars, tourists, and interested laymen across North Africa, the Levant, the Arabian Gulf, Spain, and elsewhere where the memory of this period serves important rhetorical (and often political) purposes. It's a story that people tell themselves largely for themselves—a collective autobiography based on hints of past glories and of course the suppression of distasteful elements of historical reality. My interest is not in rewriting or rehearsing this story from the olden days until the present or in offering an interpretation of the music as a social text à la Clifford Geertz (1973) but rather in tracing the stories *within* the stories, the stories in the shadows of these grand narratives, especially as they resonate today in Syria, Morocco, and Spain. Investigating the force of music (including what are today called Andalusian or Arab-Andalusian musics) is an important task of the musical ethnographer in the contemporary Mediterranean space. Tracing musical circuits around the Mediterranean Sea

Chart of the Mediterranean Sea, Richard William Seale, 1745.

promotes a more complex reading of what cultural practices in the region can teach us not only about the Mediterranean and its cultures but
about culture itself. Unmoored from territorial anchorings in fragile and
contested nation-states, culture appears as a more fluid, protean, labile,
and dynamic force not for promoting "identities" but for consolidating
potentials, swirling together subjectivities and their contradictions, and
floating—or drowning—hopes and desires.[2] Reflecting on the journeys
(sacred and otherwise), pilgrimages, itineraries, and circuits of music
and musicians in the variegated Mediterranean space (at times utopian,
at others dystopian) ultimately challenges us to reorient and reconfigure
our understandings of culture in modernity.

This exploration into the cultural imaginary—what I will be calling
a rhetoric—of al-Andalus takes us from Syria to Morocco and Spain, retracing, in effect, the movement of the populations and culture that settled Iberia but also enacting a temporal and geographic remove from the
site of its origins. I focus on musical performance and discourses of al-
Andalus in Aleppo, Damascus, Fez, Tangier, Tétouan, and Granada:
major nodes of rhetorical repair and anchoring points in a complex web
of associations, circuits of meaning, and dropping-off points. Although
organized geographically, the text should be approached as a sonorous
tissue that transcends these geographical orientations to reach across
and around the Mediterranean basin, where these cultural forms emerge
and circulate. In this manner I seek not only to map out a cartography
of Andalusian music but to chart a new understanding of culture in motion, culture as motion (Bohlman 1997; Chambers 2008; cooke 1999;
Stewart 2007).[3]

SOUNDING CULTURES

Literature has been a privileged site for the analysis of the ambiguities
and instabilities of national and postcolonial identities (see, among others, Bhabha [1990] 2013; Chatterjee 1993; Said 1993), as well as an arena for
debate about the Arab contribution to European literature (see Menocal
[1987] 2011). Recent works have explored the contours and contradictions of modernity in the Mediterranean region in terms of literature,
architecture, and even cuisine (Chambers 2008; Jirat-Wasiutynski 2007;
Matvejevic 1999). Musical practices, too, act powerfully to announce

and effect social transformations and serve as powerful tools to analyze social and cultural changes as well. In fact, a number of recent studies have focused on musical performance in the Mediterranean area as a means for constructing and confronting cultural projects both within and beyond the confines of the nation-state (see Cooper and Dawe 2005; Magrini 2003; Plastino 2003). Analysis of musical practices—putting an ear to what Iain Chambers (2008, 48) describes as the Mediterranean "echo chamber"—can tell us a lot about the cultural creativity and dynamism of the region. In sounding the Mediterranean, musical performance serves as an analytical tool rather than merely as an object of analysis. To paraphrase Chambers (2008, 47), what we need is not so much the anthropology of music but music as anthropology (see also Shannon 2012b, 775).[4] Moreover, sounding the Mediterranean reveals the continuities and breaking points around the Mediterranean basin and allows us to theorize its cultures not as distinct identities but as interacting, overlapping, mixing, resurging, and ebbing waves. Music offers, as Chambers (2008, 42) puts it, a "cultural testimony" to the complexity of subjectivities in and about the Mediterranean geoimaginal space, one of indeterminacies, contradictions, hopes, desires, frustrations, and unfulfilled destinies. Protean in nature, music animates the cultural imaginary and transports ideologies of selfhood and person; music also creates or disciplines bodily habits through the practices of performing, listening, and dancing. Music has the power and force to create states of being in the world that allow for the construction, reenactment, and contestation of communal memories and histories in music certainly but in other media as well.[5]

Music's special force derives from its ability to animate imaginal spaces and—perhaps more importantly—to penetrate and traverse margins and boundaries of the self, of bodies and entire nations and regions. Music offers a veritable soundtrack to the transnational movements of people, ideologies, capital, and mass media images (à la Appadurai 1996). Music goes wherever people travel, but it also travels where they cannot go or where they might hope to go, sounding at the same time spaces of hope, desire, and longing. This is an apt description of the new cultural dynamics of the Mediterranean basin, where music has come to mark boundaries between people even as it transgresses them, transforms them, reinterprets them. Like the waters of the Mediterranean itself, music identifies boundaries at the same time that it marks the potential for their amelioration and reconfiguration. In this way musical practices construct, reconfigure, and challenge cultural imaginaries by offering a space for the sounding of memories and desires and for the creative play with identities, margins, and boundaries.

Performing and listening to music confronts us with the transient and ambiguous nature of boundaries, for music permeates boundaries, even when they are heavily patrolled, policed, and managed; music challenges the "border-consciousness" of nation-states (Chambers 2008, 5) both in the Mediterranean and elsewhere. In Europe, whose modern identities were forged through the subjugation of alterity, musical practices can reveal a desire for the Other mixed with distaste. This is clear in the general European disdain for the southern and eastern Mediterranean populations, though not for their shorelines and sounds: literature and history reveal the evolution of a genealogy of desire/disdain for this region, from medieval and early modern fear of Saracens and Turks to contemporary polemics against Arab, Maghrebi, and, in the context of the enlarging of the European Union, other populations on Europe's imagined margins: Slavs, "Gypsies," Turks (once again), Africans, and so on.[6]

MUSIC, THE RHETORIC OF AL-ANDALUS, AND NOSTALGIC DWELLING IN SYRIA, MOROCCO, AND SPAIN

Performing al-Andalus investigates the rhetorical uses of al-Andalus in contemporary Syria, Morocco, and Spain. Focusing on the performance of varieties of what are called Andalusian music in these three contexts, the book explores the ways musical performance contributes to the creation of senses of place, collective memory and amnesia, and hopes and desires for the future. In other words, it is an examination of the role of musical practices in promoting rhetorics of what Amanda Lagerkvist (2013) terms "nostalgic dwelling"—ways of inhabiting and articulating lived experience in places embedded with a heightened awareness of the past. Although I explore these themes in the context of the Mediterranean, I engage debates about culture, nation, and memory beyond these loose borders. To do so I make use of some key terms and concepts as organizing themes for the analysis of the three case studies. The most important of these terms are *performance* and *nostalgia*. Given their various definitions, I begin by outlining my use of these terms and show how they relate to the broader project of understanding the role of music in cultural politics. In addition, I explore how performance and nostalgia are interconnected with discourses and practices of authenticity, festivalization, and globalization.

PERFORMANCE

This study takes performance as its central theme and major theoretical trope. Drawing on the "broad spectrum approach" advanced by Richard Schechner (2007) and the NYU Performance Studies school in general (see Kirshenblatt-Gimblett 2007), I conceive of performance not only in terms of the actual musical performances I attended—from concerts to festivals to lessons and master classes—but also in terms of discourse about music (what people say about music, narratives about music and society), performative speech acts (statements that "do something"), and everyday life occurrences that perform something in the sense of linking private motivations to public actions.[7] Performance, then, becomes a master trope for exteriority and a principal context for—and form of—ethnographic research. If we proceed on the basis that we cannot know what is going on in an individual's mind, we must therefore base our analyses on astute study of observable performances: the "restored behavior" or "showing doing" that is the subject of ethnographic inquiry (see Schechner 2007).[8] Therefore, as in my earlier study of music making in Syria (Shannon 2006), we will meet in these pages not only musicians and music aficionados but also artists, writers, poets, and people from a broad swath of society in Syria, Morocco, and Spain. Of course, I will also focus on actual performances and describe and analyze the aesthetic features of such performances as a way of making concrete otherwise abstract principles of the music system.[9] Moreover, analysis of actual performances allows us to understand not only the nuances but also the contradictions of cultural life both within each case study and across them. For it is in the eliciting of contradictions more than unified stories of coherence that the project of ethnography assumes its greatest role.

One productive area of research in recent studies has been the performance of class, race, gender, and nationality in a variety of genres and media. Drawing on the insights of anthropology and the study of performance and gender—and the performance of gender (Butler 1990)—we now understand identities as cultural constructions rather than as sets of innate capabilities and characteristics; one's gender, class, and racial or ethnic identities arise as a result of specific historical and cultural conjunctions and are continually being shaped by measures not only to express but to manage and control them. In this way we can understand our identities and subjectivities as performances (enactments of cultural scripts and codes) and as performative (re-creating and often challenging these scripts and codes). To take just four recent examples, the works of Kelly Askew (2003), Paulla Ebron (2003), Veit Erlmann (1996b), and David Guss (2001) reveal the utility of the concept of performance for the study of how local, national, and even regional identities are constructed and negotiated through performances ranging from music to mass media to festivals. Askew analyzes how the performance of popular music and related practices such as poetry and textiles get harnessed to nationalist agendas in Tanzania. She demonstrates how the music called Taarab reverberates with the contradictions of the modernizing nation and encodes the social history of Tanzania in its very sounds.[10] Ebron explores how the Mandinka *jali* (griot) in the Gambia performs the very idea of Africa. In a wide variety of contexts, she reveals how the *jali* serves not only as a musical performer but also as a curator of tradition and an important arbiter of what it means to be African for African nationalists at home and in diaspora, for tourists, and for the global consumption in the world-music scene.[11] For his part, Erlmann, in a wide-ranging study of *isicathamiya* (night songs) of South Africa, focuses on the performance of class and race among male a cappella singers and migrant laborers. His work deconstructs the complex interactions of musical sounds, song lyrics, dance forms, and even dress in the creation of Zulu subjectivities, including understandings of selfhood, home, and the nation.[12] Finally, Guss focuses on the role of festivals in rural Venezuela as sites not only for the enactment of traditional forms but for the performance, creation, negotiation, and contestation of tradition itself. In the face of enormous cultural variation and divisions of race, ethnicity, and class, Guss shows how the twin processes of folklorization and festivalization work to promote ambivalent ideologies of national belonging.[13] These are just four recent examples of the ways musical practices (including song, dance, and poetry) can be harnessed on festival stages to political projects of community and nation building. They reveal the importance of a focus on performance in understanding how internal differences can be conscripted into projects of nation building and serve as important sites for consumption practices and semiotic and political struggle.

MEMORY AND NOSTALGIA

The second major theoretical underpinning of the text is the concept of nostalgia and its relationship to processes of collective memory making. The performance of Andalusian subjectivities in my three case studies is intimately tied to the production and circulation of social memories not only about the Andalusian past but also about the present and future of Middle Eastern, North African, and Mediterranean societies. While it is a commonplace to suggest that music serves as an archive of social memory, storing and rehearsing in performance the traditions of the ancestors, recent anthropological and ethnomusicology studies of music making show the complex ways in which communal and cultural memories are enacted, selected, forgotten, repressed, and otherwise managed through musical performance.[14] In addition, music accesses and constructs what Paul Connerton (1989) calls "habitual body memory," which forms a template for the elaboration of social memories. In the absence of reliable archives or suppressed histories, musical performances, because of their physical, embodied nature, provide access to hidden histories (and hidden transcripts) and repertoires of knowing that supersede or evade the scriptural authority of the official archive.[15]

In my three case studies, not only does the performance of Andalusian music interact with local, national, and global memory practices (for the management and negotiation of collective memory is now a global enterprise), it also produces distinct forms of nostalgia and nostalgic remembrances of place. In her important book *On Longing: Narratives of the Miniature, the Gigantic, the Souvenir, the Collection* (1984), Susan

Stewart notes that nostalgia typically orients itself to referents that are
outside the sphere of experience of the remembering/nostalgic subject.
As a consequence of this displacement, nostalgia presents itself typically as "a sadness without an object, a sadness which creates a longing
that of necessity is inauthentic because it does not take part in lived
experience. Rather, it remains behind and before that experience" (Stewart 1984, 23). Given its close association with illness and melancholia,
nostalgia (especially in European literature) carries distinctly negative
connotations as old-fashioned, quaint, and even delusional. However,
following Svetlana Boym (2001, 2007), I understand nostalgia to be a
quintessentially modern phenomenon—that is, tied intimately to the
processes and contradictions of modernity—rather than a traditional
or archaic form of wistful remembrance. Boym (2001) asserts that to
conflate nostalgia with longing and remorse alone is to misunderstand
its complex history and to underestimate its currency today.[16] She dis-
tinguishes two main varieties of nostalgia: restorative and reflective. The
former emphasizes the *nostos,* the home, and attempts to reconstruct a
(lost or imagined) home, whereas the latter emphasizes the *algia,* the
pain of longing, and defers the return home in lieu of an ironic attachment to a lost past. In addition, restorative nostalgia does not appear as
nostalgia per se, that is, as a longing, but instead as tradition, heritage,
and the truth—not dissimilar to what Guss (2001) argues in the context
of cultural performances in Venezuela. For this reason, many revivalists,
cultural nationalists, and religious movements engage in forms of restorative nostalgia; by remembering, they are preparing the conditions for a
return. By contrast, reflective nostalgia does not call for a return of lost
truths, eschews any sense of heritage and revival, and acknowledges the
"ambivalences of human longing and belonging and does not shy away
from the contradictions of modernity" (Boym 2007, 7). In reflective nostalgias, one finds an almost philosophical reflection on history, time,
and the conditions of modernity rather than "the recovery of absolute
truth" (9).

In addition to these two main varieties of nostalgia, the restorative
and the reflective, Boym suggests other varieties of nostalgia: retrospective nostalgia, which is what we normally think of when we consider
nostalgic practices; prospective nostalgia, which is future directed;

ersatz or feigned nostalgia, a longing for things that were never lost in the first place; and anticipatory nostalgia, a sort of future past that anticipates a longing for "the present that flees with the speed of a click" (Boym 2007, 10). These varieties are not mutually exclusive, and, as we shall see, they interact in interesting ways in the contexts of Syria, Morocco, and Spain. Nonetheless, even when they share the same object, they produce very different projects having different narratives, different rhetorics.

These varieties of nostalgia bespeak complex engagements with notions of time and place. It is productive to link nostalgic dwelling to what the French historian François Hartog (2003) terms "regimes of historicity." According to Hartog, a regime of history can be understood "in a restricted sense, as the way in which a society considers its past and deals with it. In a broader sense, the regime of historicity designates 'the method of self-awareness in a human community'" (2005, 8). Following the work of numerous historians and philosophers, Hartog identifies three primary regimes of historicity: the classical, the modern, and what he terms the "presentist." While the classical understood the past as exemplary for both the present and future, the modern regime, which arose in the aftermath of the French Revolution (Lorenz 2010, 75), is future oriented and driven by a teleology of progress and perfectibility whose "natural" locus is the nation-state. Today, after the fall of the Berlin Wall and the collapse of Soviet Communism, the linear, progressive understanding of time characteristic of the modern regime of historicity and its linkage to the nation-state have given way to fragmentation of subjectivities, the "collapse of the future," and what Hartog (2005) calls the rise of a "presentist" regime of historicity (see also Lorenz 2010, 82). In this latter regime, analysis of the past has given way in academic and popular history to the study of memory and heritage; for this reason, many scholars attribute the popularity of academic memory studies to the late 1980s and 1990s, as exemplified in the work of Pierre Nora (1989), Andreas Huyssen (2003, 2012), and many others.

The close linkages between historical shifts in academic interests and (often revolutionary) social change indicate the relevance for the concept of the regime of historicity in the understanding of nostalgic practices in the three case studies I am exploring. Indeed, Boym tellingly asserts that "outbreaks" of nostalgia often follow significant social change, including revolutions. A contemporary world rife with revolutionary moments and significant social and economic challenges has produced "a global epidemic of nostalgia, an affective yearning for a community with a collective memory, a longing for continuity in a fragmented world. Nostalgia inevitably reappears as a defense mechanism in a time of accelerated rhythms of life and historical upheavals" (Boym 2007, 10).[17] As I write this text, Syria is undergoing revolutionary changes that influence how history there is constructed and memorialized, how the present will be understood in the future. Yet even in the more stable situations of Morocco and Spain, fundamental challenges to the political and economic order in what Boym (2007) refers to as "off modern" sites—that is, sites that are marginal to the center stage of Euro-American modernity—have created the conditions for memory cultures and politics that produce nostalgic responses, from the reflective to the restorative.

In what follows, I focus on the development and cultural valence of the rhetorics of al-Andalus in three specific locales. By rhetoric I mean a set of discursive practices that aim to persuade rather than merely to identify a set of conditions. This is how Kenneth Burke defined one aspect of rhetoric in *A Rhetoric of Motives* ([1950] 1969). A rhetoric is a discourse, a set of ideas and associated practices fundamentally tied to the creation of knowledge and the production of power, as Michel Foucault ([1972] 2010) identified it, but a rhetoric is also a project for a future, an act of persuasion, a promise. I suggest that the Syrian, Moroccan, and Spanish rhetorics of al-Andalus can be analyzed not only as constructing sites of memory, what Nora (1989) called *lieux de mémoire,* but also as forming terrains for the elaboration and negotiation of what Lagerkvist (2013) terms "nostalgic dwelling." In thinking about the relationship between place and memory, I draw on Lagerkvist's study of memory and mass mediation in the construction and performance of Shanghai as a city and as an idea. Using the work of Boym, among others, Lagerkvist argues that nostalgia in Shanghai is a form of future-directed memory making; that is, it is a "nostalgia for the future," a programmatic and highly mediated process whereby imaginings of a past (through such images as postcards, material objects, photographs, and the like) are conscripted into the project of constructing a future present. In the words of Ackbar Abbas (2002, 38, cited in Lagerkvist 2013, 102), this is not "Back to the Future" so much as "Forward to the Past." In a similar fashion, we can understand the recent histories of such sites as Damascus, Fez, and Granada as illuminating and echoing past future-oriented projects of nostalgic dwelling. Not coincidentally, all three sites are registered as UNESCO World Heritage sites, indicating the ways in which nostalgic dwelling in these sites is linked to global circulation of ideas of authenticity, cultural ownership, and nostalgic consumption.[18]

Through analysis of narratives and musical performance, I will explore the "chronotopes of nostalgic dwelling" (Lagerkvist 2013, 111) in Syria, Morocco, and Spain that reveal different if complementary projects of modernity and attendant nostalgias and regimes of historicity.[19] Briefly, in Syria we see the operation in recent history of a reflective nostalgia in which the longing for a lost paradise is the *algia,* or longing for something that was never really a home to begin with. In this way, performing al-Andalus becomes a way of remembering a past future of what might have been. It articulates an ironic and, ultimately, critical statement on the current state of Syrian society both during the time of my research in preconflict Syria and today. At the same time, with the increasing violence and the growth of jihadist ideologies in Syria, we also see the rise of varieties of restorative nostalgia not only for an imagined past (in combination with a sort of reflective nostalgia) but for a future Islamic state. In Morocco the performance of Andalusian music primarily engages a reflective nostalgia for a less distant past temporally and spatially. Given many Moroccans' strong sense of actual connection to medieval Spain, musical performance enacts a temporary reenactment of that past but not for the purposes of restoring it so much as for reflecting on what might have been. There are some elements of restorative nostalgia at work, especially as cultural entrepreneurs convert the reflective into the restorative as a way of accessing greater cultural and often financial capital. In such cases, al-Andalus, to borrow from Claude Lévi-Strauss (1964, 1966), is "good to think"; that is, it fits well with a cultural logic of nostalgic remembrance and consumption in contemporary Morocco. Finally, in Spain we find a curious mixture of restorative and reflective nostalgias, in addition to what Boym terms *prospective nostalgia,* a nostalgia for the future; the symbolic and material contests over Granada and similar sites (Córdoba's Mezquita mosque-cathedral comes to mind) and the ongoing debates about the place and role of Islam in Spain today are to a large degree contests over types of memory and nostalgia. Whereas reflective nostalgias and chronotopes of dwelling promote rereadings of history and a negotiation of the meaning of such places as the Alhambra and Córdoba's Mezquita, restorative nostalgias in these same sites aim to retake what was once lost and restore it for future generations (mainly of Muslims). In this way, the struggle for European self-identity plays out in the symbolic struggle for these polysemous sites of memory and memory making.

This raises a question: Is there a link between forms of artistic and everyday performance and what Boym defines as restorative nostalgia? Schechner ([1985] 2010, 36) defines performance as "restored behavior" or "twice-behaved behavior"; it is "restored" because it is the recollection of an earlier behavior or act that is re-presented, re-created in performance and hence restored. Boym argues that "to understand restorative nostalgia, it is important to distinguish between the habits of the past and the habits of the *restoration* of the past" (2007, 14, original emphasis). Drawing on Eric Hobsbawm and Terence Ranger's notion of invented traditions (1983), Boym argues that in many modern memory cultures, newly created cultural traditions are often characterized by a "higher degree of symbolic formalization and ritualization than were the actual peasant customs and conventions after which they are patterned" (2007, 14). This yields a series of seeming paradoxes in the performance of Andalusian traditions in my three cases. Boym notes: "First, the more rapid and sweeping the pace and scale of modernization, the more conservative and unchangeable the new traditions tend to be. Second, the stronger the rhetoric of continuity with the historical past and emphasis on traditional values, the more selectively the past is usually presented" (2007, 14).

In light of these ideas, I suggest that performing Andalusian music in Syria, Morocco, and Spain can be interpreted as a means of performing and shaping rhetorical stances toward the past that influence projects oriented toward the present and the future. These projects can be understood as forms of nostalgia, and in the particular places I investigated, they have produced forms of "nostalgic dwelling" that draw variously on reflective and restorative nostalgias. What forms does this nostalgic dwelling assume? As we will see in the three cases, these forms can be as diverse as rhetorically indexing an Andalusian heritage in Syrian literature, performing Andalusian subjectivities in Moroccan music, and drawing on the Andalusian past for present consumption in Spanish music and architecture.

GLOBALIZATION, AUTHENTICITY, AND THE STAGING OF MEMORY

Another important theme across the text is the relationship of the Andalusian musical traditions of Syria, Morocco, and Spain to the memory cultures of globalization.[20] None of these practices is outside of and distinct from the processes of globalization and then somehow "related" to them. Rather, they are and have been produced in a world marked by the global circulation of capital, images, peoples, ideas, and technology, to borrow from Arjun Appadurai's (1996) handy if limited vocabulary for analyzing globalization.[21] "Globalization" is not some cloud hovering over the earth's societies and cultures that then zaps them with some sort of cosmopolitan ray, altering them irreparably. Just as we cannot understand the rise of the modern world without taking into consideration the rise and operations of capitalism (Mintz 1986; Wallerstein [1974] 2011; Wolf 1982), so we cannot understand the operations of cultural practices today without considering the extent to which they are already impacted by global processes or by the dictates of neoliberalism. Examples of the pervasive logic of globalization among local cultures include the elaboration of notions of tradition and heritage, often as a result of nationalist cultural politics based in restorative nostalgias; the ways performance practices globally have been "mediatized" (Auslander 1999) to assume more or less generic forms, including festivals, videos, and recordings, as well as general expectations in the course of performance; the increasing financialization of musical practice itself as an outgrowth of the securitization and financialization of the neoliberal order (Harvey 2007); and, borrowing once more from Appadurai, the flow of ideas, peoples, images, and the like from one locale to another.

One important node in the circulation of globalized memory cultures is the festival stage. As the traditional infrastructure of musical performance—for example, expansive private courtyard homes and palaces—attenuates or disappears, most overt, scripted performances of Andalusian music today occur during or in preparation for festival concerts. As Guss (2001), among others, has noted, the festivalization of culture is often a response to anxieties of loss and cultural amnesia, as well as the invention of tradition; festivals are therefore part and parcel of the construction of globalized memory cultures in such places as Damascus, Fez, and Granada. The festival stage becomes, then, a "site of memory" (Nora 1989), like the monument, flag, archive, and museum (Lagerkvist 2013, 32–33). Are festivals and concerts the "social framework of memory" (Halbwachs 1992) in late capitalist societies? How do music festivals and other performances produce social and cultural memory in such places as Syria, Morocco, and Spain? This work aims to address these questions through close ethnographic work in these three contexts.

A related phenomenon in the global circulation of mediatized nostalgias is the heavy emphasis on questions of authenticity. In fact, it is a seeming contradiction that the more cultural practices are commoditized in global circulations, the more "authentic" they become. As many scholars have noted (Marcus and Myers 1995), commoditization is often at the heart of the production of authenticity. Fred Myers (2002) shows that in the case of Aboriginal acrylic paintings, long-standing cultural practices were conscripted into local, national, and then global cultural projects of modernity and nation building, in the process becoming authenticated on the national and world stages. The production of authenticity—or, rather, the authentication of cultural products—is the result of the complex and contradictory "traffic" between artists, entrepreneurs, and scholars, who are sometimes the same people (Bunten 2006; Marcus and Myers 1995; Shannon 2003c, 2011; Sharman 2006; Stoller 2006). In addition to residing in the commodity form, the discourse or, to follow Adorno (1973), the "jargon" of authenticity is often negotiated through discourses of the body and affect, as in the importance of sentiment in the production of authenticity in Arab music, Arabesk, and flamenco (Leblon 1995; Mitchell 1994; Racy 2004; Shannon 2006; Stokes 2010).

OVERVIEW OF CHAPTERS

In chapter 1, I provide an overview of Andalusian history and music, stressing what has evolved as the standard narrative of the story (Davila 2013), its biases and inconsistencies. I then review the current state of scholarship on the various musical cultures of the Mediterranean that lay claim to the Andalusian heritage. While the focus of the book is on the Andalusian (or Andalusian-inspired) musics of Syria, Morocco, and Spain, I make reference to performance practice in Algeria and Tunisia, as well as to diasporic Maghrebi and Sephardic Jewish performance. Much has already been written on Sephardic musics and musicians in Europe and Israel, and given that there are currently few if any living Jewish performers in Syria and Morocco and only a handful in Spain, I make only passing reference to this important music, whose links to the historical development of the musics we today call Andalusian and even Arab are well studied.[22]

In chapter 2, I tackle the Andalusian legacy in Syria. I outline the ways in which musicians and others remember al-Andalus through their performances and situate musical performance within the larger fabric of cultural and political life that, beginning in the 1960s, began to stress the historical and imaginary connections to medieval Spain. In Syria, al-Andalus serves as a touchstone of pan-Arab identities, undergirding the Ba'thist ideologies of secularism and pan-Arabism (now under threat, given the conflict in Syria) that have been central tenets of Syrian state ideologies. The music and associated literary forms support the idea of a pan-Arab nation, as well as Syria's role at the heart of ancient and modern Arab national aspirations.

Chapter 3 brings us across the Mediterranean to Morocco, with its rich and distinct Andalusian cultural heritage. In Morocco, al-Andalus has somewhat different cultural referents. The music called al-Ala and associated poetic and even culinary and architectural forms perform the connection many Moroccans feel to the Andalusian history in Spain. For many Moroccans, Andalusian culture is a direct descendant of the cul-

tures of those populations expelled from Iberia during the waves of reconquest. Rather than stress the historical, ideological, and even imaginative links between themselves and the deep history of al-Andalus in
the Arab East, Moroccans understand the Andalusian connection as a
genealogy that ties them directly to Europe and European culture. The
orientation is northern, not eastern. Moreover, whereas in Syria Andalusian culture promotes pan-Arab secularism, in Morocco it has strong
associations with the cultural elite, the monarchy, and Islam. In this way,
the music sounds regimes of value and power with very different cultural
valences from the performance of al-Andalus in Syria.

Chapter 4 explores the ways in which the idea of al-Andalus and Andalusian culture plays a role in contemporary Spain. In the post-Franco
era, Spain has striven to come to grips with its heterogeneous past. At the
same time, it has confronted a multicultural present. Arab-Andalusian
music has come to mark both an embrace of this past and a relatively
tense return of deeper cultural conflicts over the role of Islam in Europe.
In the contemporary Spanish contexts, the musics of North Africa and
the Middle East, sometimes performed in conjunction with folk and
popular musics of Spain, become sonic markers of the bridges that span
the cultures, histories, and peoples of Spain and also of the boundaries
that separate them. It is the tensions of these bridging and boundary-
making zones of contact that I sound through analysis of musical practices in Granada.

The book closes with a discussion of the evolution of the rhetoric
of al-Andalus in the twenty-first century, especially in the aftermath
of the attacks of September 11, 2001, and a now global war on terror. I examine the ways the rhetoric of al-Andalus has inspired different projects
of reconciliation and recovery, both liberal projects for a reconstituted
multiculturalism (or even postmulticulturalism) based on the medieval
notion of coexistence (*convivencia*), as well as illiberal projects for the
establishment of an Islamic state in the Middle East and the reconquer-
ing of Iberia in the name of jihad. I conclude with a *finalis* that reflects
on the differences in how the Andalusian musics of Syria, Morocco, and
Spain are performed and how the Andalusian heritage is remembered
and reinvented in these Mediterranean spaces. Analysis of music and

discourse about music are critical for an understanding of the operations of cultural memory and "memory cultures" in diverse transnational contexts. What unites these diverse cases is the role of the cultural imagination in constructing narratives of community and collective memories that allow participants to envision, in often contradictory ways, what life in the new Mediterranean can be like.

ONE

In the Shadows of Ziryab

Narratives of al-Andalus and Andalusian Music

OVERTURE: WE ARE ALL SONS OF ZIRYAB

One afternoon in Granada I join a friend in Plaza Nueva, located at the foot of the old "Moorish" quarter of the Albaicín. He manages a little tourist shop that specializes in *artesanía* (arts and crafts), mostly imported wooden boxes and glassware from his native Algeria, as well as trinkets from Morocco and elsewhere. We had met the day before when, walking around the Calle Calderería Nueva, I heard the voice of the great Egyptian singer Umm Kulthum issuing from his shop. It was too much to resist, so I went in, and we began talking about music and life in Granada. After half an hour or so we agreed to meet in the main square the next day. At the appointed hour I find him in front of a news kiosk. Because he finds the Albaicín to be "sinister" he prefers for us to head today to the newer side of town. Not only is it more pleasant to sit there, he claims, but he wants to introduce me to a friend who runs a music store nearby where I am sure to find all sorts of CDs for my project on Andalusian music. Not long after we finish our freshly squeezed orange juices at a pleasant café near the Fuente de las Batallas, we walk over to the store, a small shop stacked high with recordings. The proprietor welcomes us both warmly, and we get to discussing the ins and outs of Andalusian music. She has a large collection of what she considers to be "Andalusian music," including many of the recordings from Eduardo Paniagua's Pneuma label dealing with one or another aspect of the Andalusian musical heritage, some Syrian and other Levantine recordings, and stacks of recordings of *flamenco puro, nuevo flamenco,* fusions of Arab and flamenco music, and so on.[1] "The whole nine yards!" I think. I imagine that she must have understood that I am interested in musics from the Spanish region of Andalucía—a common confusion—so I tell her that I am mostly interested in the *Arab*-Andalusian music, not flamenco, which is closely associated with this region in Spain and especially with the city of Granada. "They are the same!" she replies. "They are all sons of Ziryab! Paco de Lucía, Tomatito, these guys [indicating a local group of Arab performers]. ¡Son todos hijos de Ziryab!" With that she puts a disc in the CD player, and, motioning for me to sit down on a stool near the cash register, we proceed to listen to the many sons of Ziryab.

The idea that all these musical cultures—from Levantine to North African to Spanish, from Arab-Ottoman to "Gypsy" to fusion—have their origins in the person of Ziryab is a popular one. The Ziryab origin story is shared, to one degree or another, by many musicians, audiences, and even scholars not only in Spain but across the span of the Mediterranean circuits I explore in this volume, and beyond. It constitutes a key or charter myth of the Andalusian musical legacies. This chapter provides an overview of the mythologies and histories of al-Andalus that inform our present reimaginings of this past time and place. I focus on the standard narrative that structures representations of Andalusian culture today across the Mediterranean region, especially the tale of Ziryab as a musical progenitor and the spread and development of Andalusian musics in the aftermath of the fall of Granada in 1492.[2] While this book focuses on the Andalusian and Andalusian-inspired musics of Syria, Morocco, and Spain, I also discuss Andalusian performance practices and cultural memory in Algeria, Tunisia, and Libya, as well as among Sephardic Jews around the Mediterranean. My aim in doing so is both to review the histories and musics of the Andalusian Mediterranean and to highlight the ways in which the mythological character of the present understandings of the past promote the complex imaginaries and rhetorics of al-Andalus. "Andalusian music" per se does not exist, that is, as a unified musical practice with a fixed repertoire and a traceable genealogy. Rather, to borrow from Claude Lévi-Strauss (1964, 1966), it is "good to think"; that is, for musicians, audiences, cultural programmers, and scholars in and of the Middle East, North Africa, Mediterranean regions, and beyond, the very idea of an Andalusian heritage retrievable through musical performance subscribes to a logic of nostalgic consumption that makes cultural (and often financial) sense. This provocative assertion will be borne out through analysis of the varied histories of al-Andalus and the musics called "Andalusian" that form part of a broader trans-Mediterranean, indeed global, circulation of ideas and practices associated with medieval Spain. The label "Andalusian" was largely a colonial artifact but one that, like so many labels (think of jazz or any other style of music), has been very productive. As we shall see, labeling a musical culture "Andalusian" has the potential to reinforce secular pan-Arab ideologies or Islamist ideologies, just as it may shore up notions of ethnic and cultural distinction by asserting multiple and contradictory claims to the past, the present, and the future.

Confronting these multiple meanings of al-Andalus leads me to ask: What depths of cultural memory and other affective resources do these networks and circuits access and empower? In other words, what is the work of al-Andalus and Andalusian music in the contemporary Mediterranean? Why are these musical and imaginative circulations important today? And what is it about the contemporary Mediterranean that allows for the development, spread, and power of the *idea* of a shared Andalusian heritage to effect change? To answer these questions requires an itinerant, "nomadic" approach (Deleuze and Guattari [1980] 1987) to the histories and mythologies of al-Andalus. To understand how the musical legacies of al-Andalus, including the legend of Ziryab, contribute to the rhetorical work of al-Andalus in the modern era requires attention to the narratives of rise and decline, ebb and flow, conquest and return voyage that not only these musics but the story of al-Andalus trace for Syrian, Moroccan, Spanish, and increasingly global communities of musicians, artists, intellectuals, and tourists.

AL-ANDALUS BETWEEN HISTORY AND
MYTHOLOGY: THE STANDARD NARRATIVE

The story of al-Andalus is eminently one of exile, conquest, and movement: if not rise and decline, then ebbing and flowing, like the sea that
partially forms its boundaries, defines its points of access, and sets its
limits. "Al-Andalus" is the Arabic name for those areas of the Iberian
Peninsula that came under Muslim rule beginning in the early eighth
century and, in the aftermath of the Christian conquest (in Spanish
known as *la reconquista*), ending with the fall of the Kingdom of Granada in 1492 and the subsequent expulsion of Muslims and Jews from
Spain as late as 1610 (in Spanish referred to as *la partida*).[3] It is important
to note that al-Andalus does not refer to a fixed place or time but rather
to a fluid and shifting geographical, historical, political, and cultural
cartography. As an object of nostalgic consumption in music, literature, cinema, popular culture, and scholarship, al-Andalus serves as a
chronotope of authenticity (Bakhtin 1981; Shannon 2005). That is, al-
Andalus constitutes a time-place endowed with an aura of the authentic, yet one with an ambiguous referent: sometimes the whole of Spain;
sometimes the southern Iberian and Moroccan sides of what Fernand
Braudel called a Euro-African "bi-continent"; sometimes the Spanish
autonomous region of Andalucía, including the modern Spanish cities
that bear the names of the medieval city-states (or *ta'ifa* kingdoms) of
Córdoba, Granada, Málaga, Sevilla, Valencia, and so on (Braudel [1972]
1995, 117, 164, cited in Gilmore 1982, 178). For this reason we must acknowledge from the outset the coexistence of multiple, overlapping, and
at times contradictory imaginings of al-Andalus, yet the multiplicity of
these imaginings attests to the power of the concept, the very idea of
al-Andalus, to animate projects of collective memorializing and myth
making.[4]

We can identify these contradictions from the very beginning both
in al-Andalus's history and in its modern historiography. While most
Occidental sources refer to the coming of the Muslims (Arabs, Berbers,
and others) as the conquest of Iberia, medieval Arabic chronicles usually refer to their arrival as a *fath*, or "opening." The idea of an opening

rather than an invasion, conquest, or colonization carries very different connotations and invokes a different, more teleological narrative.
Though the date of this opening is usually given as 711 CE, it actually
began a little earlier, in 710, when Berber generals crossed from Morocco
to Tarifa to intervene in the Visigoth civil war.[5] The full-scale "opening"
continued in April 711 with the landing of the Berber general Tariq Ibn
Ziyad on Gibraltar. This latter crossing is what led to the defeat of King
Roderic (Rodrigo), the capitulation or flight of the Visigoth forces, and
the subsequent settling of much of Iberia in the ensuing eight years by
Berber and Arab colonists—what we now know as the "Moorish Conquest of Iberia," an Arab-Muslim conquest that was also a Berber, Arab,
Muslim, and Christian opening. Another aspect of the standard narrative states that the opening of al-Andalus was also a liberation of Iberian
Jewry, who suffered under Visigoth oppression but found more tolerant
rulers in the Muslim colonizers.

The earliest political and cultural entity we know of as al-Andalus
was the Umayyad Emirate, founded in Córdoba by the Syrian Umayyad
prince 'Abd al-Rahman al-Dakhil, "The Immigrant." In 750 'Abd al-
Rahman escaped the massacre of his family at the hands of 'Abbasid
partisans in his palace in Rusafa, Syria, and made his way across North
Africa to Iberia, settling in Córdoba. By then al-Andalus was already
in the process of becoming a land not only of Syrian-Arab princes but
also of North African Berbers and Arabs, as well as Jews and Christians,
some coming from the Arab lands and North Africa, others having been
present in Iberia from before its opening to Islam. The ethnic, religious,
and class composition of al-Andalus and its political fortunes varied
dramatically from one era to another as waves of migrants, armies, settlers, and vanquished ebbed and flowed through the Iberian Peninsula
and across the Pyrenees, the Strait of Gibraltar, and even the Sahara for
more than eight centuries. This fluidity cannot be captured by the term
invasion or *conquest* or, for that matter, *opening*.

As the standard narrative would have it, the Islamic opening of
Christian Iberia prepared the ground for the development of a cultural
and scientific efflorescence rivaling and even surpassing the achievements of the storied 'Abbasid Dynasty based in Baghdad. Baghdad, seat
of the famous caliph Harun al-Rashid (763–809) and then the center

of the Muslim world, was famous for the Bayt al-Hikma (House of Wisdom), at the time the most important library and center of learning in the Islamic world, if not the whole world. We also know it today as a setting for some of the tales of *The Book of a Thousand and One Nights*. Yet Córdoba in its brief period of splendor (ca. 756–1031) would outshine even Baghdad.[6] As the late scholar of al-Andalus María Rosa Menocal notes in her best-selling *The Ornament of the World* (2002b, 33), one example of the cultural dynamism of al-Andalus was Córdoba's library, which by the eleventh century was thought to have contained over four hundred thousand manuscripts at a time when the largest library in Europe beyond the Pyrenees held fewer than four hundred. The extent of this library's collection serves as a metaphor for the broad scientific, philosophical, literary, culinary, architectural, musical, and other advances that characterized this period of life in al-Andalus, especially during the Caliphate of Córdoba (929–1031); the metonymy between Córdoba the city and seat of the caliphate and the entirety of al-Andalus as a cultural and political entity dates to this period. Córdoba was also the adopted home of Ziryab, so in the standard narrative the music finds its origins and apotheosis here as well. Even if later periods were not to see an equivalent efflorescence, and indeed the time and place of its apogee remain ambiguous, cultural developments in such cities as Toledo, Sevilla, and Granada have led generations of Arabs, Muslims, scholars, poets, and others to think of al-Andalus as representing an historical golden age.

Continuing with the standard narrative, after the fall of the caliphate in 1031 after a devastating civil war, there developed in its shadow what are called the *ta'ifa* kingdoms, independent but militarily weak city-states that included many of the regional capitals of the former caliphate: Granada, Toledo, Sevilla, Valencia, Badajoz, Saragossa (Zaragoza), Málaga, Tortosa, and, much weakened, Córdoba itself. In the words of the thirteenth-century Andalusian poet al-Shaqundi, the fall of the Caliphate of Córdoba resulted in "the breaking of the necklace and the scattering of its pearls" (quoted in Fletcher 1989, 27).[7] These scattered pearls were to develop their own rich cultural traditions. Given their political weakness—disunited politically, separated geographically, and often besieged militarily—the *ta'ifa* kingdoms often survived by ally-ing themselves with Christian states, often in opposition to their Muslim neighbors, in return for peaceful coexistence and military security. In some way, the relative weakness of the *ta'ifa* kingdoms encouraged their cultural development, as rivalries among the various rulers meant that patronage was spread more widely than in the more centralized Córdoba, which stood as a (tarnished) model of cultural development. Thus the various *ta'ifa* courts hosted a menagerie of poets, statesmen, craftsmen, scholars, and jurists who added significantly to the cultural legacy of al-Andalus (Dodds, Menocal, and Balbale 2008; Fletcher 2006; Wasserstein 1985). It is important to note that this efflorescence occurred in the absence of a central authority and in the context of cooperation and complicity among Muslim and Christian leaders, often employing the services of Jewish intermediaries.

Indeed, one of the best-advertised features of life in medieval al-Andalus is what is now known as *convivencia* (coexistence or living together; in Arabic, *al-ta'ayyush*).[8] This now well-known concept—featured in everything from academic symposia and trans-Mediterranean political and cultural projects to Spanish tourist brochures—describes the ability of the Muslims, Jews, and Christians of al-Andalus to live together peacefully from the early Umayyad period, through the Caliphate of Córdoba and *ta'ifa* kingdoms, up to the fall of Granada. Along with its architectural and literary splendors, the sociopolitical legacy of *convivencia* supports the idea of al-Andalus as a lost paradise.[9] In a time when Jewish sages such as Maimonides wrote their masterpieces in Arabic, Christian princes decorated their homes and even tombs in the Mozarabic style (Spanish *mozárabe,* from the Arabic *must'arab,* "Arabized"), and Muslim translators conveyed the wisdom of the ancient world to medieval Europe, it is tempting for more than one community to look back on this period with a mixture of mourning and even nostalgia, especially given the modern legacy of intercommunal hatred and violence.

Some scholars cast doubt on the extent of *convivencia* in al-Andalus, claiming that contemporary projects impose their own beliefs in multicultural tolerance on a world where the modalities of subjectivity were very different; medieval Iberia was not without its share of pogroms, massacres, and institutionalized discrimination in the form of *dhimmi,* or "protected status" populations (Catlos 2001; Cohen 1994; Fanjul García 2004; Fernández-Morera 2006; Fletcher 2006; Harvey 2005). Others argue that al-Andalus was, for its time, a model of relative harmony, if not interfaith coexistence. Andalusian *convivencia* remains one of the enduring cultural legacies of al-Andalus, relevant not only for narratives of the past but for a variety of contemporary projects of multiculturalism that draw on it—indeed, that have helped to construct it as a modern phenomenon. For many, the idea or even promise of *convivencia,* like the story of al-Andalus itself, is good to think as well.

THE LOSS OF AL-ANDALUS AND HYPERNOSTALGIA

Doors open and close, inviting or preventing access and movement, creating passages or erecting barriers. Indeed, the Muslim *fath,* or opening, was destined to last nearly eight centuries, though not without numerous closings, reopenings, and a (not entirely) final closure. Not surprisingly, the Arabic sources use a somewhat less poetic term to refer to this closure: *suqut* (fall), which refers both to the fall of individual cities and to the end of al-Andalus as a political entity.[10] Yet even the fall of al-Andalus (*suqut al-andalus*) refers to different and shifting places and times: for example, Córdoba in 1236, Valencia in 1238, Seville in 1248, and, most famous of all, the fall of Granada in 1492, by which time Muslim sovereignty was limited to this city and some surrounding territories. Moreover, if we are to believe contemporary historiography and popular nostalgic commemorations, the capitulation of Granada and the fall of al-Andalus did not in fact mark a full closure, for al-Andalus (and Andalusian peoples, both *moriscos* and *mudéjars*) continued to live on in architecture, music, fashion, cuisine, literature, popular culture and the arts, and even to some degree genealogy in the decades after the fall of Granada and to this day.[11] Therefore, al-Andalus refers to a waxing and waning, ebbing and flowing entity on the shores of the Mediterranean, exercising a force palpable even in our times. Indeed, al-Andalus has never seemed more relevant and invoked as today. Why might this be the case?

Three main developments have made al-Andalus relevant for our times: colonial and nationalist sentiments, commemorations of the sesquicentennial of the fall of Granada, and the aftermath of 9/11 and the so-called War on Terror. The continuing relevance of al-Andalus is its utility in modern narratives of selfhood and community: al-Andalus is "good to think" in many ways, and for many peoples. For some, the story of al-Andalus is a cautionary tale of spectacular rise, complacent hubris, growing lassitude, and eventual corruption and fall—not dissimilar to the medieval Andalusian geographer Ibn Khaldun's theory of societal development in *The Muqaddimah* (1969). For others, the rise and fall of al-Andalus reveal the complexities and shifting alliances characteristic of medieval Iberian politics. In this view, Muslim princes and Christian sovereigns sometimes fought, sometimes allied themselves against a common foe, but the eventual fall of al-Andalus resulted from the growing strength of the Christian forces and the relative weakness of the Muslim kingdoms as a result of political, cultural, and even geographical realities that favored the Christian kings, if not Christianity itself. Still others see in the fall of al-Andalus a metaphor for the struggle over Islam, with the rigid puritanism of the Almoravid (1056–1146) and Almohad (1129–1268) Dynasties (the conservative Berber Muslims who swept from the Atlas Mountains in the eleventh and twelfth centuries to take al-Andalus) at odds with the more refined and also more tolerant version of Islam characteristic of the Caliphate of Córdoba or the splendors of Granada (see Menocal 2002b).[12] Thus al-Andalus, in its rise, efflorescence, and decline and eventual fall, has tended to serve contemporary projects. Perhaps the most important common denominator of these variegated Andalusian imaginary geographies is the idea that al-Andalus represents a golden age and, with its fall, a veritable lost paradise.[13]

The idea of al-Andalus as a lost paradise has engendered a form of nostalgic remembrance of the past that deeply colors contemporary treatments of al-Andalus. Such depictions have a long history in Arabic letters. For example, medieval texts represent al-Andalus as a land of marvels in the same vein as the medieval Arabic literary genre known as *fada'il,* or "merits" literature, which valorized sites and cities in Islamic culture (Stearns 2009, 360). In the Andalusian *fada'il* texts, even the pre-Islamic land is described as a vast and fertile garden (362), and al-Andalus is described as a land of running waters, verdant fields, fragrant trees, and melodious birds. These are important themes in the literary and musical legacies of al-Andalus up to the present. Al-Andalus is also described in this early literature as a land of *jihad* or religious struggle, a theme that has assumed importance in the contemporary Mediterranean (363–364). In this view, al-Andalus is conceived to be a battleground for Islam: for example, twelfth- through fourteenth-century texts argue for its importance as a frontier of the Islamic faith, and some even suggest that to die in al-Andalus is equivalent to martyrdom (364).[14] The religious thread continues in medieval texts that foretell the fall of al-Andalus, setting this event in a millennial context as evidence of God's plan (365). Thus, the medieval Arabic texts portray al-Andalus as a land of marvels, both secular and sacred, and this paved the way for later treatments of al-Andalus as a lost paradise, either secular or sacred.

Medieval Arabic texts frequently treat the theme of the loss of al-Andalus in ways that scholars have described as nostalgic; lament over the fall and loss of al-Andalus was to become a chief theme in Andalusian literature for centuries, engendering what some scholars refer to as a nostalgic vision of the past (Elinson 2009). With the advance of the Christian reconquest, leading poets and statesmen of the day composed elegiac poetry as testimonials to their sense of loss. These typically took the form of "city elegies" (*ritha' al-mudun*), in which poets lament the loss of their cities using modified structures of classical Arabic poetics to express a unique cartography of memory based in loss and abandonment.[15] These city elegies memorialize Andalusian lifeways by evoking the rich gardens, flowing waters, and fertile orchards and fields of al-Andalus— common themes of the *fada'il* literature—which they contrast with what they perceived to be the sterility and dryness of post-*partida* life (Elinson 2008, 94). A well-known example still recited and sung today is the fourteenth-century Lisan al-Din Ibn al-Khatib's poem *Jadak al-ghaythu,* which describes the blessings of life in al-Andalus metaphorically as rainfall in a garden. Selections from the poem were transformed into the compositional form of the *muwashshah* (see below), and it remains among the most commonly performed songs of this genre in modern Syria. There are many other examples from the Moroccan, Algerian, and Tunisian repertoires as well (Guettat 2000).

The writing of elegies and lamentation for the lost cities and civilization of al-Andalus continued throughout the period of the reconquest and well past the fall of Granada and the final expulsions as generations of Arabs, Muslims, and others who had no direct connection with medieval Iberia came to understand al-Andalus as in some ways a paradise whose loss they bemoaned nostalgically. However, while it is both tempting and common practice to describe these expressions of loss as evidence of an enduring nostalgia, I argue, following Svetlana Boym (2001), that the nostalgic view of al-Andalus is a distinctly modern one. What we encounter in the earlier poems is a vision more informed by lament and longing, themes already well developed in the classical Arabic tradition. We see the operations of this more modern conception of nostalgia not so much in medieval as in modern texts on al-Andalus. Even the notion of al-Andalus as a lost paradise is not found in the earlier texts but appears only in the late nineteenth century. For example, the seventeenth-century historian al-Maqqari (d. 1631), author of a well-known history of al-Andalus (al-Maqqarī 1968), does not use the language of nostalgia or even longing to describe al-Andalus (Stearns 2009, 366–367). Even when other postreconquest writers refer to al-Andalus in longing terms, it is usually in the context of the loss of Islam, not of the cultural or natural treasures therein. The nostalgic stance develops much later, and by the late nineteenth century, in the context of the rise of European colonialism and the waning of the Ottoman Empire, we encounter increasingly nostalgic depictions of al-Andalus as a lost paradise. In fact, the very idea of al-Andalus as a lost paradise might be traced to the works of Arab and Muslim travelers to Europe who paid visits to Andalusian sites (369). Indeed, Martínez Montávez (1992) traces the idea of al-Andalus as a lost paradise to the works of Egyptian philologist and politician Ahmad Zaki, who traveled to Spain in 1892 after attending a conference of Orientalists held in London and then wrote about his experiences. In his work, Zaki (1990) discusses al-Andalus not in terms of the loss of past Muslim glory but as a model for modern Arab and Islamic society; in it, "the reader encounters al-Andalus not as a past to be lamented, the memory of which should be elegized, but as a call for political and social action in the present" (Stearns 2009, 370). Zaki's work was widely read and inspired others to make the trip to Spain, and the twentieth century witnessed the growth of a subgenre of Arabic letters devoted to not only eulogizing the Andalusian past but recovering it for use in the present and future. As we shall see later, the same was true for Spanish and other European authors as well.

Scholars agree that European colonialism and Arab nationalism played major roles in the development of this genre of writing—past looking but future oriented. Twentieth-century nostalgia for things Andalusian owes a significant debt to colonial discourses of heritage and authenticity that in many ways constructed al-Andalus as an object of European fascination. With the expansion of European colonial sovereignty over North Africa, al-Andalus came increasingly to be used as a lens through which European colonizers, scholars, artists, and travelers understood their relationship to North Africa and the realm of Islam (Davila 2013, 28–29). The long and often troubled relationship between Orient and Occident has generally been mediated by certain gate-keeping concepts, from the older Orientalist tropes of the violent, sensual, and childish "Oriental" subject to modern ideas that emphasize common ancestry and shared history as a means for justifying colonization as a civilizing mission, especially in the Spanish and French experience.[16] As an extension of the Orient planted at the borders of Europe, al-Andalus thus came to represent a conceptual bridge linking Orient and Occident. This is evident in the writings of Washington Irving, especially his *Tales from the Alhambra* (1832), but also in the musical compositions of Isaac Albéniz (1860–1909) and Manuel de Falla (1876–1946), the poetry and scholarly writings of Federico García Lorca (1989–1936), and other works from the nineteenth and early twentieth centuries that drew inspiration from the monuments and narratives of al-Andalus. If these earlier works depicted al-Andalus as a bridge between cultures—East and West, Orient and Occident—at the same time al-Andalus came to be seen as a geopolitical barrier, even a shield against the Oriental Other. Especially in the post–Civil War era, Spain's colonial incursions into North Africa were a way not only to claim a link to Spain's Moorish past but, more importantly, to bolster its European credentials, joining the other European powers in their colonial scrambles in Africa (Aidi 2006, 72). Spain's entry into the project of Europe was uncertain partly because its relative economic underdevelopment was tied implicitly and explicitly to its Arab and African past. The standard narrative of al-Andalus thus came to serve

Spanish fascists, liberals, and neoliberals alike, though in very different and yet powerful ways.

However, it is important to note that the colonial nature of modern nostalgia for al-Andalus is also strongly evident in twentieth-century Arab and Muslim literary production from this period. For example, the nostalgic poems of the Egyptian poet Ahmad Shawqi and the Urdu and Persian poet Muhammad Iqbal, writing in the 1920s and 1930s, respectively, express anticolonial and nationalist sentiments through the adoption of a nostalgia for the lost paradise of al-Andalus (Noorani 1999). Both writers made visits—pilgrimages, in a way—to the major Andalusian cities: Shawqi in 1919 to Granada at the end of a five-year exile in Spain, and Iqbal to Córdoba in 1933, where he may have been the first Muslim to pray in the famous Mezquita since the *reconquista* (237). The texts that resulted from these visits, Shawqi's "Siniyya" ode and Iqbal's poem "Masjid-i Qurtubah," owe their inspiration as much to "the colonial situation in which they were produced as to the splendors of Islamic Spain" (237). Both poets used the Andalusian sites to call for a cultural renaissance and development in their respective countries, and both were to go on to engage in and inspire anticolonial struggles. In these cases, their reflective Andalusian nostalgia was harnessed to the restorative work of anticolonial nationalism. In a similar vein, modern novelistic portraits of al-Andalus also serve as commentaries on contemporary Arab society and its discontents. A number of well-known twentieth-century Arab authors have drawn on the trope of the glories of al-Andalus to promote a pan-Arab nationalism rooted in a shared, glorious history.[17]

I take up this theme later in relation to the rhetoric of al-Andalus in modern Syria, especially in the context of post-1970s economic development principally in the Arabian Peninsula and Gulf as a result of the rise in oil wealth. The newfound riches in the era of petrodollars inspired greater interest in an earlier golden age as a model for a current and future one. It is not a coincidence that Arab investment in Spain, especially in real estate, has grown exponentially since the 1970s, more so in the south than elsewhere (Segal 1991). Saudi and other Arab royalty have built elaborate vacation palaces in Marbella's "Golden Mile" in the Costa del Sol that rival the Andalusian palaces of yore. Tellingly, the Saudi royal palace in Marbella is called al-Nahda, which means "Revival" and refers as well to the period of Arab literary renaissance of the late nineteenth and early twentieth centuries. In this period, Arab nostalgia for al-Andalus as a lost paradise developed not only as a melancholic mourning over lost glory but as a source of inspiration for present and future community. In other words, al-Andalus became a project at once transnational and postnational. Since the 1970s, nostalgia for al-Andalus as a lost paradise has drawn inspiration from and inspired reactions to another Arab loss: Palestine. Indeed, the discourses of nostalgic lamentation over the loss of a golden age and the hypernostalgic longing for a return to Palestine increased after the losses of 1948 and 1967, what in Arabic are respectively called al-Nakba (the Catastrophe) and al-Naksa (the Setback). The loss of Palestine nourished at times reflective and backward-looking and at other times restorative and forward-looking nostalgic remembrances of al-Andalus fed by Arab petrodollars (Bisharat 1997).

Finally, these forward-looking nostalgic remembrances and performances continue today, propelled by the sesquicentennial celebrations of the fall of Granada (commemorated in 1992) and in the contemporary world in which the idea of al-Andalus has become a tense discursive (and architectural and musical) battleground for the negotiation of modern Spanish, Arab, and, by extension, Mediterranean identities and political subjectivities.

ANDALUSIAN MUSICS AND MUSICAL MYTHOLOGIZING

While most commonly celebrated for their architectural, literary, and scientific achievements, the peoples of al-Andalus developed rich poetic-musical traditions that remain important elements of the urban musical cultures of North Africa, among diasporic Sephardim, to some degree in the Levant, and now increasingly in modern Spain (Davila 2013; Glasser 2008, 2010; Poché 1995; Reynolds 2000a; Shannon 2007c). The musical cultures of al-Andalus also partake of the standard narrative of the rise and decline of al-Andalus that serves larger projects of modern nation building. In other words, like the story of al-Andalus, the music is "good to think," and like the story of al-Andalus, the narrative of the origins and early development of music in the Iberian Peninsula remains shrouded in ambiguity. This ambiguity is due in part to the loss of important early manuscripts and the lack of reliable information on musical performance in al-Andalus, so that we have no musical notation and scant literary documentation of musical performance in this era. Although musical practices among contemporary musicians who lay claim to the Andalusian legacy might shed some light on medieval musical performance, we should, as Dwight Reynolds (2009) argues, treat such associations with great caution due to the probability of considerable development and differentiation over the centuries both during the time of al-Andalus and in the postexpulsion diasporas. The fact that many contemporary musicians make these associations itself becomes an important part of the analysis of the cultural work of al-Andalus and Andalusian musics in the modern era.

The very term "Andalusian music" is both vague and misleading. Indeed, Andalusian music does not exist; rather, the term references a loose category that includes the urban musics of North Africa and the Levant, Sephardic musics, flamenco, and a variety of fusions of these and other musical genres and styles.[18] As an indication of its modernity, the term Andalusian is not found in musical compilations and texts until the late nineteenth and early twentieth centuries, even if the term *andalusi* was used to refer to the geographical location of the past civilizations and to the diasporic populations resulting from *la partida* but not to the music per se. It is my contention and that of some scholars (Davila 2013; Poché 1995; cf. Glasser 2012) that the label Andalusian arose in the shadow of colonialism as a result of the enthusiasm of Western musicologists in finding what they discerned to be survivals of the medieval European musical past in North African colonies and not as an autochthonous term linking the modern with the medieval practices. While the major medieval sources do not use the term *andalusi* when referring to the music, the early modern sources do, including the eighteenth-century *Kunnash al-Ha'ik* (Bennūna 1999)—the ur-text for the Andalusian musical tradition in Morocco—which describes the rhythms and modes as derived from al-Andalus; hence we can surmise that the Andalusian attribution derives from not much earlier than the late eighteenth century. Moreover, many modern sources reject the label as inappropriate both because there is no evidence of the early use of the appellation and because the term Andalusian implies both a continuous link to the past and a concomitant denial of contributions to musical practice in the centuries following the decline of al-Andalus (see al-Fāsī 1962). In other words, Andalusian is a nostalgic label, one that, like lamenting a lost paradise, relies on an imagined geography (in this case, poetic-musical) to promote a contemporary project. In contemporary usage, the labels Andalusian and Arabo-Andalusian refer to a vast body of poetic-musical genres and performance traditions across North Africa and the Levant and beyond that share, in addition to an ideology of relatedness to medieval al-Andalus, numerous song texts, genres, and musical structures that point to family resemblances despite five centuries of differentiation. Like "jazz" and "classical," "Andalusian" describes a category of consumption that covers a variety of diverse musical practices that stretch well beyond North Africa and the Levant.

Like the story of al-Andalus itself, the story of its music is shrouded in ambiguities. Little is known about the early history of musical practice in Iberia on the eve of the Islamic "opening" of Iberia, though there is some evidence of musical contact across the Mediterranean predating this period, as musicians and other artisans had traversed the Strait of Gibraltar for many centuries (Reynolds 2000a, 63). Moreover, since the conquerors remained a minority within the Iberian Peninsula, musical practice probably remained a mixture of Arab and Berber poetic and musical practices overlaid onto Visigoth and Proto-Romance musical structures, though we have no documentary evidence of the musical cultures of this period and place (60–61). Given the cultural dominance of Levantine Arabs in the early years of the opening, their musical practices no doubt strongly influenced the early growth of music in al-Andalus as court musicians, especially female and male slave singers from Baghdad and Medina, made their way to the Iberian Peninsula and circulated among the cultural elite. We can surmise that popular music (that outside the sphere of influence of the court) remained strongly marked by pre-Islamic indigenous practices, though we have no record of this (60–63).

The link between the various musics labeled Andalusian—from the Levantine, North African, and Spanish—rests on the idea that all these musical cultures can be traced back to Ziryab; they are all *hijos de Ziryab*.

Ziryab is widely considered to be the progenitor of Andalusian musical cultures in all their forms. This heroic personality is thought to have brought his musical and poetic genius—not to mention sartorial, culinary, and other innovations—with him across the length of the Mediterranean from Baghdad to Córdoba, and his legacy lives on today globally. Ziryab is the nickname of Abu al-Hasan 'Ali bin Nafi', who according to legend was an apprentice musician to the great Ishaq al-Mawsali at the court of the ninth-century 'Abbasid caliph Harun al-Rashid. "Ziryab" means "dark nightingale" in Persian and probably refers to the man's dark complexion, his renown as a singer (hence the bird reference), and the possibility that he was a freed slave of African origin (Davila 2009; Reynolds 2000a, 64–66, 2008). As the best-known version of the Ziryab tale goes, the young musician outperformed his master at one of the caliph's *jalsat,* or "gatherings," performing so well on an *'ud* (Arabian lute) and singing with such mastery that he gained the caliph's favor. This so enraged Ziryab's teacher that the upstart prodigy was forced to flee Baghdad to escape his mentor's wrath, a veritable death sentence. Ziryab, at the invitation of the Umayyad caliph, headed west to Umayyad Spain, and, according to legend, around the year 822 he crossed the Strait of Gibraltar and entered Córdoba accompanied by the Jewish court musician al-Mansur al-Yahudi (al-Mansur the Jew; see Shiloah 2007).[19] Once there he found favor with the caliph 'Abd al-Rahman II and, so the story goes, founded the first school of music, added a fifth string to the *'ud,* taught a corpus of several thousand songs, and developed distinct music structures, including the rudiments of the *nawba* (or *nuba,* "suite") form, common in contemporary Andalusian musical traditions. He is also thought to have set trends in fashion and high culture in what was still the relatively undeveloped outback of early ninth-century al-Andalus. If you eat asparagus, play chess, wear different clothing for the different seasons, and have bangs, thank Ziryab, for he is thought to have introduced these practices to medieval Spain, from where they spread to the rest of Europe (Reynolds 2000b; Shannon 2007a).

Zoom forward some six centuries, and, according to popular and scholarly narratives of Andalusian musical and cultural history, with the fall of Granada in 1492 and the subsequent expulsion of Muslims and Jews from Iberia, Andalusian Muslims and Jews (including *moriscos, marranos,* and *conversos*) made their way to North Africa, with the large majority settling in present-day Morocco, Algeria, and Tunis; some went as far as the Levant and Ottoman lands, including the Balkans.[20] Following well-worn pilgrimage and trade routes, the Andalusian refugees brought with them their culture and music.[21] The standard narrative claims that this music has echoes of the music created by Ziryab, so that today what we hear are echoes of al-Andalus among his "sons." This notion of contemporary Andalusian music deriving in whole or in part from the ninth-century innovations of Ziryab leads us to ask how this figure has come to play such an important rhetorical role in histories of the music, since recent scholarship has cast serious doubt on many aspects of the Ziryab story. As Reynolds (2008) and Davila (2009) argue, the Ziryab legend represents a redaction of historical sources and an amalgamation of musical and extramusical transformations that came to be ascribed to one cultural hero. In fact, almost no biographical information on Ziryab is found in the medieval texts, including the tenth-century sage al-Isfahani's encyclopedic *Kitab al-aghani,* which relates largely anecdotal information about him. Most accounts are at least at a century's remove, if not greater (Davila 2009; Poché 1995; Reynolds 2008; Shannon 2007a; Wright 1992).[22] Both Reynolds (2008) and Davila (2009) compare the existing manuscript evidence on Ziryab the man and point out numerous inconsistencies and gaps in the legend. Reynolds posits two main acts of editing and embellishment—one as early as the eleventh century, the other in the seventeenth—that reduced the polyphony of the earlier sources to a glorious (if monotone) legend. Davila's analysis of the earliest sources reveals how these acts of collating, editing, and suppressing the evidence about Ziryab the man promoted the idea of Ziryab the myth—the Ziryab who lives on today in the historical and cultural imaginary of Andalusian music. Moreover, the efforts to burnish the role and character of Ziryab may have reflected early modern efforts to paint al-Andalus as a golden age and lost paradise (Reynolds 2008, 166). Might modern nostalgia for al-Andalus have its roots in seventeenth-century writings?

Like other legends, the Ziryab story is mostly accepted as historical fact by many in Syria, Morocco, and Spain, as well as more generally in the Western treatment of Middle Eastern, North African, and even

European musical and cultural history, even among scholars (see, e.g., Manzano 1985, 41–46). Ziryab serves as a symbolic starting point for histories of Andalusian music and a marker of both the indebtedness of al-Andalus to Levantine culture and its subsequent divergence. Moreover, the Ziryab legend fits well not only with the Carlylesque "great man" view of history (Carlyle 1888; see Davila 2013) but with the aforementioned modern North African and Arab concerns with national identity, anticolonial struggle, and postcolonial development. In other words, Ziryab, like the notion of a lost paradise or golden age, serves as a modern discursive trope (White 1978). For my purposes it is less important what Ziryab may have created or the extent to which he may have influenced Iberian and post-Iberian Andalusian cultures than that for enthusiasts of Andalusian music, Ziryab is "good to think." That is, they hear their own cultural roots and heritage in his legend, even when the musics they perform and point to as evidence sound different. This is important because Andalusian music participates in a larger set of modern rhetorics that link contemporary practices with medieval antecedents.

ANDALUSIAN MUSICAL CULTURES AFTER ZIRYAB

The actual post-Ziryab history of the musics of al-Andalus has been traced by a number of scholars (Davila 2009, 2013; Reynolds 2000a, 2008). Most rely on a standard genealogy linking writers from the twelfth through the eighteenth century. The Tunisian writer Ahmad al-Tifashi (d. 1253) provides one of the earliest if fragmentary treatments of Andalusian musical and poetic practices, as well as the first comparative treatment of poetic-musical practice between the Levant, North Africa, and al-Andalus. In his *Mut'at al-asma' fi 'ilm al-sama'* (Pleasure for the ears in the art of listening), al-Tifashi argues that Ziryab's influence had waned by the eleventh century in the face of musical styles developed by the Andalusian sage Ibn Bajja (Abu Bakr Ibn Yahya al-Sayigh, known in the West as Avempace; d. 1139), whose works are now lost (see Davila 2009, 2013). Al-Tifashi famously wrote that Ibn Bajja "combined the music of the Christians with that of the Arab East" (Reynolds 2000a, 65–66), thereby creating a uniquely Andalusian style. He further notes that in the thirteenth century, Ibn al-Hasib of Murcia furthered Ibn Bajja's style and composed songs and theoretical texts that were the basis of all the music heard in the al-Andalus and North Africa of his day, though nothing survives of Ibn Hasib's work. Scholars concur that the Almoravid and Almohad Dynasties most likely witnessed the gradual convergence of musical practice in al-Andalus and North Africa due to the presence of numerous North African emigrants in Iberia when al-Andalus was effectively a province of Morocco. North African historians of the era referred to the *'udwatan,* or "two banks," of the Muslim dynasties, the North African and the Iberian. The flow of people across the Mediterranean from one bank to the other meant significant mutual influence in all domains of expressive culture, including literature and song. This was to continue in the post-Almohad era and during the centuries leading to the fall of Granada, and likely well after (Fuchs 2009). Connections with the Arab East were more tenuous but nevertheless important in introducing Andalusian poetic and musical forms to the Levant following long-established pilgrimage and trade routes; for example, the Andalusian Sufi masters Muhyi al-Din Ibn al-'Arabi (d. 1240) and Abu al-Hasan al-Shushtari (d. 1269) traveled and settled in the Arab East and may have introduced specifically religious forms of the *muwashshah* to the region; Syrian musicians and scholars often claim that it was Ibn al-'Arabi who introduced this Andalusian poetic-musical genre to Syria when he arrived in Damascus in the early thirteenth century.[23]

Sources on musical life in al-Andalus from the thirteenth century to the fall of Granada and final expulsions of Muslims and Jews from Iberia indicate the development of fixed musical structures, a large poetic-musical repertoire and instrumentarium, and growing independence from the traditions of the Arab East (Davila 2013). The Egyptian Ibn Sana' al-Mulk's (d. 1212) *Dar al-tiraz* (House of brocade) constitutes the first comprehensive treatment of the *muwashshah* genre from both a musical and a poetic perspective (Reynolds 2007). The influence of Andalusian music on the musical cultures of Christian Iberia remains debated, though examination of the medieval and early modern European instrumentarium reveals clear borrowing from Arab-Andalusian music and suggests more extensive influence in form and content, and Andalusian music remained vital in Spanish and Portuguese courts even after the final expulsion of the *moriscos* (Ferreira 2000).

The musical practices of these and earlier Andalusian refugees is widely thought to form the basis of the urban musical traditions of North Africa today and to a far lesser extent some of the musics of the Arab East. An important development in the history of Andalusian music in the post-Iberian era was the compilation of songbooks (variously called *kunnash, majmu'*, or *safina*) that aimed to preserve the traditions in diasporic contexts; we can in fact consider these documents among the earliest examples of a postexodus Andalusian memory culture. The most important of these is the *kunnash* of the Tetouani jurist Muhammad Ibn al-Husayn al-Hayik (also al-Ha'ik), who compiled his work in Fez at the end of the eighteenth century. Later editions of this and other collections form the basis of contemporary musical practice in North Africa today, especially in Morocco, and often form the core of musical training at conservatories (Davila 2013).

ANDALUSIAN MUSICS OF THE MEDITERRANEAN:
A BRIEF LISTENER'S GUIDE

The North African and Levantine musical systems, while to a large degree distinct with respect to tonality and rhythm, share many similarities in instrumentarium, nomenclature, and overall structure and therefore exhibit a strong family resemblance. It is common in (ethno) musicological scholarship to differentiate the two regions, both because the musical and other cultural traditions can be distinct and because the influence of Ottoman and other forms on the Arab East was stronger than in North Africa; indeed, many musicians I interviewed in Morocco thought that the musics of Syria and Egypt were "Turkish," while their traditions, especially the Andalusian, were more authentically "Arab." However, both the Levantine and North African musical traditions are based in suites of (mostly) Arabic-language poetic texts set to music. The tonality is modal in nature rather than diatonic, meaning that the songs are composed in distinct musical modes having predefined musical and extramusical associations. While the organization of the musical suites, elements of performance practice, and the modal qualities of the North African and Levantine musics may be distinct, uninitiated listeners would indeed be correct to hear a family resemblance between them even if aficionados of one tradition or another, even within a defined national context, would note important differences.

Two areas of distinction are important. On the one hand, there is surprisingly little overlap in the poetic texts used in the Syrian and Moroccan traditions, though each claims that the majority of the texts are of Andalusian composition or inspiration. In fact, the nature of the poetic repertoire is far more complex than this simple Andalusian attribution, and even where there are shared texts between Morocco and Syria, they are performed in different ways. Moreover, many of the texts in the North African Andalusian traditions were composed in the postexilic era, belying the claim that these musical cultures are repositories of Andalusian heritage preserved essentially unchanged; for example, a significant percentage of the Moroccan al-Ala tradition consists of songs composed in the last three centuries in Moroccan dialectical Arabic, in the genre known as *barwala* (Davila 2013). In addition, Davila (2015) demonstrates that the majority of known authors of texts in the suite *Ramal al-maya* were either North African or Levantine, not medieval Andalusian. On the other hand, the musical cultures of the Levant and North Africa are modal, but the modes used have very different intervalic characters, even when they share the same or similar names; for example, the Levantine mode *rast* and the Moroccan mode *rasd* are very different. The Levantine modes share important ties with Ottoman, Persian, and even northern Indian modal musics, while the Moroccan (and to a degree Algerian and Tunisian) have similarities with Berber, European, and sub-Saharan African modes.[24] The precise intervallic nature of each mode, the modes' interrelationships into families of modes, and their relationship to the modes of other Arab and North African musical cultures have been the subject of debate among communities of performers, aficionados, and scholars for almost a century and continue to this day.

ANDALUSIAN MUSICAL GENRES AND STRUCTURES

The musical form most closely associated with the Andalusian musical legacy is the strophic form called *muwashshah* (see Davila 2013; Heijkoop and Zwartjes 2004; Reynolds 2000a; Shannon 2007c). The word *muwashshah* derives from the Arabic word *wishah* or *wushah,* a type of embellished sash or scarf worn over the shoulders by women in the medieval period. By extension, the word *muwashshah* means "embellished" or "decorated," referring to the embellishment in the poetic texts (what medieval Moroccan texts called *shughl*, "work").[25] The *muwashshah* is thought to have first arisen in al-Andalus between the ninth and eleventh centuries as a poetic-musical genre, though the origins of this and other strophic forms such as *zajal* and their relationship to Arabian, Persian, and early Romance literatures have been the subject of scholarly debate for over two centuries (see Davila 2013; Monroe and Liu 1989). Though early sources attribute these forms to individual creators, they most likely developed as a result of extensive experimentation in multirhyme and multipart forms having roots in the courtly traditions of the Arab East and the popular musics of Iberia, among other sources.

Modern musical practice diverges from the classical poetic tradition. Unlike the *qasida* (the monorhymed Arabian ode) and similar genres, the *muwashshah* follows a multipart division between three parts: an opening section, a middle section, and a final section.[26] The traditional *muwashshah* consisted of a series of four or five stanzas with two alternating melodies following one of two main patterns.[27] In the modern era, it has become common to sing only a single stanza with opening and closing sections, creating a tripartite melodic structure in which the opening and final sections follow the same melody, while the middle section has a distinct melody, often in a different musical mode. As Reynolds (2007) notes, passages in the thirteenth-century *Dar al-tiraz* suggest that this structure may have characterized medieval compositional and performance practice. While some scholars claim that in medieval practice the initial section was repeated as a refrain at the end of each strophe, little evidence from medieval and modern sources supports this claim outside the Jewish *piyyutim* tradition (Seroussi 1986; Shiloah 1995).

A defining characteristic of Andalusian musics is their organization into suites, called *nubat* in North Africa and *waslat* in the Levant. As early as 'Abbasid Iraq, the *nuba* implied turn-taking among musicians performing standard sequences of songs. None other than Ziryab is credited with bringing this practice to al-Andalus and organizing each suite into a slow opening section (*nashid*), followed by slow tempo (*ba-*

sit), medium tempo (*muharrak*), and fast tempo (*hazaj*) sections (al-Shāmī 1984a; Shannon 2007c).[28] The organization of suites in terms of the sequence of slow, medium, and fast tempi characterizes the organization of North African and Levantine suites today (Shannon 2007c). Medieval sources, drawing on classical Greek humoral theory, associated the musical modes with specific times of the day, bodily humors, celestial configurations, seasons, and colors (Shiloah 2001). Claims that in the early Andalusian tradition there were originally twenty-four modes, one for each hour of the day, are not supported by evidence, and today fewer than half this number are performed in the various North African traditions; the Moroccan repertoire is organized into eleven *nubat*, though the use of supplemental modes in performance practice brings the total number of modes to twenty-five (Davila 2013, 148–149). Even in the time of al-Tifashi (the thirteenth century), the *nuba* consisted of a fixed sequence of songs, and this practice is followed in contemporary North African traditions; the structure of the Levantine wasla allows for more variation in the organization of songs, as well as for the possibility of composition of new forms, something not acknowledged in North Africa even if practiced (Shannon 2007b).

In terms of tonality, extant sources provide little information about tonality and rhythm in medieval Andalusian music (Shannon 2007a). Since at least the time of al-Ha'ik, North African Andalusian traditions have utilized a series of modes (*tab'/tubu'*) that differ from the Arabian *maqam* system of modes tradition in the near absence of microtonality, as well as in their melodic treatment, use of modulation, and compositional practices. Rhythmic cycles in medieval Iberian and North African traditions follow sequences of four or five rhythmic patterns, which are in many respects different from those used in the Levant, though both are organized as repeatable sequences of duple and triple meters. Some scholars suggest that medieval Iberian musical practice may have developed independently from eastern Arab music, which displays marked Ottoman and Persian influence (Shannon 2006; Shiloah 2001). As for the instruments used, evidence from medieval Iberia survives in textual and iconographic sources, including the illustrations for the thirteenth-century *Cantigas de Santa Maria*. The primary instruments used in the medieval period were the *rabab* (the rebec, a

boat-shaped fiddle); various forms of the *'ud* (a four-course lute); percussion instruments such as *al-duff* (the *adufe,* or frame-drum), *al-tabl*
(the *atabal,* or kettledrum), *naqqara* (nakers, small kettledrums), and *al-*
tar (a large frame drum); wind instruments, including *al-buq* (*albogue,*
or hornpipe), *al-nafir* (*añafil,* trumpet), and *zamr al-nay* (reed flute);
and instruments with no known modern equivalent, such as the *urghun*
(organum).[29] Chief among instruments in both medieval and modern
practice, the human voice served as the central instrument given the
importance of song texts and poetic forms in Andalusian musical traditions. Purely instrumental music in the form of preludes served to
introduce the singing of poetry; this association remained relevant until
well into the twentieth century in the Levant and even to this day in
North African traditions.

ANDALUSIAN MUSICAL TRADITIONS
TODAY: NORTH AFRICA

Distinct regional traditions arose in the North African littoral in the
post-Iberian era, drawing on existing forms and developing into what
are known as the Andalusian musical cultures in modern Morocco,
Algeria, Tunisia, and Libya. Traces of the Andalusian poetic and musical heritage can also be found in the Arab East, including Iraq and
Yemen, though not with the same associations of direct inheritance
as found in North Africa, where *andalusi* marks in some areas a distinct cultural identity (Bahrami 1995). Many North Africans trace their
musical heritage through genealogies of migration from specific cities
in al-Andalus, what has come to be one of the most important tropes
of authenticity in the North African contexts. Whereas Fez is thought
to have received the traditions of Granada and Valencia, Tétouan wel-
comed that of Granada, Tlemcen developed that of Córdoba, Tunisia
that of Seville, and Tripoli those of Seville and Córdoba. There is scant
evidence for regional song styles within al-Andalus to support these
claims, though the associations are strong, for example, in the Gharnati
(Grenadine) musics of Rabat and Oujda in Morocco and in Tlemcen in
Algeria (Glasser 2008, 2012). Moreover, popular claims tend to support a
view of the musical traditions of North Africa as essentially unchanged
since the fall of Granada, which denies the now well-documented post-

Iberian contributions to Andalusian music from the last several centuries and continuing into the present. Sufi confraternities may have played an important role in preserving texts and melodies of North African Andalusian musics, as did the formation of numerous amateur associations (*jama'iyat*) in the twentieth century (Glasser 2008; Reynolds 2008; Shannon 2007c). With independence, most North African nations made the Andalusian musical repertoire part of their national cultural patrimony. As a result, Andalusian repertoires were standardized and codified into official songbooks, and national music conservatories today serve as the primary context for learning the inherited performance practices. One result has been the classicization of the music and concomitant restrictions if not outright prohibitions on new compositions in the older forms (Shannon 2007b).

Each of the North African traditions follows the suite structure of medieval performance practice, arranging repertoires of poetic texts into more or less fixed sequences based on melodic mode (*tab'*) and rhythmic cycle (*mizan*). Algeria, Tunisia, and Libya exhibit increasing degrees of Ottoman and eastern Arab influence on structure, tonality, rhythm, and performance practice (Ciantar 2012; Guettat 2000). In Morocco, Andalusian music is generally known as *al-musiqa al-andalusiyya*, *al-tarab al-andalusi* (Andalusian *tarab*), or *al-ala* (instrumental music, as compared with *sama'*, "audition," i.e., the music of the Sufi confraternities, in which instruments typically were not used). Since at least the late nineteenth century, performance practice has remained conservative, closely following the known variations of the songbook (*kunnash*) compiled by al-Ha'ik, supplemented by oral traditions in the three primary centers of *al-ala* music performance: Fez, Rabat, and Tangier/Tétouan.[30] These are associated with genealogies of each orchestra (*jawq*) and its leaders. Despite ample evidence for composition by leading artists in the twentieth century, most contemporary musicians and aficionados argue that adding to the repertoire is neither acceptable nor practiced (Shannon 2007b). The repertoire of more than a thousand songs includes the genres of *muwashshah, zajal, qasida,* and *barwala* (a variety of colloquial Moroccan poetry) arranged into eleven *nubat* utilizing twenty-five modes, and five rhythmic sequences. In addition to *al-ala,* Moroccans recognize the *gharnati* (Grenadine, sometimes *al-*

tarab al-gharnati) traditions of Oujda and Rabat and the *malhun* tradition as important elements of Morocco's Andalusian heritage (Glasser 2008). A typical Moroccan *ala* ensemble features *rabab, 'ud, tar, kamanja* (violin, played off the knee), and vocalist (*munshid*); other instruments are frequently added, including the *qanun* (lap zither), *nay* (reed flute), and different lutes and drums. Occasionally piano, clarinet, saxophone, and transverse flute can be found in modern ensembles, though the practice is debated.

The Andalusian music in Algeria is centered in three major urban centers: Tlemcen, where it is called *sana'* (craft) or *gharnati;* Constantine, where it is called *ma'luf* (customary, traditional); and Algiers, where it is also called *sana'* (Guettat 2000; Poché 1995). The traditions of Tlemcen and Constantine are thought to be the older and most distinctive of Algeria's Andalusian traditions, though all share basic elements. The repertoire, like the Moroccan, which consists of over a thousand songs, is organized into twelve complete *nubat* for the traditions of Tlemcen and Algiers and ten for that of Constantine. A total of twenty modes are known across the three Algerian traditions, though only twelve are associated with complete *nubat,* for which they are named. Performance of the Algerian *nuba* follows a suite structure similar to that of Moroccan *al-ala,* with instrumental preludes and five main vocal movements. Algerian Andalusian music ensembles comprise, in addition to the essential instruments of the Moroccan repertoire, such instruments as the *kwitra* or *kwithra* (long-necked four-stringed lute), *snitra* (mandolin), and *'ud 'arbi* (four-stringed lute).

In Tunisia, the Andalusian music known as *ma'luf* is performed in the urban centers, especially the capital, Tunis (Davis 2004). Tunisian Andalusian music in general exhibits more Levantine and Ottoman influences than the musics of Morocco or Algeria, including song texts, modal and rhythmic structure, and performance practice; for example, Tunisian *ma'luf* features use of microtonality and genres of clear Ottoman provenance such as the *bashraf,* an instrumental prelude. The over seven hundred known pieces of the *ma'luf* repertoire are organized into thirteen suites (called *nubat,* as they are in Morocco and Algeria) and performed in five rhythmic cycles (also known as *mizan*). Additional suites borrowed from the Arab East are often performed in conjunction with the *ma'luf* repertoire. A total of thirteen modes are used in Tunisian *ma'luf,* though two or more additional modes from the eastern Arab *maqam* traditions are often used as well. Tunisian *ma'luf* ensembles consist of *munshid* (vocalist), *rabab, 'ud 'arbi, tar,* and *naqqarat* (small kettledrums).

Andalusian music in Libya is known variously as *ma'luf* or *fann* (art; Ciantar 2012). Relatively unknown compared to the other North African traditions, Libyan *ma'luf* draws on a mix of North African, Levantine, Bedouin, and Berber musical traditions as a result of its geographic position between Maghrib and Mashriq. This diversity of origin is also reflected in the repertoire, which includes genres more characteristic of Levantine musics. As in the rest of North Africa, Sufi confraternities played a role in the preservation of Libyan *ma'luf,* and it remains a staple at religious festivals and in public performances in larger urban centers, chiefly Tripoli and Benghazi. The repertoire of over two hundred songs is organized into twenty-four *nubat* incorporating thirteen musical modes. Each *nuba* is known by the first line or hemistich (*dakhla/tashtira*) of the primary poetic text of that song sequence rather than by mode, as in the other North African traditions. The primary instruments utilized in Libyan *ma'luf* include the *ghayta, bandir/bindir* (frame drum), *shatkh* (*darbukka*), *naqqarat, tar, kinji* (vocal soloist), and *raddada* (chorus).

ANDALUSIAN MUSICAL TRADITIONS TODAY: THE LEVANT

In the contemporary Levant, Andalusian music refers to songs and song texts thought to derive from medieval Iberian poetic and musical forms (Shannon 2003a). In practice, the Andalusian label refers primarily to the *muwashshah,* which comprises one segment of a larger multigenre suite known as the *wasla* and which is usually performed individually, contrary to North African traditions in which *muwashshahat* are usually performed sequentially without a pause. Modern Levantine performance of the *muwashshah* is based largely in the collection of Muhammad Shihab al-Din (1795/1796–1857), *Safinat al-mulk wa nafisat al-fulk* (The ship of state and the treasure of the ark), which contains over 350 song texts (see Reynolds 2004). In Aleppo, Damascus, Beirut, and Cairo, the *muwashshah* constitutes an important element of the *wasla* suite of songs and is still utilized as a compositional form whose melodic structure follows a basic tripartite form (*dawr, khana,* and *ghita'*) reminiscent of earlier Andalusian poetic structures (see above and also Shannon 2003a).

While the *muwashshah* has served largely as a conservatory genre in Egypt, in Syria it remains a more central component of modern musical life. Syrian Andalusian music comprises several hundred songs organized into twenty-three suites arranged by mode and comprising a wide variety of rhythmic cycles in complex arrangements of duple and triple meters. The complete repertoire includes instrumental overtures, instrumental improvisations, and the vocal genres of *qasida, muwashshah, mawwal* (a colloquial ode), *dawr* (a multipart colloquial song), and what are known as *al-qudud al-halabiyya* (light songs based in contrafactum compositions, where well-known melodies are given new lyrics, often in colloquial Arabic). The overall repertoire is immense and continually changing as new generations of artists set classical and modern poetic texts to compositions in the tripartite melodic structure of the *muwashshah.* Although national conservatories teach the *muwashshah,* usually referred to as the "Andalusian" *muwashshah,* this genre remains a living heritage in more traditional forms of performance, such as private evening musical gatherings (*sahrat,* sing. *sahra*) and in the performance of the Sufi *dhikr.* Levantine ensembles perform the Andalusian repertoire on the instruments of the standard Oriental *takht* ensemble: *'ud, qanun, nay, kamanja,* and *riqq* (tambourine). Ensembles seldom use instruments such as transverse flute, saxophone, trumpet, mandolin, or piano, as is the case in some North African traditions.

SEPHARDIC ANDALUSIAN MUSICS

The long tradition of Jewish performance of the Arab and Arab-Andalusian musics of North Africa and the Levant is continued in Israel, among the remaining Jewish communities in Arab lands and Turkey, and among diasporic Jews, especially the Sephardim (Seroussi 1991; Shiloah 1995). Performance practice includes the Arab-Andalusian repertoires, specific Hebrew liturgical forms, and songs from Ottoman and Balkan traditions in a variety of languages, including Arabic, Hebrew, Ladino, Judeo-Spanish, Judeo-Arabic, Turkish, and others. Andalusian

Jews (usually called Sephardim) took with them their musical and poetic forms, which were based closely on Arabic poetics and musical practice, into their diverse diasporic communities in North Africa, the Levant, and the Ottoman Empire. The existence since the nineteenth century of Arab and Sephardic Jewish communities in the New World has meant that Andalusian musical forms can be found throughout the Americas, from Canada and the United States to Venezuela, Brazil, and Argentina, though traces of the latter are not well documented. Composition of liturgical and paraliturgical forms such as *baqqashot* and *piyyutim* having a relationship to the medieval Iberian and post-Iberian musics continued in this period (see, among others, Katz 1968; Kligman 2009; Seroussi 1986; Shiloah 1995). While some Jewish communities exist across North Africa and in very small numbers in the Levantine Arab states, none in Syria, Morocco, or Spain performed Andalusian music in public during the time of my ethnographic research (1996–2013), and therefore this ethnographic study of music making does not include information on living Jewish performers of this tradition.

Modern Spain and Portugal have seen a resurgence of interest in Iberia's heterogeneous pasts, resulting in a renewed interest in the study of medieval Andalusian musical traditions and their re-creation and modern adaptation in performance, especially of such repertoires as the *Cantigas de Santa Maria* (see Ferreira 2000).

TWO

The Rhetoric of al-Andalus
in Modern Syria, or,
There and Back Again

We thread our way through the crowd of evening shoppers in the Souq al-Buzuriyya, passing the rows of barrels of aromatic spices and nuts, as well as Ghraoui's, my favorite chocolate shop, which dates to the late nineteenth century. There's no time to stop tonight, however, for Hussein and I are headed to Khan As'ad Pasha to hear a concert of Andalusian music. Hussein is a well-known 'ud player from Hama who had relocated to Damascus to pursue teaching and performance opportunities. We arrive a little late, and the Ottoman khan, or caravanserai, the largest in Damascus, has already filled up. With intricate domes soaring over the halls surrounding its expansive courtyard, the eighteenth-century structure is a good venue for a musical performance: acoustically rich and capable of hosting a large audience. Tonight's concert is part of the Andalusian Music Festival, sponsored by the Instituto Cervantes (a Spanish cultural center) in Damascus, and it features ensembles from Morocco and Spain. The Moroccan group, Ensemble Ibn 'Arabi (named after the Andalusian sage), directed by Tangier-based qanun player and scholar Ahmed El Khaligh, features performers of the 'ud, kamanja, nay, and percussion, as well as a vocalist.[1] They specialize in Islamic chant (in-

shad) and Sufi songs (*sama'*), as well as instrumental music from North Africa. Wearing flowing white gowns in the stately khan, they are the very picture of authenticity.

They begin their performance with a bow and salutation to the "noble shaykhs of Damascus" (*shuyukh dimashq al-afadil*) followed by a short suite of songs, including some *muwashshahat* attributed to Ibn 'Arabi and concluding with a few well-known Islamic chants. The music is somber if lively and to my ears pleasant, and the sounds echo in the courtyard. The audience, a mix of mostly urbane Damascenes and curious passersby, as well as not a few musicians, seems engaged enough, and some people sing along with the chants, though there is also the usual milling about and banter that happen at these sorts of events. Having arrived a little late, Hussein and I stand toward the back of the crowd and are soon joined by other latecomer friends. After the first song is over he leans toward me and remarks on the Moroccan flavor of the music, that the music is a mix of Arab and North African styles. After they finish he pronounces the *qanun* player in particular as *hilu,* using the all-purpose Syrian-Arabic term for "good." He is less impressed by the *'ud* player but, perhaps out of professional courtesy, declines to offer any substantial criticism other than to say, "The Moroccan modes are limiting. They only play Western modes. The Arab modes have more possibilities."

As we talk with friends the Spanish group begins to set up. It is the Ensemble Mudéjar, founded in the early 1990s by vocalist and *salterio* (psaltery) player Begoña Olavide.[2] In addition to Olavide's psaltery, which is similar to a *qanun,* the ensemble features performers on *'ud, nay,* and frame drums, in other words, essentially similar to a traditional Arabian *takht* ensemble. They perform a suite of what they call Arab-Andalusian music (*música arábigo-andaluza* or *música andalusí*) and sing in a variety of languages, including Arabic, Spanish, and Ladino (Judeo-Spanish). As they play the song "Rifqan 'ala qulaybi ya man ablah" my friends seem at once interested and perplexed.[3] The musicianship is good, and to my ears the vocals are lovely, but for them something seems a little off. When the song is over I ask them what they think. "It's just flamenco using our instruments!" says one friend, a teacher at the Damascus music conservatory. "Her pronunciation is wrong and the modes are all European," claims another. *"Hilu,"* says Hussein again, "but it's *hajin* [mixed, hybrid] and not as authentic as our music."

My Syrian friends heard the songs from Spain as distant echoes of their own music, returning, as through an echo chamber, darkly to remind them of their connections to a land long lost to them: al-Andalus. The Ensemble Mudéjar had taken great strides to research and develop an extensive repertoire of the musical styles of medieval Iberia, including those of Muslims, Jews, and Christians, and also reproducing the instruments themselves (the luthier Carlos Paniagua re-creates medieval instruments based on iconographic depictions), striving for authenticity in their presentation and in the emotional tenor of the songs.[4] However, to the ears of my Syrian friends, the music was not authentic. At best it was *hilu,* but overall it was just another "flamenco" performance, a hybrid where they wanted the "pure" original. Indeed, as we shall see, the contemporary presence of al-Andalus in Syria actuates a congeries of often contradictory associations with Syrian self-identity and notions of authenticity.

AL-ANDALUS IN SYRIA

The so-called Andalusian musics of Syria resonate within a broader cultural context, for modern Syria, though far removed in time and space from medieval Iberia, is nevertheless rife with images and evocations of al-Andalus: in literature, given the rich poetic legacy of al-Andalus, but also in painting, vernacular architecture, television and cinema, popular discourse, and of course the musical forms called "Andalusian." Syrian music serves as a powerful vehicle for the expression of pan-Arab sentiment.[5] Despite Syria's geographical remove from Iberia, al-Andalus remains an important referent for Syrian musicians; this is especially the case for the *muwashshahat,* which are generally understood to be of Andalusian origin and in Syria are called *al-muwashshahat al-andalusiyya.* Performed across North Africa and in the Levant, the *muwashshahat* serve in Syrian popular culture as metaphors for the Arab past, a past enjoying a curious presence today. Aside from its aesthetic merits, the *muwashshahat* more than any other genre in the Syrian musical repertoire link contemporary Syria to al-Andalus. Moreover, they play a defining role in what I call the rhetoric of al-Andalus in modern Syria, that is, a set of ideas and practices that are "good to think" in the context of a modernizing nation. Andalusian music, in its performance, reverberates with an Arab-Andalusian memory culture, evoking the genius of Arab culture in both Iberia and the Levant.

To understand the relationships among modern Syrian culture, medieval Iberia, and contemporary "Andalusian" musical performance in Syria we must inquire into the rhetorical realm in which discourses about al-Andalus circulate and acquire meaning. What role does al-Andalus play in the modern Syrian cultural imaginary? Why should a time and place seemingly remote from the Arab East continue to exercise influence some five centuries after its decline? Why do the Andalusian associations with the music reverberate in Syria today? In other words, what work does al-Andalus do in modern Syria? How is al-Andalus good to think?

This chapter explores the dynamics of the Andalusian legacy in Syria by exploring the interpolation of Syria in al-Andalus and al-Andalus in Syria. I begin with a discussion of the role of the *idea* of al-Andalus in modern Syria, tracing some genealogies of the term from the early twentieth century to today. I focus initially on the presence of al-Andalus in the popular Syrian imaginary, then turn to focused discussions of the literary and historical ties of modern Syria to medieval Iberia. Finally, I address the ways in which musicians and audiences remember al-Andalus through musical performance. To address the question of why Syrians emphasize the idea that their musics have a connection to al-Andalus, I situate Syrian "Andalusian" music within the larger fabric of cultural and political life that from the 1970s came to stress the historical and imaginary connections to medieval Spain. In brief, in Syria al-Andalus serves as a touchstone of pan-Arab identities, undergirding the Baʿthist ideologies of secularism and Pan-Arabism that have been central tenets of Syrian state ideologies for over five decades and that now are dissolving with the conflict in Syria. The so-called Andalusian music and associated literary forms in Syria (chiefly the *muwashshahat*) reinforce Syria's self-proclaimed role as the heart of ancient and modern Arab pannational aspirations. While al-Andalus played a role in some early expressions of Arab nationalist and pan-Islamic sentiments, in Syria the valorization of the Andalusian heritage seems not to have played an important role until the postindependence era, and especially after 1970 as a result of a complex conjunction of developments, including the political dominance of the Syrian branch of the Ba'th Party, the rise of oil wealth in the Arabian Gulf countries, and the plight of the Palestinians, whose losses resonate in important ways with the loss of al-Andalus. Performance of Syria's Andalusian music today thus resonates with the modern work of al-Andalus as a metaphor for past Arab glory and future hopes. Drawing on the Umayyad connections between Syria and Iberia and the confluence of Syria in al-Andalus and al-Andalus in Syria, Andalusian music sounds the historical consciousness of a modernizing Syria. Yet, consumption of the Andalusian heritage is more than a nostalgic retreat to the past; rather, it serves as a powerful medium of critique for the present. The implicit cultural critique of "Andalusian" culture in Syria is the key to understanding not only Syria's relationship to al-Andalus but the continuing relevance of al-Andalus in contemporary Syrian cultural politics today and into the future. The present conflict has yielded competing reflective and restorative nostalgias for a preconflict Syria marked by an idealized multiculturalism and for a future (also idealized) pan-Islamic state, both drawing inspiration from earlier nostalgias for al-Andalus.

The standard narrative of·al-Andalus is one of rise, efflorescence, and decline, of opening (*fath*) and fall (*suqut*). While we know that this is hardly the entire story, nonetheless the standard narrative of Andalusian history exercises a powerful hold on the popular and to a large degree even the scholarly imagination of medieval Iberia. This is because al-Andalus is "good to think" in a variety of ways: as a golden age of cultural development, as a much lamented lost paradise, and as a "culture of tolerance" (Menocal 2002a). As in the standard tale of nostalgic remembrance, the majority of Syrians with whom I spoke during my field research prior to the onset of war and the vast majority of texts I consulted on al-Andalus and Andalusian history, literature, and music conceive of al-Andalus as a pinnacle of cultural achievement. In a departure from the standard narrative, however, many Syrians I interviewed also emphasized the Arab and even Syrian dimensions of al-Andalus, elements that either play a minor role or are left out altogether in most North African and Spanish renditions of the standard narrative. Syrians see themselves at the heart of the story of al-Andalus: as its founders (if not its "openers"), as contributors to its development and glory, and as recipients of its treasures once it fell. They understand the story of al-Andalus as essentially one of Syrian-Arab cultural roots taking blossom in a new land and then, after years—indeed, centuries—of development, coming back home to their native soil with the exile of Moors from Spain and their eventual resettling across the Mediterranean, including in the Levant. The Syrian version of the Andalusian saga begins in Damascus with the Umayyad Dynasty (661–750 CE), under whose aegis al-Andalus was first "opened" and under whose leadership it first came to fruition during the Umayyad Caliphate of Córdoba (929–1031). It is these Umayyad (read "Arab") roots that many Syrians consider to have been the dynamic heart of Andalusian culture, the fruit of which came back to Syria in the post-*partida* era. In this way the dominant Syrian narrative of al-Andalus grafts a return voyage to the standard narrative of rise and fall. As a result, the Syrian narrative becomes one of a voyage of Arab culture—there and back again, or Syria in al-Andalus and al-Andalus in Syria. The notion of a return is important on three fronts: it links modern Syria to medieval and early modern Iberia, it serves as a touchstone of cultural critique in the modern age, and it resonates with the Palestinian problem.

The pan-Arab, Umayyad dimensions of the Andalusian imaginary in Syria are evident in much popular discourse on al-Andalus.[6] On one of my first visits to Damascus I met the well-known novelist and editor Fadil al-Siba'i (b. 1929, Aleppo). We met briefly outside his home in central Damascus as I was heading to a concert with a friend. We stopped to say hello, and he asked about my work in Syria. When I mentioned my interest in music and especially in the poetic-musical genre of *muwashshah,* considered to have been invented in al-Andalus, he raised his eyebrows and said, "Ah, al-Andalus! You mean the Andalusian *muwashshah!*" He went on to talk enthusiastically about *firdawsuna al-mafqud* (our lost paradise), referring to the Arabs' loss of a paradise of culture, learning, and tolerance—much like the standard narrative of rise, efflorescence, and fall. On another occasion we met at his home and talked more about his interest in things Andalusian. While al-Siba'i is best known as a novelist, he worked for many years as a lawyer and civil ser-

vant and founded an independent press, Dar Ishbiliya (Seville House),
which focuses on editions of well-known Andalusian texts and Arabic
translations of works on al-Andalus. He himself has cultivated a deep
personal interest and expertise in Andalusian science (especially agriculture) and literature; his vast collection includes many publications from
Moroccan, Algerian, Tunisian, and Spanish publishers. When I asked
about his deep interest in medieval Iberia, he suggested it was "natural"
(tabi'i) for him as a Syrian-Arab to feel this link because of his familial
connection to medieval Iberia. When I expressed surprise (masking a
certain amount of doubt) about this connection, he asserted that his ancestors originally came from the Arabian Peninsula, had settled in Syria
many centuries ago with the opening (fath) of Bilad al-Sham (Greater
Syria), then joined one of the various waves of immigrants to al-Andalus,
possibly settling in Ishbiliya (Seville). With the fall of that and other
cities, they had come home again to Syria, retracing in some ways the
route of the muwashshah genre itself, at least as it is portrayed in Syrian
discourse. The voyage of al-Andalus—the there and back again of the
Syrian idea of al-Andalus—was embodied in his personal history, even
if it started, as he claimed, "fifteen hundred years ago in the Hijaz."[7]

At the time I found it curious that a modern Syrian novelist would
trace his roots deeply in Arabian and Andalusian history. However, for
al-Siba'i, as for many others, these are intertwined stories, an Arabian-
Syrian-Andalusian nexus with great rhetorical power. Not long after this
discussion I could not help noting the curious presence in modern Syria
of the Andalusian past. For example, numerous restaurants, hotels, and
stores carry names related to al-Andalus. In Damascus I found Hotel
Granada, Córdoba Hotel, Seville Gifts, al-Andalus Sweets, al-Andalus
Hospital, and al-Andalus Coppersmith. In Aleppo there are al-Andalus
Street, an entire neighborhood named al-Andalus, and several estab-
lishments with names linked to al-Andalus: the al-Andalus Institute
for Languages and Computers, al-Andalus Elegance (a clothing store),
al-Andalus Bookstore, al-Andalus Hairdresser, and even al-Andalus
Chicken (though it probably referred more to the al-Andalus neighborhood than to the bird). I came across many other examples of the popular use of Andalusian referents in urban design and commerce, even a
village between Hama and Homs called Granada (Gharnata), as well

as statues to major Andalusian cultural figures, including one of 'Abd al-Rahman I (al-Dakhil), the founder of Umayyad Spain, erected on the occasion of the conference held in Damascus in 1986 called "Min al-Sham ila al-Andalus" (From Syria to al-Andalus).

On a trip in 2004, I attended an exhibition by the expatriate Syrian painter Sami Burhan entitled *Takriman lil-Andalus* (In honor of al-Andalus). Burhan (b. 1929) is among the foremost modern Arab artists and one of the first to incorporate the art of calligraphy and calligraphic design into the fine arts. He studied calligraphy at a young age, then trained in Aleppo, at the École des Beaux-Arts in Paris, and at the Academy of Fine Arts in Rome. He resides in Italy but comes to Syria for exhibitions and to visit family and friends. The show, held at Gallery al-Sayed, a spacious and well-lighted space for art that hosts exhibitions of local, regional, and international artists, consisted of a selection of Burhan's oils and watercolors using Arabic calligraphy to address Andalusian themes, among them *al-Andalus* and *Tulaytula* (Toledo).

Burhan escorted me around the gallery, pausing before selected works so he could explain them to me. Stopping before his painting *al-Hubb* (Love), he told me it came from reading Muhyi al-Din Ibn al-'Arabi's famous statement "adinu bi-din al-hubb" (I follow the religion of love)—today understood as a testament not only of faith but of nonsectarian tolerance and ecumenicism. He then explained that his work requires contemplation because it operates, like all art, at two levels: the apparent (*khariji*) and the interior (*batini*).[8] On the surface one sees a composition and may not understand it, Burhan intoned in his warm voice. Yet, by careful listening one can hear its "silent music," using a phrase with which the late Fateh Moudarres had explained his own very different works (Shannon 2006, 22).[9] I raised the connection of his work to Moudarres's and noted the similarities among Syrian painters of a certain generation. He corrected me to state that while his work is indeed Syrian because of his origin, it is also distinctly "Arab," even global. "Anyone can paint those portraits of Bab Touma or the old courtyard homes," he claimed, referring to the Orientalist-style paintings common in many commercial galleries.[10] "French, Italian, whatever. It makes no difference. But *my* work is unmistakably Arab, even in Italy, where I have lived for over forty years. Everyone recognizes my work as *Arab*. It has

Statue commemorating 'Abd al-Rahman I (al-Dakhil) for the conference "From Syria to al-Andalus," Damascus, 1986. *Photo credit: Faedah Totah*

Scripture 2. Sami Burhan, 1985. *Photo credit: Cimaglia and Alessandra Pedonesi* / Saudi Aramco World / SAWDIA

that mark of Arab identity [*huwiyya*] even if it participates in globalization [*'awlama*]" (personal communication, January 2004). When I asked about the link to al-Andalus, he told me that he began with the Ibn al-'Arabi quotation and then created works inspired by other Andalusian figures: Ibn Tufail, Wallada, and others.[11] "This is why the exhibition is called *In Honor of al-Andalus.* It's dedicated to the creative spirit of that golden age."

For both al-Siba'i and Burhan (close friends, it turns out), al-Andalus is a living presence, whether in Syria or in Italy, but it is first and foremost an Arab presence. Even when they draw on Islamic elements—al-Siba'i in his work on Islamic sciences in al-Andalus, Burhan in his inspiration by Ibn al-'Arabi and Sufi thought—their primary cultural orientation is Syrian-Arab. Al-Andalus is, for them as for so many others, a highpoint of Arab culture and an extension of the cultural developments first begun under the Syrian Umayyad Dynasty. Moreover, it is an access point for entry into the contemporary world, one characterized by the global circulation of forms, ideas, and media (Appadurai 1996). Al-Andalus for these older artists not only represented a past—their past—but reverberated with their understanding of Syrian-Arab society and culture, thereby linking personal biography with national social and political history.

The frequent evocations of al-Andalus and things and places Andalusian struck me as curious, because most cultural orientation in Syria is decidedly eastern: historically, Syria is more closely tied to other Levantine, Arabian, Ottoman, and Persian cultures than to the far West (al-Maghrib, including al-Andalus). More common than the Andalusian referents are those that evoke Syria's connection with the ancient pre-Islamic Syrian and Mesopotamian civilizations and the (Damascus-based) Umayyad period. Damascus features shops, streets, buildings, and statues evoking such literary figures as Abu Nuwas, al-Mutanabbi, and al-Ma'arri, as well as hospitals and pharmacies linked to the great Muslim scholars al-Razi and Ibn al-Haytham;[12] the latter also has a park named for him in the Syrian capital (and a popular restaurant for *fatteh,* a sort of chickpea and hummus stew).[13] The invocation of past glories also finds expression in the numerous references to the ancient Mesopotamian and Levantine civilizations: Sumerian, Babylonian, Aramaic,

Assyrian, Chaldean, Canaanite, and so on. I once saw an ad for a computer store that featured a desktop computer on a glass table reflecting cuneiform tablets, with the phrase "Building on the achievements of our forefathers" (see Shannon 2006, 25). Unlike in other Arab capitals, there are in Damascus very few references to European, North American, and other international place-names or concepts: the Versailles restaurant, Lina's Paris Cafe, Le Baron, Aroma, Butterfly, Casablanca, Piano Bar, Tao Bar, and the like (see Salamandra 2004). These various orientations—eastern, ancient, Andalusian, European, international—index Syria's civilizational depth and diverse heritage (*turath*). While al-Andalus is not the major reference point, it serves as an important metaphorical orientation, like these others, and moreover serves as an especially powerful link to Syria's Arab and Muslim heritage. Yet there is a subset of referents to the Andalusian past in the Syrian present. They constitute what I will call an Andalusian imaginative horizon (see Crapanzano 2003). What is Syria's connection to medieval Iberia? What might account for the development of this Andalusian imaginative horizon in Syrian popular culture?

Though separated from the Iberian Peninsula by the length of the Mediterranean, Syria has strong historical and cultural links to al-Andalus. It was the Umayyad prince 'Abd al-Rahman al-Dakhil, fleeing the massacre of his family at the hands of Abbasid usurpers, who established the first kingdom of al-Andalus, a sort of shadow caliphate designed and envisioned along the lines of the Umayyad Caliphate of Damascus (see Menocal 2002a). Not only were the rulers of the early Andalusian kingdoms Umayyad Syrians, but large numbers of Syrians made the voyage to al-Andalus at the time of the conquest and over the following centuries, seeking mercantile opportunities, knowledge, or political refuge (ironically, these are the same reasons modern Syrians find their way to Spain). Córdoba and its famous sites—the Mezquita mosque-cathedral and ruined Madinat al-Zahra—testify to the Umayyad presence in al-Andalus, one that modern Syrians understand as a distinctly "Syrian" presence.[14] The ties between modern Spain and modern Syria are complex and date to the 1950s, with the signing of treaties and cooperation and trade agreements between Spain and Syria, Lebanon and Jordan.[15] Spain is also home to a growing Syrian expatriate community alongside its vast Arab émigré communities, mainly in the province of Andalucía (chiefly Málaga and Marbella) but also in Madrid, Barcelona, and elsewhere.

One would think that, given its role in the contemporary public sphere, al-Andalus would have played an important role in earlier manifestations of Syrian nationalism, the Arab revival (*nahda*), and pan-Arab national thought. However, with few exceptions, al-Andalus, medieval Iberia, and Islamic Spain do not appear in the texts of early Arab nationalists (Khalidi et al. 1991).[16] My research through archives of newspapers and cultural magazines in Syria from 1900 to 1970 yielded very little related to these topics other than a handful of nostalgic travel memoirs and histories that reiterate the standard narrative.[17] In fact, even in popular Syrian literature there is scant mention of al-Andalus and its heritage until well into the 1970s. The Andalusian past has almost no presence in Syrian thought and cultural politics throughout the first two-thirds of the twentieth century. Older writers, teachers, and journalists confirmed my suspicion: of course, al-Andalus was known, and students for decades had memorized important Andalusian poems and knew the outlines of Andalusian history, but few people spent much time writing about al-Andalus as a cultural reference—as either a glorious past or a future model. Even Fadil al-Siba'i, an enthusiastic promoter of all things Andalusian, founded his Dar Ishbiliya publishing house only in 1987, even though he had been publishing stories since the late 1950s. The first conferences held in Syria on al-Andalus or Andalusian topics were held in the 1980s; the first symposium on the relations between Syria and al-Andalus was held in 1986.

Even if it seems to have played little role in the early formation of nationalist thought in Syria, the role of al-Andalus in contemporary Syria can only be understood in light of the vicissitudes of postindependence thought in Syria, for al-Andalus serves not only as a reminder of a golden age and lost paradise but also as a cultural standard for the modern era and even the future. The Arab and especially Umayyad dimensions of al-Andalus are key to understanding how it came to play a role in modern Syrian cultural politics and why it remains a powerful index or point of repair even today. Al-Andalus not only reminds Syrians of imagined past glories but serves as a potent tool for refashioning their understanding of modernity (see Shannon 2006). In this sense, al-Andalus, as an archive of memory (Taylor 2003) and as a living performance practice, is a powerful tool for self-criticism and by extension criticism of existing power structures. I illustrate this important move through a brief overview of Arab and Syrian nationalism to show how the idea of al-Andalus has been harnessed to promote new social forms, some tied implicitly and explicitly to pan-Arab (Ba'thist) ideologies, others to Islamist ideologies, and some to new forms of Arab identities. In the end, we need to understand the role of al-Andalus in Syria today as producing a form of what Adonis ([1985] 1992) described as "double-dependency"—on the modern West and on the Arab past (see also Shannon 2006, 77).

AL-ANDALUS IN SYRIAN NATIONALIST THOUGHT

Historians of Syria concur that Arab nationalism was essentially an oppositional movement tied to the decline of the Ottoman Empire, the advent of Turkish nationalism, and, to an extent, the rise of Zionism (Barakat 1993; Hinnebusch 2001; Hopwood 1988; Khoury 1983, 1987, 1991; Mufti 1996). Arab nationalism in its various incarnations sought to rally the Arab peoples under one flag based on historical, cultural, geographical, linguistic, and affective ties. The aim of such movements was partly to continue the nineteenth-century *nahda* project of cultural renaissance, reform, and renewal, as Barakat (1993, 161) argues, but it also served as a project whose aim was to consolidate the power of the traditional urban elites in eras of transitions. With the decline and fall of the Ottoman Empire and the advent of European (French) colonial rule (ca. 1920–1946), urban notable families, primarily in Damascus, sought means both to bolster their position with the new external power and to curry favor with an increasingly resentful population.[18] As Khoury writes, "Nationalism provided the kind of ideological cohesion and emotional appeal that urban leaders needed to be politically effective between the wars." For the urban notables, "nationalism never was a revolutionary idea with profound social content; rather it was an instrument to win French recognition without upsetting the status quo." The tenets of Arab nationalism in this early period remained relatively simple: glorifying the Arab past and appealing to the sentiments of peoples accustomed for centuries to the yoke of tyranny. In this context, the call for a unified Arab nation "was an attractive and compelling ideology" in the wake of the collapse of the Ottoman empire (Khoury 1991, 22; see also Khoury 1983, 1987).

The politician, writer, and historian Shakib Arslan (1869–1946) espoused a variety of Arab nationalism that some call "Islamic nationalism" (Cleveland 2011). Arslan believed that the best hopes for the Arab nation were to be found under the continued umbrella of the Ottoman Empire and under the leadership of a reformed vision of Islamic statecraft. Arslan penned an extensive history of al-Andalus, *al-Hulal al-sundusiyya fi al-akhbar wa al-athar al-andalusiyya* (The silk brocade garments in the annals and ruins of al-Andalus) (Arslān 1936). The subtitle claims that his work is "an Andalusian encyclopedia that covers all that has been written on that lost paradise," in this way drawing on earlier notions of al-Andalus as a lost paradise articulated by al-Maqqari and presaging later versions of this in the modern period. Arslan both was inspired by and collaborated with well-known Islamic reformers, including Jalal al-Din al-Afghani and Rashid Rida. For this reason, his text needs to be read parallel to his major work, *Why Did the Muslims Fall Behind and Others Progress* (Arslān 1975), as well as with the journal he edited, *La national arabe.*[19] The latter, despite its title, promoted an Islamically informed notion of Pan-Arabism in contrast to the secular nationalism that was developing in this same period and that would ultimately win out (see Haddad 2004; Kassab 2010, 29–31). Even if he advocated an "ideological complementarity" between Islamism and Arab nationalism (Haddad 2004, 110), in many ways the contradictions in Arslan's work also presage the continuing struggle between secular and Islamic forms of national and pannational solidarity that marked Syria's and the wider region's histories throughout the twentieth century and into the twenty-first century.[20]

In the turbulent decades after the decline of the Ottoman Empire, the energies of Arabism became harnessed to the project of forming and ruling a country that had not seen independence for many hundreds of years except briefly in 1920 under the Hashemite king Faysal (Khoury 1987, 35–36). Among the more important of these trends were the establishment of Antun Sa'ada's protofascist Syrian Socialist Nationalist Party in 1932 and the founding in 1947 of the Ba'th Party by Michel

'Aflaq and Salah al-Din Bitar (Hopwood 1988; Mufti 1996; Seale 1987). Both organizations advanced distinct visions of Arab unity: the former envisioned a "Greater Syria" based on geographic contiguity, while the latter promoted a grander vision of pan-Arab unity based on cultural ties and political aspirations; this is encapsulated in the Ba'thist motto, *Wahdah, hurriyah, ishtirakiyah* (Unity, freedom, socialism). With the establishment of the state of Israel in 1948, the idea of Pan-Arabism became intimately connected to anti-Zionism (and vice versa), as well as to political self-interest, as was the case in the many Syrian coups d'état in the 1950s (see Khalidi et al. 1991, 181; Mufti 1996, 48–50). According to Mufti (1996, 63), Pan-Arabism's golden age in Syria was ca. 1954–1964, a period that coincided with the growth of the state and its institutions; regional alliances, primarily with Iraq and later the ill-fated union with Egypt; and the continuing Palestinian quest for self-determination. This era ended with the Ba'thist coup in 1963 and their final ascent to power in 1970 with Hafez al-Asad. Under al-Asad, the idea of Pan-Arabism found a strong advocate in Damascus, partly as a response to the Palestinian problem, partly as a ruse to consolidate power by playing off adversaries under the guise of Arab unity.

This situation changed dramatically for Syrians in the 1960s and 1970s. If al-Andalus played little if any role in articulations of national aspirations in the early twentieth century, by the last third of the century it had become ubiquitous, so that by the time of my field research, the Andalusian past had a strong presence in contemporary Syria. Why might this be the case? What would account for the ideological role of al-Andalus in this late period of Syrian history? While we can trace Arab interest in al-Andalus as a golden age to writings from the early modern to late nineteenth and early twentieth centuries, in fact, it would appear that mid-twentieth-century political concerns couched in literary interventions account for the renewed interest in the Andalusian heritage not only as a sign of an Arab golden age but as inspiration for renewal in the present.[21] As Noorani (1999, 238) points out, in the work of many earlier travelogues, al-Andalus and its history provide a refuge from the ills of the present, one marked by British and French colonial oppression and societal decline. For later writers, the political context of nationalism was more important, and al-Andalus came to stand both as a chronotope of authenticity and as a foil against which to read the Arab present, even one "of colonialism, racism, sexism, political and intellectual repression, religious intolerance and militancy, class stratification and economic inequities that continue to plague the modern world" (Granara 2005, 60). According to William Granara, the type of nostalgia developed in these works is both restorative and reflective. That is, on the one hand, al-Andalus appears as a mythologized golden age devoid of controversy and contradiction, and on the other, it stands as a mirror reflecting an idealized if fragmented image of the homeland that blends a nostalgic view of the past with a lament for the present state (Granara 2005, 62). "Reflective nostalgics," writes Svetlana Boym, "see everywhere the imperfect mirror images of home and try to cohabit with doubles and ghosts" (2001, 251). The idea of al-Andalus played little role in early modern Syria because it had little in the way of value; it did little work. By the early 1960s, this changed, and al-Andalus came to serve as a useful rhetorical tool in modern Syria. We can account for this by reference to four factors: the influence of Syrian literature of the 1950s and 1960s, especially the poetry of Nizar Qabbani; the rise to power of the Ba'th Party and its aggressive pan-Arab ideology; the Palestinian problem, the loss of which resonates with the lost paradise of al-Andalus; and the rise of petrodollars in the Arabian Gulf, which funded the dream of a recovery of Andalusian glories. In this matrix of poetry, politics, and finance, al-Andalus came to represent not only a golden age of past valor but a model for present and future action. It was a nostalgia for the present moment (Jameson 2002).

AL-ANDALUS IN SYRIAN LITERATURE: NIZAR QABBANI AND SALMA AL-HAFFAR AL-KUZBARI

The rhetorical force of al-Andalus in modern Syria owes an enormous debt to the literary works of Nizar Qabbani and Salma al-Haffar al-Kuzbari, who set the stage for later developments in Syria of an Andalusian "imaginative horizon" (Crapanzano 2003) that structures how the past is understood and how the present and future are constructed. Like the writings of the poet Zaydan, Egyptian poet Ahmad Shawqi, Lebanese painter Moustafa Farroukh, and others, Qabbani's and al-Kuzbari's were facilitated by actual visits to Andalusian sites; later nostalgic writings

in Arabic are not limited to those with personal knowledge of the Andalusian sites. Like the earlier works as well, theirs were influenced by
the larger political context: not colonialism, however, but Pan-Arabism,
especially in light of the defeats in the Arab-Israeli wars. This allowed for
the sort of reflective nostalgia that Granara finds in the earlier works but
also a restorative and even "prospective nostalgia" for a future Andalusian utopia (a theme picked up in much post-9/11 writing). The immediate context was the gradual loss of Palestine (marked by the wars of 1948,
1967, and 1973), which resonated with an Arab population coming to
terms with the challenges of postcolonial state building. In this context,
the idea of al-Andalus as a golden age was "good to think" for the simple
reason that it allowed access to a glorious past (mythologized as such)
and promoted it as a basis for moving into the future.

Of the two authors, who were close friends, it was Qabbani who
would enjoy greater fame, though al-Kuzbari wrote of her experiences
first. Al-Kuzbari's novel 'Aynan min ishbiliyya (Two eyes from Seville,
1960) was based on her travels in Spain with her husband, the Syrian
ambassador to Spain in the 1960s. Al-Kuzbari, daughter of a former Syrian prime minister, and Qabbani, then working as cultural attaché at
the Syrian embassy, journeyed to Córdoba and Granada in May 1963, a
voyage that would result in the composition of some of Qabbani's more
important poems. Qabbani gathered the poems he composed during
his time in Spain in Al-Rasm bil-kalimat (Drawing with words, 1966).
Among his many works, it was his poem "Gharnata" (Granada) that has
had the greatest influence. Based on the May 1963 visit to the Alhambra,
"Granada" is a landmark poem, like Shawqi's "Siniyya" ode, "Granada"
echoes Syrian nationalist hopes and also posits a claim on modern Spain
through the medieval heritage, come to life in the form of the Syrian-
Arab past irrupting in the Spanish present: "For the Arab, Spain is an
unbearable historical anguish. Under each stone of hers sleeps a caliph,
and behind every wooden door of hers there peek two black eyes. In the
gurgling sounds of the water fountains in Córdoba's houses you can hear
a woman weeping for her knight who never returned. To visit Andalusia
is to travel in a forest of tears. Not once did I go to Granada and stay in
the Alhambra Hotel but I found Damascus sleeping with me on my Andalusian pillow" (Qabbānī [1983] 2000, 107, see also Alkhalil 2005, 189).

Qabbani's poem would become standard fare for Syrian schoolchildren from the 1960s onward (Alkhalil 2005, 204), and it struck a chord in a Syrian public highly attuned to poetry and deeply versed in the rhetoric of loss. As a result, the idea of al-Andalus as an Arab golden age began to circulate more frequently in the following years, and it continues to do so.[22] During this period Syrian society attempted to regroup after a number of serious challenges: losses in the Arab-Israeli conflict (despite seeing the October 1973 war as a "victory"), the rise of Islamism at home (and the resulting devastation visited upon the city of Hama in 1982), the achievement of economic stability (at the expense of commercial development and personal freedoms), and Syria's growing presence internationally (as a regional actor and in its emergence from the shadow of the ill-fated Soviet Union). The idea of a great Umayyad Arab past as a cultural referent for the present made sense for Ba'thists, and while Qabbani was far from being a Ba'thist ideologue, he was a committed Arab nationalist, and his works celebrated not only women and sensuality, as is well known, but also the beauty of Syria, especially of his native Damascus. There is a decidedly political tenor in much of his work of the post-1967 era. This is evident not only in his numerous works on Damascus, with their nostalgic remembrances, but in his decidedly political poems, such as *Hawamish 'ala daftar al-naksa* (Margins of the notebook of the setback, 1967). It was not a stretch for the poet of Damascus to become a poet of Córdoba and Granada through historical and, in his poetic imagination, contemporary aesthetic links. In light of the disastrous results for the Arabs of the Palestinian conflict, Qabbani's poetry drew on these historical ties to create a contemporary space in which al-Andalus was "good to think" for a population coming to terms with its place in the region and the world and with its own history.

Qabbani's and Kuzbari's works not only resonated with a modernizing, pan-Arab political project but found poignant echoes in the loss of Palestine. Indeed, the defeats in the Arab-Israeli conflicts—the Nakba (Catastrophe) of 1948 and the Naksa (Setback) of 1967, as well as the "victory" of 1973—reverberated strongly throughout the Arab world, and in Syria these losses were felt as a betrayal of trust. Many scholars have written of these wars as turning points in Arab society (al-'Azm [1968] 2011; Barakat 1993), and the issues faced by Palestinians (their suffering under occupation, their right of return, the recovery of their lands) and Syria's own cause (the return of the Golan Heights) have remained constant points of reference in contemporary Syrian cultural politics (culture and politics). Politically, until the outbreak of civil strife in 2011, Syrian politicians, especially the Ba'th Party, used the discourse of Palestinian rights and the hoped-for return of Palestine (or the establishment of a Palestinian state and the return of the Golan) as rallying points for Pan-Arabism, often cynically while oppressing their own people and doing little to advance the Palestinian cause. The Palestinian issue reverberates strongly with the metaphor of al-Andalus as a lost paradise. Modern Arabic literature abounds with references to the Palestinian issue that make direct and indirect reference to the loss of al-Andalus.[23] In addition, like Andalusian refugees in North Africa, Palestinians in Syria often maintain the deeds and even keys to their lost homes in Palestine. A few thousand kilometers away, in Morocco, I found that many Moroccans of Andalusian origin also claim to possess the keys to the homes they lost in the fall of al-Andalus. In both instances, there is a desire for return, a more immediate desire in Syria that bespeaks a restorative nostalgia, and a more rhetorical desire in Morocco that indicates a more reflective nostalgia. Palestine stands as a lost paradise for the Palestinian refugees in Syria, as elsewhere in the Palestinian diaspora, and also as a long-dreamed-of destination of return.[24]

But more than popular support for Pan-Arabism, Ba'thist ideologies, and pro-Palestinian sentiment, it was perhaps the influx of wealth from the oil-rich Arabian Gulf nations that funded the realization of what had previously been only dreams: the resettling of al-Andalus and its elevation to not only a lost paradise of past glory but a (utopian) vision of a future state of glory in the Arab world itself, a sort of new al-Andalus. If the 1970s saw the rapid growth in nation building in the Arabian Gulf (in particular the Gulf Cooperation Council [GCC] states), the 1980s witnessed investment of Arab wealth on an unparalleled scale around the world, including in Spain.[25] Arab investment in Spain was concentrated in trade goods, including Spanish arms (Segal 1991) and real estate, often, though not exclusively, in the province of Andalucía (the eponymous home of al-Andalus), where oligarchs and potentates, including shadowy characters such as Rifa'at al-Asad, exiled brother of the late dictator Hafez al-Asad and uncle to the current Syrian president, Bashar al-Asad, erected fabulous palaces and formed real-estate empires along the "Golden Mile" of Marbella. G C C money also financed the building of the Great Mosque of Granada (which opened in July 2003), the first mosque to open in Spain since the fall of Granada. At the same time, large numbers of Syrian intellectuals worked in the gulf as teachers, journalists, and businessmen, bringing the optimism of the new gulf economies to bear on critical questions of Arab identity.

In this mixture of petrodollars and cultural confidence, with a decidedly conservative and Islamic orientation, the idea of an old-new Andalusian was born, and we see the rise in a cottage industry of Andalusian-inspired projects, from the architectural to the cinematic to the musical. A conference held in Damascus in 1986 was called "Min al-Sham ila al-Andalus" (From Syria to al-Andalus), and from 1996 to 2010 the Instituto Cervantes in Damascus hosted a biannual international Andalusian music festival. The Jama'iyat al-'Adiyat (Archaeological Society) in Aleppo, directed for many years by Muhammad Qujjah, organized conferences on the Andalusian figures Ibn Hazm (2002) and Lisan al-Din Ibn al-Khatib (2003), among other events related to Andalusian history, often in coordination with the Instituto Cervantes in Damascus and the University of Aleppo.[26] The Arab-Andalusian links remain present in powerful ways, even when the associations between cities like Aleppo and Granada are ambiguous. Indeed, as the emcee for a Sabah Fakhri concert I attended in Aleppo in 1997 remarked, the city is the "jealous guardian of the Andalusian traditions," even though very few Aleppine families claim direct Andalusian ancestry.[27] In 2006 Aleppo was selected as a Capital of Islamic Culture.[28] Among the many conferences and events were those that treated the connections between al-Andalus and Aleppo, including the poetic and the musical; Muhammad Qadri Dalal, the celebrated Syrian musician and scholar, gave a lecture on Aleppo's religious song, whereas others spoke of the *muwashshah* and its role in Aleppo.[29] From the 1980s through the early twenty-first century, al-Andalus was in the air as an ever-present element in Syrian self-understanding both of its past and of its present and future orientations. As journalist Jean-Pierre Perrin argued in a critical appraisal of an exhibit at the Institut du Monde Arabe in Paris,

al-Andalus is no longer only in Andalucía.... And if contemporary
Andalucía does not feel particularly bereft of the Arab world..., it, however,
feels itself indeed to be an orphan of al-Andalus. Not only the intellectuals,
artists, and writers, those always haunted by this sacred and irretrievably
lost Atlantis, but also the common people of Cairo, Damascus, Marrakech,
and Baghdad, for al-Andalus is still in the collective unconscious of the Arab
peoples. For them, it was a golden age, so much so that they feel dispossessed
of it.... In Arab cities, al-Andalus is everywhere. (2001)[30]

AL-ANDALUS IN SYRIAN MUSIC: SOUNDING
A LOST PARADISE REGAINED

The links between the Andalusian past and the Syrian present and future were made clear to me by one of my music teachers in Aleppo. During a voice lesson when we were working on an "Andalusian" *muwashshah*, I asked him why Syrians celebrate al-Andalus when it was so far
removed in time and space.[31] He thought for a moment and then replied,
"al-Andalus was for us a golden age ['*asr dhahabi*], but it is also a source
of solace [*raha*] as well, especially in an era of political, economic, and
cultural decline [*tadahwur*]."[32] As for the music, he argued that it is essentially earlier Arabian song forms that underwent development in Spain
and then came back home to Syria after the fall of Granada. For him,
the music was at heart Arab music with an Andalusian flavor or tinge.[33]
Nonetheless, it not only sonically represented a past golden age but also
sounded a then-present situation of decline. In this narrative, which in
a way is shared by many but not all Syrian culture brokers, al-Andalus
appears as a kind of fantasy land—a resort where the Arabs lingered and
played for some eight hundred years before being tossed out.[34] Moreover,
in the Syrian collective memory, as expressed in popular and musical
evocations, al-Andalus serves as a symbol not only of Syrian-Arab political and cultural glory, whose loss they lament, but of a hoped-for progress and desire for a better future. It is important to stress here the political role of the idea of Syria in al-Andalus and, by extension, of al-Andalus
in Syria, since the connections speak not only to nostalgic memory of the
past but also to a critical engagement with the present and even a hoped-
for future (one not easily envisioned, given the current conflict). In other
words, nostalgic dwelling in preconflict Aleppo was a way of articulating
not only a vision of a lost paradise but also a politically charged program

for the recovery of that lost Syrian home in al-Andalus for the purposes of creating a better future. It was a prospective and reflective nostalgia, with a hint at what Boym (2001) has termed anticipatory nostalgia for what were the fleeting moments of possibility. In an Aleppo scarred by conflict and devastation, nostalgic dwelling has without a doubt assumed new meanings. As the well-known Andalusian *muwashshah* puts it, "Your delight was only a dream in sleep or drowsiness" (lam yakun wasluka illa huluman fil-kara aw khilsat il-mukhtalisi).[35] But more than a past dream, al-Andalus today stands as a testament to potential future development, a critical standpoint for assessing the present, and a guidepost for creating a new society, "for al-Andalus . . . reminds us of glories that were created by the great forefathers of a people looking for a place, indeed a margin, on a map-made complex."[36]

I turn now to analysis of the music itself. The musical genres called "Andalusian" in Syria have an ambiguous relationship both to the musics of medieval Iberia and to those musics called "Andalusian" in North Africa today. Whereas in Morocco musicians can demonstrate links between Moroccan Andalusian music (what is principally known as *al-ala*) and the practices of medieval and post-*partida* Iberia, Syrians cannot easily make the same claims. In fact, the musics called "Andalusian" in both contexts are in many ways different, even though they share fundamental structures and aesthetic orientations. My interest, however, is not to trace musical and poetic influences between Iberia and Syria, or to demonstrate the Arabness of Iberian music, or to prove that either the Syrian or the Moroccan is more authentically Andalusian or Arab but to understand the rhetorical and ideological uses of al-Andalus in modern Syrian music. In preconflict Syria, the use of the Andalusian appellation in music supported and "sounded" state ideologies of Pan-Arabism and also plays a role in the cultural politics of heritage production and consumption. Moreover, in what follows I demonstrate that the music called "Andalusian" in Syria, like its counterparts elsewhere, sounds out contradictions in these ideologies by reverberating with networks that transcend the limited scope of the Ba'thist state and echo pan-Islamic and even pan-Mediterranean cultural networks. "Andalusian" music in this way comes to serve as a vehicle for redeeming Syrian culture, first by sounding the cultural achievements of a purported golden age / lost paradise and then by serving as a model for a utopian vision for a post-Asad Syria. Hence, the Andalusian pasts in Syria are sounded as Andalusian futures. This is the work of al-Andalus in Syria.

The rhetorical uses of al-Andalus in modern Syria arose as the result of a confluence of political and cultural currents dating to the 1960s. The music called "Andalusian" also rides on these same currents and at the same time helps to energize them anew; in the language of M. H. Abrams (1953), the music is both a "mirror," reflecting the broader sociopolitical context, and a "lamp," illuminating the pathways of power and promoting change in cultural forms, not only reflecting them. Music engages with society in such a way that music sounds society's dynamics and contradictions. In many ways, performance of "Andalusian music" in Syria preceded the rise of interest in things Andalusian in literature, granting music, as numerous scholars have indicated, a certain primacy in the social analysis of political and economic formations (Attali [1977] 1985). The music highlights (even predicts) tensions and anxieties in society as a whole, so that we can turn to music to understand these deeper currents of change; for this very reason, cultural theorist Iain Chambers asserts that we need "not the sociology of music, but music as sociology" (2008, 47).

This section provides an overview of the music called "Andalusian" in Syria, especially the genre of *muwashshah,* and offers an interpretation of its rise and continued vitality as a performance and compositional genre as a result of the cultural politics explored above. Even where the links between Syria and al-Andalus are tenuous, stressing the Andalusian dimensions of the music allows it to be appropriated into the larger pan-Arab projects of the state. In this context the music plays an ambiguous role, serving at once as a soundtrack of Pan-Arabism via reference to the Andalusian golden age but also as a cautionary tale and reminder of contemporary Arab problems through the same reference to a lost paradise. The Andalusian *muwashshah* as performed in modern Syria (up to the era of the rebellion) thus served until recently, and may serve again, as a powerful critical tool for performing Arabness.

In Syria and the Levant in general, the performance of the Andalusian *muwashshah* is a staple of the traditional Arab musical suite known as the *wasla.*[37] In Syria these songs are known as *al-muwashshahat al-*

andalusiyya, or "Andalusian *muwashshahat,*" even though many if not most of them were composed not in medieval al-Andalus but in the Levant and Egypt in the previous two centuries.[38] The Andalusian appellation acknowledges these songs' probable origin, as well as the fact that many (though certainly not all) of the lyrics to the Andalusian *muwashshahat* performed in Syria are based in poetic texts first composed in al-Andalus between the tenth and fifteenth century. However, many of the song lyrics draw on texts by Levantine poets, from ancient to modern times, and Syrian artists today still compose new *muwashshahat,* unlike their counterparts in North Africa, where composition of new songs is considered inappropriate (see Shannon 2007b). For this reason, the *muwashshah* is better thought of as a living compositional form than as a fixed genre that cannot be altered or even composed in.

Melodically, Syrian *muwashshahat* are firmly rooted in the modal and rhythmic cycles of what in the twentieth century came to be called "Arab" music, although this music has much in common with Ottoman and Persian musical cultures (see Shannon 2006, 92–93; Touma 1996). In this regard, its musical structures are distinct from those utilized in North African Andalusian musics, though the relationship between them remains debated, and most listeners would hear a family relationship between them in terms of structure (they are suite based), tonality (modal), rhythm (complex), instruments, texts, and general aesthetic parameters, including the concept of *tarab* (see Shannon 2003a, 2003c, 2005, 2007b). Syrian ensembles that perform "Andalusian" *muwashshahat* utilize variations of the ensemble known as the *takht,* comprised of the *mutrib* (vocalist) accompanied by *oud* (Arabian lute), *qanun* (lap zither), *nay* (end-blown reed flute), *kamanja* (violin), and percussion instruments such as the *riqq* (tambourine) and *tabla* (goblet-shaped drum). Moroccan and other North African Andalusian ensembles utilize similar instruments but with significant variations. Some Aleppine writers claim that the musical structure of the Andalusian *muwashshahat* predates al-Andalus and has variously Arabian or even Syriac roots (Shannon 2003a); moreover, in this view the poetic forms, rather than arising in Iberia, coevolved in the *mashriq* and *maghrib* (Qalaʿhji 1988). At a minimum, this discourse claims that the musical and poetic structures, at heart Arabian, were refined in al-Andalus but after the fall came home again to Syria. This idea appears in some common retellings of the Ziryab legend that have the legendary progenitor of Andalusian music stopping in Syria (specifically in Aleppo) on his flight from Baghdad to Córdoba. The insertion of Aleppo into the standard Ziryab story promotes the rhetorical linkage of Aleppo to al-Andalus and establishes the city at the heart of the Andalusian saga. The incorporation of Syria into the Ziryab legend speaks volumes about how many Syrians see the Andalusian heritage: as essentially Arabian, as an extension of Syrian culture, and not as North African or Iberian. In some ways, the return voyage of modern Syrian artists to al-Andalus mimics the mythical voyage of Ziryab, which has become a standard trope for understanding not only the origins of Andalusian music but the pan-Arab connections between Iberia and Arabia.[39]

As in the narrative of Fadil Siba'i, the modified Ziryab legend was performed musically in Spain by two visiting Syrian artists. In 2001 'ud player Hussein Sabsaby performed at the opening event for the exhibition *The Splendor of the Córdoban Umayyads,* held in the ruins of Madinat al-Zahra.[40] The exhibition, which ran from June through September 2001, featured weekly concerts of musics of the "Three Cultures" and was attended by both the Syrian president and the Spanish king. Sabsaby described the performance as a collaboration between himself on 'ud and Spanish flamenco artists, both a guitarist and a vocalist, in order to demonstrate the links between Syrian-Arab music and Spanish flamenco. To his ears they were related, and in fact he went on to perform and record with a Syrian flamenco guitarist. This is no surprise, since Sabsaby was a student and devotee of the Iraqi 'ud master Munir Bashir (1930–1997), who produced a recording of solo 'ud improvisations entitled *Flamenco Roots* (1998; for more on these presumed associations, see also Leblon 1995; Noakes 1994).[41] In fact, the rhetoric of al-Andalus as essentially Syrian-Arab is performed musically in compositions, recordings, and concerts. Syrians commonly understand Spanish flamenco to derive from "their" music, and in fact whenever Arab music is mixed with popular and classical European musics, even when they are early music styles, many Syrians hear them as "flamenco." There have been a number of Syrian experiments that feature guitar and 'ud, or 'ud played in the style of "flamenco" guitar (loosely understood), meaning strumming and sometimes chordal playing not characteristic of traditional Arab-style *'ud* playing. For example, in 2006 Sabsaby recorded a CD with guitarist Tariq Salihiyya entitled *Hanin* (Longing). One of the tracks is "Min wahy al-Andalus" (Inspired by al-Andalus), which Sabsaby says he composed after he performed at *The Splendor of the Córdoban Umayyads* exhibition. Sabsaby's website describes "Min wahy al-Andalus" with reference to al-Andalus as a place of civilization, entertainment, and so on—the standard narrative.

Seven years later, the young female Syrian *'ud* player and singer Waed Bouhassoun performed in Granada on January 31, 2008, to open the "Damascus: Arab Capital of Culture" festivities.[42] In the presence of the Syrian first lady and the Spanish queen, Bouhassoun performed in one of the rooms of the fabled Alhambra; according to Spanish musician friends, this is an extremely rare opportunity. In addition to highlighting a talented young woman performer from Syria as a symbol of progress and openness, the festival also demonstrated the rhetorical ties between Syria and Spain. Even more pronounced than having a Syrian perform at the Cordoban Umayyad exhibit—since, after all, the Umayyad Dynasty in Iberia was of Syrian origins—the decision to open the festivities in Spain was remarkable. It literally inserted Damascus (and, by extension, Syria and the Arab world) into Spain at the heart of one of the most symbolically charged architectural spaces in the Mediterranean and Middle Eastern regions. Both the Sabsaby concert of 2001 and the Bouhassoun performance of 2008 confirmed the Syrian rhetoric of al-Andalus, namely, that the "original" and "authentic" Arab culture (metonymically associated with Umayyad culture) was the heart of the development of Andalusian culture. Bouhassoun literally sounded the close affective and rhetorical links between Syria and Spain with her *'ud*.

These are but two examples of the broader musical associations of Syria and al-Andalus. The Andalusian *muwashshahat* remained a staple of traditional performance practice in Syria throughout the twentieth century and into the twenty-first on the stage, in the Muslim rite of *dhikr* (Shannon 2006, 205), and in conservatories and private homes.[43] However, these "Andalusian" songs received scant attention in the first half of the twentieth century, just as al-Andalus was scarcely on the map for intellectuals and journalists: newspapers and cultural publications of the period focused on Western music or on the careers of rising stars like Umm Kulthum. However, by midcentury, as the Syrian nationalist rhetoric of al-Andalus began to develop, the radio stations of Aleppo and Damascus (established in the late 1940s) initially featured almost daily programming of Andalusian *muwashshahat,* usually a mix of Syrian, Egyptian, and occasionally even North African compositions, but the vast majority of songs were of then-contemporary pan-Arab musics. In fact, on-the-air programming of the "Andalusian" repertoire had faded by the mid-1950s as the Arab world entered what is widely considered the Golden Age of modern Arab song with the ascendancy of artists like Umm Kulthum, Asmahan, Muhammad 'Abd al-Wahab, and, a bit later, 'Abd al-Halim Hafez and many others. It is notable that Umm Kulthum only recorded two *muwashshahat* in her long career, and none after the 1930s, favoring modern genres such as the *taqtuqa, ughniyya, qasida,* and monologue (Danielson 1997; Shannon 2006).[44] At a time when Nizar Qabbani was visiting and eulogizing the ruins of al-Andalus, Andalusian or Andalusian-inspired songs found a brief home on the air before being sidetracked by modern songs.

However, even if they did not feature as prominently on radio broadcasts, the *muwashshahat* would not die out. On and off the air, by the late 1960s and 1970s a new generation of performers and composers would take up the *muwashshah,* giving it renewed life. During this period a number of private and later public music conservatories were established in Syria in which the Andalusian repertoire formed the core of the musical pedagogy (though, tellingly, most Syrian music schools have focused on European classical music). In an interview, Saadallah Agha al-Qalaa, a professor of engineering and computer science at the University of Damascus, former minister of tourism (2001–2011), and a respected musicologist and performer on the *qanun,* mentioned that his father, Fu'ad al-Raja'i, founded the first conservatory in Aleppo in the 1950s. Although an established dentist, Raja'i also composed *muwashshahat,* and the genre was incorporated into the curriculum as one of the bases for vocal and instrumental instruction.[45] In the same era, Syrian scholars and composers had turned their attention to documenting the form (perhaps as a result of anxiety over its possible loss), producing songbooks and studies of the *muwashshahat* and other genres of music in Syria (see, e.g., Rajā'ī and al-Darwīsh 1956). Still others began to compose new *muwashshahat* (something alien to the Moroccan Andalusian tradition), and in fact some of the staples of the *muwashshah* repertoire were composed in the 1960s by such Syrian composers as Majdi al-'Aqili (1917–1983); interestingly, al-'Aqili's aim was to recapture the Andalusian essence of the *muwashshah* in Syria by composing melodies that more closely matched the poetic meter than is often the case with earlier *muwashshahat*.[46] Prominent Syrian artists like Sabah Fakhri formed their entire careers around the *muwashshah,* whereas in Egypt, for example, *muwashshahat* almost died out or remained ensconced in the conservatories as part of a (largely dead) heritage. As a result, today the Andalusian genres remain at the heart of what most Syrians would recognize as their classical music more than in any other Arab country. Moreover, the ability to perform and even compose *muwashshahat* is a marker of authenticity, that is, of Syrian-Arab identity (see Shannon 2006). The numerous contemporary compositions (even in a time of war) and the continuous performance of the *muwashshahat* as a staple of musical practice and training in Syria indicate the continued relevance of this genre for Syrian musical self-understanding.

The Syrian-Andalusian connections do not exist only in those older compositions. They are performed, as I have noted, in public architecture, popular culture, and musical events, from private listening sessions to background music in hotels and restaurants, to private and public concerts. As noted earlier, from 1996 to 2010 the Instituto Cervantes of Damascus and the Spanish Embassy in Syria sponsored a biannual festival of Arab-Andalusian music. The performance by the Spanish ensemble at the Khan As'ad Pasha in Damascus in 1998, while engaging and somehow close to being Arab, was understood by my Syrian musician friends as essentially European. For these expert listeners it didn't evince enough "Oriental spirit" (*ruh sharqiyya*) to qualify as "Arab" and hence was unable to elicit the emotional reactions known as *tarab* that are typical of "authentic" Arab music in the Levant (see Racy 2004; Shannon 2006). Even though the lead vocalist sang a song in Arabic and the artists performed on many standard Arabian instruments, the music was heard at best as a pleasant, well-executed, and interesting performance but at worst as an example of "contaminated" (*hajin*) music that was in fact closer to what they understood to be "flamenco" than to "Arab" music.

In November 2000 the fourth Andalusian music festival was held in a number of Syrian cities and also celebrated the shared legacy of al-Andalus between Syria and Spain. A Syrian newspaper reported the event as follows:

> Two Syrian cities (Damascus and Aleppo) will [host] four Andalusian nights in which ancient music and songs from the days of the Moors in Spain will be presented.... The Syrian-Moroccan-Spanish connection of this cultural festival is evident: the Umayyad Dynasty based in Damascus established the Umayyad rule in Andalusia, and Aleppo, capital of the North, became the bearer of the artistic traditions of this glorious past. Morocco became a refuge to the thousands of Spanish Muslims (Moors) who fled the Spanish Inquisition after the Spanish reconquest of Andalusia. Thus, musical traditions of Andalusia were preserved throughout the centuries. Three [ensembles] from Aleppo, Morocco, and Spain will perform in this festival, using period instruments and authentic styles.[47]

Note the recourse to the Syrian-Andalusian connection via the history of the establishment of an exilic Umayyad Dynasty in Córdoba (and, by inference, the Ziryab tale as a musical and historical link) and the implicit assumption of a static, mythological temporality linking modern Syria to medieval al-Andalus to support the claims to musical authenticity. Another local newspaper ended its announcement of the same festival with these words: "Ensembles from Spain, Morocco, and Syria will present medieval music and songs [tawashih] from the Syrian, North African, and Spanish Andalusia regions from the tenth century. This will emphasize the common cultural heritage between these regions and bring back to memory the glorious past of the Arabs in Spain."[48]

These announcements make reference to the notion of a shared history; to the recovery, performance, and thus preservation of a shared heritage; and, significantly, to the memory of "the glorious past of the Arabs in Spain." The cultural referent is Arab, even when the musical thread weaves from Syria to Morocco to Spain and back again. Similar sentiments were expressed in the brochures and reports on the fifth and sixth festivals (which I did not attend), as well as in the above-mentioned conferences and roundtable discussions hosted by the Archaeological

Society in Aleppo. Al-Andalus lives on in Syria, in its music and social memory, even when—or especially when—those memories are imagined, producing what Boym calls ersatz nostalgia: nostalgia for places and events that one has never experienced.

THE RHETORIC OF AL-ANDALUS AND
THE STRUGGLE FOR THE PRESENT

The Syrian culture of memory that these various histories and events evoke is based in the notion of a glorious but lost past combined with an impatience with a desultory present and aspirations for refound glory in the future. Memory of al-Andalus as representative of Arab glories (with no reference to the contributions of non-Arabs or to the intervening five centuries since the fall of Granada) serves as a touchstone for these sorts of imaginings—past oriented, but with an eye toward the future.[49] The interplay of Syria in al-Andalus and al-Andalus in Syria must be understood as an expression of late twentieth-century anxieties over the Syrian and Arab nation in which the rhetoric of a shared cultural essence is deployed on both popular and official fronts to promote the idea of Syria as home to Arab aspirations. At the same time, this rhetoric supports reflective and even restorative nostalgias as a tool of autocritique. The evocation of a lost paradise and golden age must be understood, I am arguing, as a metacommentary on Syrian and Arab society. By the late twentieth and early twenty-first century, even before the onset of the current conflict, Syrian society was in a deep crisis of political legitimacy, let alone economic stagnation. The rhetoric of al-Andalus as a golden age of progress illuminates the contradictions of what the poet Adonis ([1985] 1992) termed the Arabs' "double dependency"—simultaneously on their glorified and mythologized past and on Western modernity for any sense of progress into the future. It is a danger to invest too heavily in either, for the risk is that a double dependency turns into a double loss of both the past and the future.

For musicians as for intellectuals, writers, and other culture brokers, al-Andalus remains a living presence, but it is first and foremost an *Arab* presence. In its cheapest forms, as in commoditized products (e.g., al-Hamra' cigarettes) and in the Syrian version of the standard narrative of al-Andalus, it reads like a Syrian version of *My Big Fat Greek Wedding*

(2002): everything good in the world has a Syrian-Arab origin, whether flamenco, frilly dresses, or *pasta fagioli* (to extend a culinary metaphor). Even when drawing on Islamic elements, such as in al-Siba'i's work on Andalusian sciences or musical evocations of Islamic mysticism, the primary cultural orientation tends to be Syrian-Arab, not pan-Islamic. Al-Andalus is, for these artists as for so many others, a high point of *Arab* culture and an extension of the cultural developments first begun under the Syrian Umayyad Dynasty. Even today, in crisis-ridden Syria, the Andalusian referents reverberate strongly, both in their Arab and in their Islamic dimensions.[50]

In these examples, we see the importance for the contemporary Syrian culture of memory of the collapse of temporalities into a singular mythic time where the tenth and twentieth centuries are experienced to some degree as simultaneous. To borrow from Mircea Eliade ([1954] 1971), the *tempus* of everyday life is infused with the aura of the *eternus* or is even collapsed into it.[51] Unlike the "homogeneous, empty time" of the modern nation (Anderson [1983] 1991, 26), these contemporary Syrian artists and intellectuals interested in heritage live in a world of simultaneous and often contradictory temporalities: homogeneous, empty time is certainly one of them, but also, among others, the eternity of the Quran; the cyclical time of origin, journey, and return; prophetic time; and oscillating time (as in Gellner's [1983, 1–85] "flux and reflux" model of social change, derived from the fourteenth-century Andalusian scholar Ibn Khaldun). Syrian modernity is fashioned through its multifaceted popular culture, which evokes and instantiates some of these heterogeneous and even discordant temporalities, anchored in shifting spatial referents: sometimes Greater Syria, sometimes al-Andalus, and often a mixture of Syria in al-Andalus, and vice versa; we might call these shifting temporal-spatial complexes, reading Michel Foucault through Mikhail Bakhtin, "heterochronologies."[52]

Al-Andalus came to play a larger role in the imaginings of the Syrian nation only when the larger forces of social and political integration were active, so that the rhetoric of al-Andalus was also a rhetoric of the Syrian nation seeking to understand itself. Literary and musical interventions played an important role in sparking these developments. Today, in the context of great dislocation, destruction, and unfathomable pain and suffering, al-Andalus may come to play another role in Syria: not only as a symbol of Syrian (Arab/Umayyad/Sunni) achievement but also as a hoped-for future redemption, as a time-space for dreaming, perchance for healing. Pre-conflict Syria now appears as a sort of golden age, and the recent rise of often ersatz nostalgic remembrance of the past along with sometimes violent programs for the renewal and reimagining of the Syria of tomorrow has created a situation in which the older rhetoric of al-Andalus may yet come to assume new valence. Any future role for al-Andalus in imaginings of a new Syria will likely revolve around long-standing tensions over the nature of Arab society and political legitimacy, and the role of Islam or any other ideological system in providing that basis. Given the current state of affairs, it likely that, should al-Andalus return to the Syrian stage, its Islamic aspects will be emphasized more than its Arab-Umayyad dimensions. In fact, this has already been the case in the rhetoric of Islamist groups in Syria, including al-Qaeda and the now powerful Islamic State (IS); as I discuss in the conclusion to this work, these and other groups draw on the rhetoric of reclaiming al-Andalus for Muslims via jihad to advance their political projects. In time, however, the rhetoric of al-Andalus, so closely tied to Arabism and to a broad understanding of community, may offer a way to reimagine the Syria of tomorrow as, to again borrow from Menocal (2000a), a "first-rate place."

THREE

The Rhetoric of al-Andalus in Morocco

Genealogical Imagination and Authenticity

OVERTURE: AL-ANDALUS IN MOROCCO

The sun has just begun to set when I hop out of my taxi and make my way past the barricades into the lobby of the Jnan Palace, a swank hotel in an elite neighborhood of Fez. The Fez Festival of Andalusian Music is about to begin, and I am characteristically a little late. I meet one of the organizers in the lobby. He presents me with my complimentary tickets and says as I rush past, "Don't worry! It hasn't started yet!" The lobby has an exhibit of musical instruments, books, photographs, and other memorabilia of Morocco's Andalusian music, so I stop to have a look. Strolling around, I run into a number of performers, aficionados, and scholars of the music who have come to be my friends, teachers, and primary interlocutors in my research in Morocco. In a way, I feel at home among them and look forward to the concert. I've forgotten my camera and recorder at the hotel and only have a small notebook with me. No matter; it means I can focus more on the event and less on the technology. I want to enjoy the music and not just analyze it.

By now, the spring of 2009, I've come to know many of the ensemble leaders and can perform songs from several of the suites. After touring the exhibit, I walk into the main hall as the concert prepares to start. The hall is enormous, easily holding a few thousand people, and it is already chock-full: young and old, men and women, mostly well dressed and relatively well heeled. I stand in the back with ʻAbd al-Malik al-Shami, a well-known aficionado (*muluʻ*) of the music and a professor of Andalusian literature at the University of Fez. The evening's program is dedicated to the memory of the founders of one of the main schools of Andalusian music: ʻUmar al-Jaʻidi and his son Muhammad of Rabat. After some opening remarks, the Orchestre at-Tarab al-Asil of Rabat, under the direction of al-Hajj Mohammed Zaki, take the stage. They are dressed in the typical costume of Andalusian musicians in Morocco: white or cream-colored robes (*jellaba*-s) topped by a red "fez" or *tarboush* hat with a black tassel, and grounded by yellow, open-heel slippers (*bilgha*).[1] The ensemble consists of some fifteen musicians performing on the standard Arabian lute (*ʻud*), violin, viola, cello, and the Moroccan two-stringed fiddle called a *rabab*; two percussionists on *tarr* (tambourine) and *darbukka* drums; plus solo vocalists. They proceed to perform the rhythmic movement *darj* of the suite *Hijaz al-kabir*. The performance lasts about thirty minutes, and the audience, after a short period of warming up, reacts enthusiastically. My companion in the back of the hall sings along to several songs before excusing himself to visit with other friends. Others come and join me for periods of time before heading off to greet other friends. It is a typical festival performance: well packaged and presented, convivial and even at times boisterous, and at the same time self-contained, even controlled.

After the first set and a short interlude, the Orchestre al-Asala of Meknes, led by Muhammad Warithi (Ouariti), comes onstage to conclude the evening. While they perform the movement *basit* from the suite *Isbihan*, I join my friend the performer and scholar ʻAbd al-Fattah Benmusa in the lobby to discuss his recent publications on Moroccan Andalusian music, as well as to discuss my participation in a scholarly colloquium that will be held in two days' time. Another friend, Mounir Sefrioui, an architect and well-known *ala* enthusiast, comes over and bemoans the fact that young people are not interested in the music anymore; he aims to fix this by "livening up" the music, making it more relevant to Moroccan youth.[2] I look at my watch. It is nearly midnight, and I worry about not being able to find a taxi back to my hotel, so I take my leave. There are three days and nine more concerts to go. Plenty of time to do some work.

Fourteenth Annual Fez Festival of Andalusian Music, Fez, 2009.

On the way home I glance through the program. In addition to list-ing ensembles from a variety of cities—from Rabat and Meknes to Fez, Tangier, and Safi—the program describes the two ensembles that per-formed that evening using the word *asil*, meaning "authentic." There is a sense that this festival is about the presentation, study, and preserva-tion of *authentic* Andalusian music through the musical performances, the exhibition, and the scholarly colloquium. Ten days later I find my-self attending another festival of Andalusian music, this time in Tét-ouan, where the emcee announces with conviction, "The music we are hearing tonight is the same music that the caliph of Córdoba heard in his palace!" I am struck by the ideological packaging of the festival, which emphasizes the "five-century history" of Andalusian music in Morocco. As in Syria, the Moroccan organizers and performers go to great lengths to stress the authenticity of their musical traditions, and the perform-ers of Andalusian music in Morocco seem intimately tied to collective memory making.

THE RHETORIC OF AL-ANDALUS IN MOROCCO: THE GENEALOGICAL IMAGINATION

If in Syria the rhetoric of al-Andalus promotes a set of postcolonial pan-Arab identities, in Morocco it occupies a different place in the public imaginary at once more historically grounded in a genealogical imagination and more closely associated with the Moroccan nation.[3] In other words, al-Andalus does a different sort of work in Morocco's cultural and political spheres. Morocco's Andalusian music, usually called *al-ala,* sonically connects Moroccans to medieval Iberia, echoing shared histories and genealogies that tie them directly to Europe and European culture. Unlike Syrian Andalusian imaginaries, the Moroccan Andalusian orientations are primarily North–South, not East–West, tracing the interactions of Moroccan, other North African, and Iberian populations and culture across the Mediterranean. Andalusian culture in Morocco also has strong associations with the cultural elite and especially with the monarchy, which draws on the Andalusian legacy in many ways to bolster its legitimacy. Finally, Andalusian culture in Morocco engages in interesting and complex ways with Morocco's Islamic heritage. In this way, al-Andalus engages "regimes of value" (Appadurai 1986a, 15) having different cultural valences from what is performed and consumed in Syria and enjoys a different rhetorical force in Moroccan society.

How and why is al-Andalus relevant in Morocco today? What role does al-Andalus play in modern Moroccan social, cultural, and political consciousness? What is the rhetorical force and value of the Andalusian legacy in Morocco, and how is cultural authenticity constructed and performed musically in Morocco? The rhetoric of al-Andalus plays an important role in the articulation of modern Moroccan national identities. Morocco's Andalusian music is a social institution with links to a wide array of centers of power and authority (state, religion, ethnicity, commerce). It exercises a strong rhetorical force in contemporary Moroccan cultural politics not only because of the links—actual and affective—between Morocco and medieval Spain but because of the operations of a genealogical imagination that continues to inscribe al-Andalus into Moroccan society. Al-Andalus therefore serves as an important leg sustaining the project of a modern Morocco because of its links to a prestigious past, a refined high culture, and a hoped-for (utopian) future. The affective and historical ties to al-Andalus are performed in Morocco's Andalusian music, which serves both as a sonic link to an idealized and prestigious past (as in Syria) and as a vital component of contemporary cultural politics that trade in the currency of a reflective nostalgia. Moreover, nostalgic dwelling in Morocco occurs principally through the framework of festivals. Indeed, as extensions of colonial and early nationalist cultural politics of heritage curation, the recent "festivalization" of Moroccan culture grants Andalusian music additional social and cultural currency and allows it to perform this role as an especially powerful sonic emblem of the nation.[4] In this way, contemporary Andalusian music in Morocco performs a dwelling in nostalgia that is very much directed at the present moment.

The story of al-Andalus runs parallel in many ways with the story of Morocco. It is significant for the purposes of my argument that the project of al-Andalus began in and for many centuries included what is now Morocco, for instance, Marrakech as the capital of the Almohad and Almoravid Dynasties, which ruled Morocco and al-Andalus from the tenth to the twelfth century. The traveler will note the similarity in the architecture of the minaret of the Kutubiyya Mosque in Marrakech, the Tour Hassan minaret in Rabat, and the bell tower of Seville's Giralda, all dating to the time of Almohad rule in al-Andalus (ca. 1121–1269). More importantly, the flow of peoples, ideas, and practices across the Strait of Gibraltar was continuous throughout this period and into the post-*partida* eras, so that we can think of North Africa and Iberia as, to borrow from Fernand Braudel (1972, 117, 164), a cultural and a political and geographical "bi-continent." The connections between the North African and Iberian sides of the strait, what were called the *'udwatan,* or "two banks," of al-Andalus, continued throughout the history of al-Andalus.[5] With the successive fall of Andalusian city-states and the flight of many thousands of refugees and immigrants to North Africa, the cultural ties between Iberia and the North African littoral even strengthened as these populations settled in areas already inhabited by Andalusian refugees from earlier migrations or established new neighborhoods and even cities upon their arrival.

While the history of the period 1500–1850 is beyond the scope of this text, it is important for our purposes to note the close association in this period between the collapse of Muslim authority in al-Andalus and the settling of Andalusian refugees in North Africa, on the one hand, and the rise of a unifying central Moroccan authority (what Moroccans term the *makhzen* versus the areas not under central control, *bilad al-siba*), on the other. The expansion of European imperial power along the Atlantic and Mediterranean coasts of Morocco, what was formerly called the Barbary Coast, played an important role in the shifting of power from sea-based pirate republics to land-based empires that in later decades set the conditions for the development of Moroccan national identity.[6] Not surprisingly, this period is also often considered to be one of decline and decadence in Andalusian music (see, e.g., Guettat 2000), though recent scholarship has shown that, in the almost total absence of documentary evidence of musical life from this period, the idea of cultural decline is most likely an extension of the common trope of civilizational rise and fall and of Great Man theories of historical agency, both of which form the core of the standard narrative of al-Andalus (for more on this, see Davila 2013). It is also, perhaps tellingly, during this period that the music today known as Andalusian assumed important Moroccan dimensions that would distinguish it from its sister musical cultures across North Africa.

The story of al-Andalus as a component of Moroccan national identity began to coalesce in the twentieth century in the context of colonial administration, anticolonial resistance movements, and nationalist political programs. Despite the relative lack of scholarship on nationalism and the nationalist movements in Morocco, scholars concur that, despite the diversity of a population differentiated by significant divergences of ethnicity, class, and region, Moroccans cultivated through the first half of the twentieth century a strong sense of national belonging.[7] Earlier colonial-era commentators on Morocco argued that the ethnic polarization of Moroccan society into Arab and Berber (itself an artifact of colonial governance) and the tensions between urban and rural populations (often mapped onto the ethnic divisions) prevented the growth of nationalist sentiment in Morocco.[8] However, more recent reappraisals reveal an important strand in Moroccan nationalism tied directly to anticolonial sentiment and to regional and international liberation movements. According to both Abdallah Laroui (1977) and Muhammad 'Abid al-Jabri (1988), the vitality of Moroccan nationalism drew to a large degree on a sense of Moroccan membership in pan-Arab and pan-Islamic communities, especially in the wake of post–World War II decolonization movements across North Africa and the Middle East, the rise of strong pan-Arabist leaders in Egypt and Syria, and, later, close identification with the Palestinian cause. These two poles, the pan-Arab and the pan-Islamic, continue to play out in contemporary national politics.

Colonial-era documents and postcolonial events suggest that the rhetoric of al-Andalus played an important role in the formation of a Moroccan national identity. Many of the nationalist leaders came from Fez, which was until midcentury the intellectual, political, mercantile, and spiritual capital of Morocco. Of these, some claimed genealogical connections to al-Andalus, as many of my interlocutors noted and as verified in registries of Andalusian *ansab* (patronymics): these include such names as Bennouna, al-Fasi, al-Kattani, and al-Wazani, among many others (see al-Kattānī 2002). The association of Andalusian families with Moroccan nationalist movements hence reinforces the elite connotations of this identity. The formative role of Andalusians in the Moroccan nation is even recognized in the 2011 revision to the Moroccan constitution, whose preamble states that Morocco's national unity and territorial integrity are "forged by the convergence of Arab-Islamic, Amazigh [Berber] and Saharan-Hassani components and enriched by 'African, Andalusian, Mediterranean and Hebrew' heritage" (Madani, Maghraoui, and Zerhouni 2012, 18). The Andalusian heritage, then, is an important part of what it means to be Moroccan today.

Who are the Andalusians of Morocco? The term *Andalusian* has multiple referents in contemporary Morocco. First and foremost, it refers to the refugees from post-*partida* Iberia who settled in or even founded cities such as Tétouan, Chefchaouen, Tangier, Fez, Rabat, and Salé, among others. These cities have strong connections historically to medieval Iberia, and in fact whole neighborhoods of Fez and Rabat, both traditional and modern, are associated with al-Andalus and Andalusians. Andalusian also refers to their culture, including music but also cuisine, dress, architecture, and even language (Bahrami 1995). Some Moroccan elites have gone so far as to remodel their large villas based on the architecture of al-Andalus, especially the Alhambra of Granada, while still others acquire (by various means) the interior decorative elements of Fasi palaces and relocate them to their modern villas in Casablanca: doors and fountains but also entire wooden ceilings and even panels of *zellij* mosaic tiles. Because the Andalusis tend to reside in similar neighborhoods (often called al-Andalus, as in Fez) and have a shared set of cultural practices and values, Beebe Bahrami (1995) has argued that "Andalusian" in Morocco is a quasi-ethnic identity distinct from "Arab," "Berber," and other ethnicities in Morocco.[9] In contemporary Morocco, the label "Andalusian" thus refers to specific geographical places (neighborhoods), populations (a quasi-ethnic group associated with elite culture), and a culture (or set of practices and styles thought to derive in some ways from medieval Iberia, including music, cuisine, architecture, dress, and language). It is the pluripotentiality and polysemous nature of the Andalusian label that affords it such power to symbolize at once a discrete and elite class segment of the Moroccan population, a set of musical and cultural practices, and an ideal—indeed, an idea—linked to a strong rhetoric.

Numerous individuals in Fez and Rabat extolled their Andalusian origins to me and claimed that this explained their "natural" affinity to the Andalusian musical repertoire. Others uncertain of their ancestry nonetheless made claims to an Andalusian background in the hopes of gaining some of the prestige that it affords. For example, in 2004 a man showed me the deed to his grandfather's home in Fez, which was located in the "al-Andalus" neighborhood of the *medina,* or old city; to him this was proof enough that he had Andalusian ancestry, even though the grandfather had settled there from elsewhere and the house was not very ancient by Fasi standards. A number of musicians in Fez claimed Andalusian ancestry, hoping that by asserting a genealogical link to al-Andalus they might be granted more authority and authenticity in their performances than non-Andalusians. Sometimes even an association with Fez was enough to bolster the claim of prestige ancestry; a brief biography of Muhammad Briouel on the back cover of his book of notations (Briouel 1985), for example, notes that he is from "near Fez." Like Aleppo for Syria, Fez emanates tradition and authenticity like almost no other place in Morocco.

One way the Andalusians of Morocco assert ties to Iberia is through a genealogical imagination that posits direct links between present families and their medieval antecedents. Indeed, many Moroccan families can trace their heritage directly to Andalusian families in Spain, and some carry patronymics that indicate this closely: for example, one study (Daoud 2004) lists over one hundred names of Tétouani families of Spanish Andalusian origin, from al-Andalusi, Cortobí, and Garnatí to Ramos, Salas, Vargas (Bargach), and Torres. Another (Hakim 1988) claims that of 365 original families of Andalusian origin, 107 families remain in Tétouan.[10] In many instances, the Spanish equivalents are clear. Other families, including al-'Attar, Del-Lero, and Seffar, among others, also claim direct ancestry to Andalusian families. Such associations are not limited to Tétouan but can be found in Tangier, Chefchaouen, Fez, Rabat, Oudja, and, with recent migrations, Casablanca, among other Moroccan cities. The persistence of this identity in Morocco can be attributed, according to Bahrami (1995), to four principal features of the Andalusians in Morocco: first, the standard narrative of al-Andalus retains cultural value today, allowing Andalusians to maintain their distinction; second, social practices such as Andalusian endogamy reinforce continuity among Andalusians in Morocco; third, the multiple connotations of the Andalusian identity in Morocco allow it to adapt to new social and cultural conditions; and finally, non-Andalusian Moroccans value the Andalusian heritage, so Moroccan Andalusians have acquired greater cultural capital than their numbers would indicate.

A related means by which Andalusians (and no doubt many non-Andalusians) rhetorically assert their ties to medieval al-Andalus is through the trope of keys to their former homes. On many occasions Moroccans mentioned that they or families they know of maintained keys to their ancestral homes in Spain. Some even claimed to have seen these keys and to bring them out annually as part of a rite of memory. Like Syrians and Palestinians reflecting on or even bemoaning the lost paradises of al-Andalus and Palestine, some Moroccan musicians refer to al-Andalus as a lost homeland. For example, in the liner notes to his CD *La clef de Grenade* (The key to Granada) (2001), the Moroccan *'ud* player Said Chraibi states, "Once a year, in Shaouen, my Andalusian grandfather used to take out the key of the house in Granada and weep. We left Andalusia a hundred years after 1492."[11] I heard similar claims many times in Fez and Rabat. Once, while visiting a (non-Andalusian) musician friend, I noted some old keys hanging on the living-room wall of his home on the coast near Tangier, tellingly called Dos Orillas (Two Banks). When I mentioned the keys and asked, only partly in jest, if they were to his ancestral home in Spain, he laughed and said, "No, they are just keys! Décor!" The use of actual or imaginary keys to claim a stake to ancestral homes (and homelands) is similar to the Palestinian discourse and practice of maintaining keys and land deeds to homes in occupied territories in the Golan and Palestine; indeed, many Palestinian refugees in Syria, Lebanon, and Jordan maintain these deeds and keys framed and mounted in their homes (see Slyomovics 1998). For this reason, there is often a strong resonance between the loss of al-Andalus and the loss of Palestine in the performance of Andalusian musics in Syria. The rhetoric of loss is not limited to Moroccan Muslim Andalusis or Palestinians, since some Sephardic Jews also claim to maintain keys to their former homes in al-Andalus (in Hebrew, Ha-Sepharad). I once spotted a compilation of Spanish Sephardic songs that featured an old key on the album cover. Finally, like the prayer concluding many a Passover seder, "Next year in Jerusalem," some older Rabati Andalusians finish their prayers with the words: "May God take back our lost paradise" (Bahrami 1995, 74), referring to al-Andalus, not Jerusalem.[12]

The key, of course, symbolizes a number of things in addition to the actual tool for opening a door lock. Keys are metaphors for memory, for disclosure of secrets and mysteries, and they are potent symbols as well of tradition and stability, for that which is undisclosed and hidden remains so to those who do not possess the keys to discovering it. The old key metonymically represents a shared discourse of loss, memory, and nostalgia. I return to this point below in the explication of the ways Andalusian music in Morocco helps to perform the nation via the construction of a "tradition" (an Andalusian heritage) that, door-like, offers access to the primary bases of cultural authority in the nation: Islam, the monarchy, and elite power brokers.

*Andalusian Music and Performance in
Morocco: Al-Ala in Performance*

In what follows, I provide an overview of the musical system of the Moroccan Andalusian music known as *al-ala*: its basic musical features, including its rhythmic and tonal organization, its song varieties, and the social and institutional basis for musical performance and aesthetics.[13] I then examine the rhetoric of al-Andalus and its relationship to contemporary Moroccan society (ca. 1995–2015) through an analysis of performance, recordings, and discourse about the music among musicians, scholars, and enthusiasts. This minor (which is to say, elite) music plays an important rhetorical role in constructions of the modern nation by sonically reinforcing the ties between an Andalusian political and economic elite with pan-Islamic sentiments and the monarchy.

Although there is some debate in Morocco about the proper name of the music—some call it "Andalusian music" (*al-musiqa al-andalusiyya*), whereas others call it "Moroccan instrumental music" (*al-ala al-maghribiyya*) or, more commonly, "instrumental music" (*al-ala*)—its origins are generally considered by performers and enthusiasts to be Andalusian, and the cities of Tangier, Tétouan, Chefchaoun, Fez, Rabat, and Oujda are considered to be those with the strongest Andalusian heritage. These cities are also the home of the majority of musical ensembles that specialize in the performance of Andalusian musics. While early modern texts, including the eighteenth-century *Kunnash al-Ha'ik,* often refer to aspects of the music as *andalusi,* the evolution of an Andalusian identity through music began in earnest with the efforts of European scholars to document Morocco's musical patrimony during the French and Spanish Protectorates over Morocco ca. 1912–1956 (al-Fāsī 1962; see also Bin 'Abd al-Jalil 1988; Davila 2013). Prior to a 1939 conference of Andalusian music held in Fez that referred to the music as "Andalusian," there are few references to the music or even the culture surrounding it as Andalusian. Nineteenth-century and most early Moroccan texts refer to it simply as *al-ala* or *nubat al-alat* (turn taking of instruments), though in Algeria the term *Andalusian* was applied as early as 1904 and may have been in use for some time before (see Glasser 2012; Yafil and Rouanet 1905). The first scholarly texts to extensively promote the idea of an Andalusian musical tradition are colonial texts (Davila 2013, 46, passim). By the 1920s French colonial authorities were referring to the music as "Arabo-Andalusian" or simply "Andalusian" (see Ricard [1931] 1987). In 1927 the French colonial Service des Arts Indigènes (Service for Indigenous Arts) organized a "census" of existing Moroccan musical traditions and then, beginning in 1928, a series of *journées de musique marocaine* (Moroccan music days) (5). These cultural programs aimed at reviving and fortifying the Moroccan traditions in the face of "vulgar" modern influences, especially those brought by musical recordings (3–4). One of these musical days programs was held in Fez and devoted to "Andalusian music." At the same time, the musicologist Alexis Chottin was brought in from the Direction Général de l'Instruction Publique (General Directorate of Public Instruction, an early form of the Ministry of Education and Culture) to lead, in addition to the new national conservatory, the Laboratoire de Musique Marocaine (Laboratory of Moroccan Music), which was a study center for the various Moroccan musical traditions, among them "Andalusian" (6). One of Chottin's lasting legacies was the initial attempt to notate the *ala* repertoire (beginning with the *nubat al-'ushshaq*), as well as to establish the basis for the conservatory tradition in Morocco (see Chottin 1929, 1931, 1939). Territories in the north of Morocco were (and some remain) colonized by Spain.[14] Spanish colonial era scholars Julián Ribera (1922) and Patrocinio García Barriuso (1940) also advanced the idea that the Moroccan music was "Andalusian," a living extension of the musical and poetic practices of medieval Iberia.

This history suggests that the very term *al-musiqa al-andalusiyya* (Andalusian music) has a probable colonial provenance. As Davila argues, "The expression *Andalusian music* probably was an artifact of oral tradition adopted by twentieth-century Western scholarship and then taken up by North African scholars" (2013, 44). The dearth of premodern references to al-Andalus in descriptions of the music suggests that "Andalusian" is a modern and not traditional ascription, something promoted by French and Spanish colonial authorities: directors of conservatories, museums, and festival organizers. Interest in Morocco's musical heritage formed part of the larger colonial cultural policies that attempted to shore up and preserve Moroccan traditions, usually at the expense of organic development, which is why Janet Abu Lughod (1981) refers to Rabat in this period as exemplifying "urban apartheid." The French approach to colonial patrimony was decidedly curatorial: study it, preserve it, perfect it, maintain it. This approach seems to have been perpetuated by Moroccans, including musicians who worked with Chottin's laboratory and those who rose through the conservatory system, which to this day focuses largely on rote memorization of the *ala* repertoire.[15] It also promoted what has blossomed into a veritable cottage industry of Andalusian studies in Morocco, including a university center for Andalusian studies and numerous private Andalusian associations and clubs, as well as the elaboration of medieval Iberian and Andalusian studies in Europe and the United States. In addition, the French, by labeling the music "Andalusian" and accentuating the connections to medieval Iberia, marked it as European, thereby denying the contributions of Moroccans to the musical tradition in the centuries after the decline of al-Andalus (see al-Fāsī 1962). The denial of Moroccan agency through the attribution of the music to medieval Europe helped to promote an Orientalist-tinged nostalgia for an Andalusian golden age, a sentiment echoed in the works of many Spanish artists in the first third of the twentieth century, for example, Federico García Lorca and Manuel de Falla. It was just another example of the well-documented colonial strategy of divide and rule that was aided and abetted by scholars, from historians to musicologists to ethnologists. *Al-ala* became and remains in a festivalized Morocco an unchanging bastion of authenticity in a sea of change, one tempestuously threatening the shores of cultural purity as early as the 1920s and of course accelerating by the end of the twentieth and beginning of the twenty-first century. The net effect was to promote a sense of distinction, one already at play among communities of Moroccan Andalusians and one that had to be preserved without great change. These attitudes have remained in force since independence in 1956, as Moroccans inherited the cultural infrastructure of the colonizers and maintained many of their policies (see Rabinow 1989). The promotion of Andalusian music to the status of a national music began at this time with the harnessing since independence of Andalusian heritage—now called Moroccan Andalusian heritage—to the bandwagon of Moroccan nationalism, often at the urging of the newly restored monarchy, which played an important role in the nationalism movement and since independence has used Andalusian music in rituals of state. I explore the importance of the monarchy to Andalusian music and the role of the music in supporting the monarchy below.

Moroccan Andalusian music shares many features with the Arab and Arab-Andalusian music of the Arab East, with whom it bears a family resemblance. In both traditions, poetic texts, primarily *muwashshahat* and *zajal,* are set to music and organized into a series of suites according to melodic mode.[16] In Morocco (and elsewhere in North Africa) these suites are called *nubat* (sing. *nuba*), though in performance practice the *nuba* is distinct from the Syrian *wasla* in many regards. Though tradition states that there were originally twenty-four *nubat*, one for each hour of the day, since at least the late eighteenth century eleven *nubat* are known in modern performance. Each *nuba* is named for one of the melodic modes (*tubu'*, sing. *tab'*), and each in turn is divided into five main rhythmic movements (*mayazin*, sing. *mizan*) based in a primary meter (*iqa'*, pl. *iqa'at*).[17] Performances usually include a selection of poems from a given movement within a single suite, followed by the performance of songs from the same or another movement but from a different suite. (This is in contrast to the Levant, where the performance of a suite usually begins and concludes within a single mode and tends to proceed from longer to shorter rhythms.) In terms of tonality, the Moroccan Andalusian modes are for the most part diatonic (making them similar to scales used in European musics); they do not incorporate the microtonal intervals common in Ottoman, Persian, and Levantine musics.[18] A significant number of the modes have a pentatonic character, similar to many sub-Saharan African musics and to North African musics of Amazighi and West African provenance, including Gnawa. Rhythmically, *al-ala* consists of five principal meters: *basit, qa'im wa nusf, batayhi, darj*, and *quddam*. Each meter corresponds to a suite of poetic texts and perhaps is more properly understood as a movement within the larger structure of the *nuba* (see Bin 'Abd al-Jalil 1983). Each meter is a simple duple or triple meter with less complexity or syncopation than the numerous rhythmic cycles used in Levantine music (though in performance practice the organization of meter between instrumentalists, vocalists, and percussionists is highly regulated and complex). In terms of the instrumentation, the Moroccan Andalusian ensemble (*jawq*) since the nineteenth century has typically used the standard Arabian *'ud*; the European violin (*kaman*), viola (*altu*), and sometimes the cello; percussion instruments (*tarr* and *darbukka*); the *rabab* (a box-shaped two-stringed fiddle); and four-stringed lutes such as the *'ud 'arbi* and *'ud ramal*, which are not used in the Levant but can be found in other North African musics. The violin is also played off the knee, unlike its use in Europe or the Levant, for this allows the performer to also sing. Some modern ensembles incorporate clarinets, saxophones, trumpets,

Concert of Moroccan Andalusian Music, *al-ala,* "Fes Hadara," Fez, 2004.

and pianos—features almost never found in Levantine music of any variety, let alone what Levantines consider their classical Arab or Arab-Andalusian music. However, the use of such instruments is scorned in Morocco by defenders of tradition even if some acknowledged masters performed on them.

Today Moroccans identify three primary schools of *al-ala* performance: Fez (also known as the conservative school), Tétouan/Tangier, and Rabat. These three schools are based in the inherited performance practices of three leading figures in Moroccan Andalusian music: Sidi Muhammad al-Brihi (d. 1940) and 'Abd al-Karim Rayyis (1912–1996) in Fez, Mohamed Larbi Temsamani (1920–2001) in Tétouan/Tangier, and Moulay Ahmed Loukili (1909–1988) in Rabat. The differences among the schools are small and tend to reflect differing interpretations of the same repertoire (often at the level of ornamentation), the use of instruments such as piano (e.g., more widely accepted in Tangier/Tétouan than in Fez), and overall aesthetic. Nonetheless, the establishment of conservatory training, based now primarily in Rabat (see Davila 2013), the wide-spread availability of reference recordings of the music, and the growth of Andalusian music festivals and related institutions have produced a degree of standardization in performance practice across the various schools. Festivals in these three cities aim to promote and preserve the music, which performers and audiences generally understand to be a survival of earlier Andalusian musical practices passed across the genera-tions through oral tradition, curated by past masters and their disciples.

The principal institutions and organizations promoting Andalusian music in contemporary Morocco include amateur associations in Rabat, Casablanca, Fez, Meknes, Oudja, Tangier, Taza, and Tétouan, among other cities, chiefly in the north of Morocco.[19] These associations spon-sor annual concerts (*hafla-*s) and festivals (*mihrajan-*s), often in con-junction with the Moroccan Ministry of Culture and Communication. They also host musical evenings (*umsiya-*s) or listening sessions (*jalsa-*s) on special occasions. In addition, a network of state-sponsored music conservatories in these and other cities provides training in vocal and instrumental performance and music theory; the principal conservato-ries are in Rabat and Fez, though branch schools can be found in many cities (see Davila 2013). In conjunction with these semiofficial and of-ficial organizations, in the 1980s the Moroccan Ministry of Culture and Communication, in collaboration with France's Maison des Cultures du Monde, released a seventy-three-CD, one-hundred-hour anthology of *al-ala* called *Anthologie "Al-Âla." Musique Andaluci-Marocaine.*[20] This col-lection aims to represent the main schools of Andalusian music perfor-mance based on the interpretations of selected masters. As a result, the collection has become an important reference for students, performers, and aficionados, both local and foreign. Of course, as a living tradition Andalusian music far exceeds the boundaries of these official settings and institutions and as a result is often a feature of wedding celebrations, especially among the elites, where *al-ala* is typically performed along with other genres, including the urban popular music known as *chaabi,* Arab pop music, and the Moroccan genre known as *malhun*—another traditional music of Andalusian origin that is more popular than *al-ala* because its lyrics are in colloquial Arabic, though it does not enjoy the same level of state patronage and prestige as *al-ala.*

In 2004 during a survey I conducted of the music market in Fez, a young Fasi cassette vendor told me that Andalusian music is "bourgeois music," and few young people listen to it. An older cassette vendor claimed, to the contrary, that I wouldn't find a house in Fez in which the Andalusian repertoire was not cherished, that is, in the "true" Fasi homes, those of the ancient settlers of the city and not the new migrants from the countryside ('aruba); he himself claimed to be a relatively "recent" immigrant, his family having come to Fez sometime in the seventeenth or eighteenth century. It was telling, however, to find that by 2005 this man's cassette shop had been converted into a shoe store. "Ah, sidi [sir], shoes sell!" was his response when I asked him about the store's conversion. He blamed the Internet, not his clientele, and in fact claimed to still have a vibrant side business trading in cassettes and CDs for his committed musical clientele. Because of this, al-ala is for all intents and purposes a minor music in Morocco today. Unlike the numerous varieties of popular music available in the Moroccan music market, from chaabi and Gnawa music, to North African and Arab (more commonly Egyptian and Lebanese) popular songs, to transnational forms of popular music from rock to hip hop and beyond, al-ala is actively listened to by a relatively small number of enthusiasts (see Aidi 2014). However, Andalusian music, even if it is a "bourgeois" music of elite aficionados, carries important cultural weight. Moreover, it is at least passively consumed by anyone tuning into Moroccan television and radio during religious holidays and occasionally state television programming on Morocco's cultural heritage. It is played in hotel lounges and some restaurants as a form of sonic decor, announcing authenticity. I recall meeting a Moroccan friend at a hotel café in Rabat prior to attending a nearby concert, and, upon hearing some strains of al-ala coming over the café sound system, he joked, "We don't have to go to the concert. We can just sit here with our coffee!"

Even if al-ala remains marginal, it seems that many Moroccan elites are turning (or returning) to Andalusian music—what many proclaimed to me to be their classical music—in defense of national culture and as a way of reappropriating tradition. For example, in a 2005 conversation, a woman member of the Moroccan Parliament—a member of the Fasi political, economic, and cultural elite—argued that many

Moroccan youth are "rediscovering" the Andalusian music and that she enjoys listening to it as well. Festivals featuring Andalusian musics, including *al-ala* and sometimes other Moroccan, North African, or Arab genres, are now commonly found around Morocco and throughout the seasons, from CasAndalous in Casablanca (December), to the Festival of Andalusian Music in Fez (April and May), to Tarab-Tanger (June), Chefchaouen (July and August), and the Festival of Atlantic Andalusian Musics in Essaouria (October). There are also ongoing concerts, programs, workshops, and festivals, for example, at the Dar al-Ala (House of Andalusian Music) in Casablanca and among aficionados in Fez. In 2004 the son of a well-known *al-ala* aficionado started the Facebook group "Amateurs de la Musique Andalouse." (His invitation for me to join this group was, in fact, my entry into the world of social media.) At the time, there were about a thousand members of the open group (meaning anyone with a Facebook account could join it). By 2015 there were almost fourteen thousand members: young and old, mostly Moroccan but also foreigners, musicians, and nonmusical aficionados alike. The group page features posts of photos and videos from concerts, master classes, workshops, and lectures, as well as discussions of master performers, the musical structure of the tradition, and from time to time song lyrics and general good wishes for Islamic and Moroccan holidays. The postings are in a mixture of Arabic and French. There are other Facebook pages and groups, some closed, such as the "Associations des Amateurs de la Musique Andalouse du Maroc" and "Groupe Chabab Cordoba de la Musique Andalouse," which have a few hundred members apiece; the open group is by comparison significantly larger and growing. What this online presence indicates is both fairly widespread (though quite obviously self-selected) interest in the tradition and also a sort of curatorial, documentary, and revivalist approach to the music. These are all important avenues for promoting the tradition, indeed, for constructing it and refashioning it.

PERFORMING AL-ANDALUS: AUTHENTICITY AND NATIONAL IDENTITY IN *AL-ALA*

In addition to its association with the monarchy's strategies of legitimation and colonialist notions of heritage and authenticity, the principal

way in which Moroccan Andalusian music performs the Moroccan nation is through its accessing deeply held notions of tradition and authenticity that are at the heart of Moroccan self-understanding, especially
spiritual (see Hammoudi 1997). The authenticity of the Moroccan Andalusian tradition is performed through a series of "interpretive moves"
(Feld 1988) made by performers, aficionados, and scholars regarding the
musical system, the aesthetics of performance practice, and the social
contexts of performance. One way that Moroccans promote the authenticity of their Andalusian tradition is through its distinction from the
musics of the Arab East, which in the ears and eyes of many are "Oriental," "Turkish," or otherwise foreign. In fact, throughout the course
of my field research I found that many Moroccan performers, scholars,
and aficionados tended to downplay the Arab aspects of the music and
instead accentuated its associations with Moroccan, pan-Islamic, Spanish, and by extension European culture. Yet, some claimed that the Moroccan Andalusian music is more authentically Arab than the music
called "Arab music" by Levantine Arabs. As mentioned above, where
Syrians hear the absence of microtonality in Moroccan music to be a
sign of its inauthenticity (i.e., its lack of authentic Arabness), some Moroccans argue that the musical modes used in Syria and the Levant are
essentially Ottoman or Turkish and that the "true" Arabian modes are
those used today in Moroccan Andalusian music; the Levantine ones
had become corrupted by association with the Ottoman Empire. For
example, over the course of weekly lessons, al-Hajj Ahmad al-Shiki, a respected performer of *al-ala* in Fez and an innovator in the revival of older
instruments such as the four-stringed *'ud ramal,* said that to his ears the
Andalusian modes are the original Arabian modes; any differences heard
today (such as that between the Moroccan and Levantine modes called
hijaz) are the result of developments that took place in the Levant after
the flourishing of al-Andalus and partly under the influence of Ottoman and Persian musical traditions.[21] In a similar vein, 'Abd al-Malik
al-Shami, professor of Andalusian literature at the University of Fez and
a well-known enthusiast for the music, also claimed that to his ears the
modes used in Morocco were closer to the original Arabian modes and
that those used in Syria and Egypt were for the most part "Turkish."
This remark was echoed by 'Abd al-Fattah Bennis, a well-known Fasi

performer who, when I asked him about the modes, said that to his ears the Moroccan Andalusian modes were the more "Arab" sounding.

Each of these respected individuals—experts in the music as performers, scholars, and promoters—based his judgment on his ears, that is, on a personal, embodied feeling. For others, including younger performers, the Moroccan and Levantine modes form two ends of a modal continuum whose gradual transformations can be traced across North Africa; they constitute different musical "dialects" of the same language and can be learned and used in different situations. Indeed, as a result of the influx of pan-Arab songs through the mass media, many Moroccan performers are mastering the eastern Arabian styles, including not only the Arabic dialects of Egypt, Syria, and the Arabian Gulf, for example, but also the modal "dialects" of the musics. This has not been universally praised, and in fact many defenders of tradition argue against the "corruption" of the local modes by performers who have developed the Levantine and pan-Arab repertoires. Ahmad al-Shiki claimed that he only performs *al-ala,* nothing more; therefore, his art is pure. During one lesson when we worked on a particular song, he said, "This song likely dates from the time of Ziryab if not earlier, given its melodic structure."[22] This was about the strongest statement concerning the authenticity of the Moroccan tradition that I was to hear.

Regarding the melodic modes, others found no relationship between the systems of *maghrib* and *mashriq*. For example, in a 2004 interview, Muhammad Briouel, the director of the conservatory in Fez and leader of one of Morocco's prominent Andalusian ensembles, claimed that the two musical systems are entirely different. When I asked about the relationship between the Levantine mode *al-rast* and the Moroccan *al-rasd* (the two words being variant spellings of the same word), he asserted emphatically that they are entirely unrelated: "Look, one ends in *t,* the other in *d*—and *al-rasd* has the letter *sad* [an emphatic *s*], and *al-rast* has *sin* [a regular *s*]." For him, the tonal system of Moroccan Andalusian music is essentially European, not Arab. The proof of Moroccan music's stronger links to al-Andalus was the ability of Moroccan and European musicians to perform together because, as he put it, "they share the same musical language."[23] For some music lovers, the relationship of Morocco's Andalusian music to other North African and Levantine traditions was interesting and formed the basis for debates about origins, influences, cultural change, and authenticity (see Bin 'Abd al-Jalil 1988). However, for others such as Briouel, the links to Europe and to Spain in particular were more important than any linkages to the Arab or Levantine musical heritage. My fascination with the modal structure of these traditions mirrors the interests of ethnomusicology, but, surprisingly, I found that few Moroccan musicians were much concerned with debates about tonality; the origins of the modes seemed a moot point for them. More than one musician told me, "I just play the music and don't think much about the modes."

This disavowal of the links with the Arab East is reinforced through Moroccan understandings of the concept of *tarab*, or the set of emotional responses to music characteristic of much Middle Eastern music. In the Arab East, *tarab* refers to states of deep emotionality and passion that index Arabness in important ways (see Racy 2004; Shannon 2003c); therefore, *tarab* is a critical vehicle for the presentation of emotional sincerity and authenticity in the context of musical and poetic performances. In 2004 I had a discussion of *al-ala* with an older scholar of the music in Fez who himself claimed Andalusian ancestry and had long-standing connections with the various cultural institutions supporting the music in Fez. I asked him about the concept of *tarab*, since an alternative name for the music is *al-tarab al-andalusi*. He argued that the *tarab* in *al-ala* is different from the *tarab* of the "Orient" (*al-sharq*, by which he meant the Arab East, Turkey, and Iran) because it derives from the courts of al-Andalus and is, in his words, closer to a European understanding of emotionality: more refined and controlled sentiments rather than the baser feelings of the East. He mentioned Egyptians weeping at concerts of Umm Kulthum as an example of the latter, what *al-tarab al-andalusi* is distinctly *not*. "We are moved by the music, but we don't lose control or weep unless it is called for." I often found him at concerts singing along with the songs, responding bodily with slight motions of the hands and torso but with none of the more demonstrative emotional conducting I had noticed in Syria and Egypt during my earlier periods of research.

On a related note, during my research I frequently heard the claim (mostly from American researchers in Morocco and their elite Moroccan associates) that the music is locally known as *musiqa al-na's,* literally "music of drowsiness" or "music that puts you to sleep." According to an American acquaintance, this is because the music is widely played in the afternoons on television and the radio, when people take their after-lunch siestas. Another claimed that it is because by its nature the music is boring and soporific, as opposed to the vivacity of more popular musics. This surprised me, because I had never heard this sentiment in Syria, where the traditional Arab music tends to be played in the evenings in conjunction with eating, but in the context of soirées, not of going to sleep. In many months of research in Morocco I seldom heard the music played in the afternoons on the radio or television, except during the festivities leading up to King Muhammad VI's nuptials, and I never heard anyone aside from foreigners and a handful of Moroccan elites make the claim that it is *musiqa al-na's.* The argument that Moroccans consider Andalusian music to be "music that puts you to sleep" seemed dubious, though at the same time quite telling, so I inquired among my musician friends and teachers in Fez and Rabat. Most of them scoffed at the idea and argued that anyone who claimed that the music was sopo-rific was, in the words of one Rabati musician and scholar, "either not educated, without musical taste, or a Berber." For his part, the performer and scholar 'Abd al-Fattah Benmusa suggested that those who think the music caused *na's* were not so much wrong as ill-informed and unedu-cated about *al-ala:* the music can indeed cause relaxation and possibly induce sleep due to its complex relationship with cosmological configu-rations, but it is also a music of joy (*farah*) and movement (*haraka*): it depends on the mode used and the time of day. Ahmad Shiki concurred: there are indeed some *tubu'* that can induce drowsiness, but it depends on the time of day.[24] In the end, the association of the music with sleepi-ness is possibly a reflection of a colonialist if not Orientalist bias about a "local" music reproduced through the discourse of Western scholars and their Moroccan (largely Francophone and Anglophone) associates. No modern text refers to the music in this way, and astute listeners (the so-called *mulu'*), scholars, and performers dismissed the idea. Nonethe-less, as several of my teachers and interlocutors noted, the idea ties into long-standing ideas about the potential effects of music on the human body and soul. As in Syria, authenticity is negotiated through discourses of emotions and affective states; in Syria, this process of negotiation is effected through the concept of *tarab* (Shannon 2003c, 2006), whereas in Morocco, where *tarab* is also used, authenticity is negotiated through the complex associations of the *nubat* with calendrical features and bodily humors.

Just as *tarab* in the Arab East is linked affectively with Sufism, especially in the affective regime of such practices as *dhikr* (Racy 2004; Shannon 2005), *tarab* in *al-ala* is associated with Islam in important ways. And as in Syria, the connections to Islam promote its authenticity and by extension its rhetorical placement in Moroccan nationalism. Many of my teachers and interlocutors argued that the Moroccan Andalusian tradition had close ties to Sufism. For example, many of the so-called schools of *al-ala* performance are closely associated with Sufi orders: the Darqawiya Sidiqiya, Harraqiyya, and Wazzaniyya of Tangier/Tétouan and the Siqilliyya and Sharqawiyya of Fez, among many others. Notably, many of these Sufi orders perform at the annual Fez Festival of World Sacred Music and the Festival of Sufi Music held in Fez, both founded by anthropologist Faouzi Skali. Moreover, some performers and scholars claimed that the Sufi orders preserved the songs due to the strong links between *al-ala* and *al-sama'* (paraliturgical a cappella singing), especially in terms of melodic line, vocal quality, and in some instances poetic texts. During an interview at his small textile shop in the *ville nouvelle* of Fez, the ensemble leader Anas al-'Attar mentioned that many of the songs of the Sufi *zawiya* were also performed in *al-ala*, demonstrating the close links between *al-ala* and *al-sama'*.[25] To illustrate this point, he pulled out from behind his desk a large and ancient-looking book of religious song texts compiled by his grandfather (leader of a prominent Fasi *zawiya* and brother of the late 'Abd al-Karim al-Rayyis, leader of the most celebrated *al-ala* ensemble in Fez, the Orchestre al-Brihi). The book, which he consulted for his work as a young ensemble leader, signaled a genealogical tie to an authentic past, one made incarnate in his *rabab*, which he had inherited from his great-uncle al-Rayyis and which served for him as the ultimate symbol of his authority and authenticity in the *ala* community.

If the connections between Andalusian music and Islam are often mentioned in cities like Fez and Tangier, ideologies of pan-Arab identity seldom factor into discussions of this music and its associated culture. Indeed, Moroccan scholars often accentuate distinctions between North Africa (*maghrib*) and the Arab East (*mashriq*). For example, Muhammad 'Abid al-Jabri (1988) discusses the uniqueness and genius of Córdoba's Andalusian-Moroccan-Islamic philosophy as compared with that found in the Levant, which he implies is derivative and inferior. Indeed, the Islamic associations of the music are especially important for many Moroccan aficionados and performers. For this reason one of the major times one regularly hears this minor music is during the month of Ramadan. In the context of struggles for political legitimacy between the state and Islamist parties (such as the Justice and Development Party), music has become a powerful sonic marker of cultural authenticity.[26] In a market saturated with popular music from Europe and the Arab East, many middle-class and elite Moroccans are turning to Andalusian music as a way of reinforcing their connections with a Moroccan national "tradition"; some Islamists have even argued that the Andalusian musical repertoires are more appropriate for Muslims to listen to, while the other genres are to be avoided as inciting sexual depravity and moral corruption. Interestingly, many of the poetic texts of the Andalusian repertoire are of the amatory genre known as *ghazal*, though these are often interpreted as having mystical significance. In this regard, the music plays an important role in the symbolic negotiation of Moroccan national identity as a signifier of Muslim piety.

The association of *al-ala* with Islam is reinforced publicly through the broadcast on radio and television of the music during Ramadan. It also has strong affiliations with the monarchy, and the palace uses the music as one sonic marker of its legitimacy. For example, during the summer of 2002 I heard the music broadcast over the mass media and in public squares in Rabat and Fez during King Muhammad VI's wedding celebrations. The monarchical connections to the music run deep: for example, in the early independence era, Andalusian music was performed at the annual Throne Day celebrations commemorating the king's accession (Davila 2013, 148–149). Moreover, the late King Hassan II was the honorary president of the Andalusian Music Amateurs Association, suggesting that the Islamic associations of the music might play a role in the panoply of practices that legitimize Alawite Dynastic rule in Morocco dating back many generations (Combs-Schilling 1989; Waterbury 1970). Andalusian music sonically marks the Moroccan royalty and Morocco's high culture and heritage, which link the nation to a celebrated medieval and European culture to which it claims to be the direct heir.

The rhetoric of al-Andalus in Moroccan Andalusian music illustrates how musical practices and discourse about music promote deeply felt understandings of selfhood and community among musicians and music lovers. Musical practices and discourse about music are also important means for promoting ideas—rhetorics—of the Moroccan nation as well, of performing the nation. As we have seen, in these constructions and performance the idea of authenticity plays an important role as a guarantor of meaning and as a benchmark of tradition. I have explored how musicians and scholars negotiate authenticity in *al-ala* through an appeal to a genealogical imagination grounding the music in medieval Iberia and through its connections with Islam and the Moroccan monarchy. In what follows I explore the negotiation of authenticity in *al-ala* performance through a discussion of how Moroccan musicians understand composition in their music, debates about local tradition in an era of globalization, and efforts to preserve and revive the tradition through performance and instrument making. These three processes are tied to underlying discourses of cultural purity and heritage at the core of many nationalist cultural politics (Guss 2001).

CONSTRUCTING AUTHENTICITY: THE TABOOS AND ANXIETIES OF MUSICAL INFLUENCE

The standard narrative of the history and development of Andalusian music in Morocco posits that a pure tradition arrived in Morocco with the expulsions and, despite some loss and decay, remained essentially unchanged until the twentieth century, when the great masters developed their schools and the tradition was finally recorded and "fixed" for posterity. However, evidence points to significant contributions by Moroccans to the corpus of Andalusian song texts and melodies from the seventeenth to the twentieth century, some accepted as integral to the corpus of songs. While we know very little about the music from the fifteenth to the eighteenth century, during this time the musical traditions of the Iberian Peninsula were in close contact with those of North Africa, so the traditions must be understood as mutually constitutive. The Moroccan additions that are accepted include the change of some (but on the evidence not all) of the lyrics of the suite *Ramal al-maya* from amatory poetry (*ghazal*) to praise poems (*madih*) of the Prophet Muhammad.[27] Another acknowledged change was the addition of the rhythmic cycle (*mizan*) called *darj* to the compilations of *al-ala* repertory that emerged in the late nineteenth and early twentieth centuries (Davila 2013). These interventions in the *ala* repertoire are acknowledged as additions or supplements resulting from social pressures, changing the lyrics of one suite to better suit the needs of Muslims, as well as from the impulse to rationalize the system, codifying what was perhaps oral tradition. A similar process was the rationalization of the organization of suites (see Bennūna 1999). In addition, there are known instances of composition within the *ala* repertoire, but these are generally understood as either reviving older practices or giving air to typically Moroccan forms of poetic expression. For example, in the 1950s, Loukili, head of the Moroccan radio orchestra, began a series of interventions in the *ala* repertoire that aimed to restore songs that had been "corrupted" through either the accumulation of mistakes in pronunciation or the improper attribution of songs to suites or rhythmic cycles. Despite Loukili's stature as a master, his corrections and renditions of the repertoire did not always meet with approval, and some performers today argue that they follow the older and more authentic tradition, errors and all. This is similar to criticism of more recent attempts to correct and notate the repertoire. In addition, scholars note that a number of the song texts of the *ala* repertoire—perhaps as much as 5 percent—are in the genre of Moroccan colloquial Arabic poetry known as *barwala* (pl. *barawal*), which does not correspond linguistically or structurally with the Andalusian *muwashshah/tawshih* or *zajal* or the Arabic *qasida* (Davila 2013). These clearly Moroccan additions to the corpus are explained as accretions that arose in the time when the music came to the shores of North Africa; oddly, the *barwala* is not usually acknowledged as central to the Andalusian repertoire. The evidence of Moroccan contributions to *al-ala* supports the claims that the music should more properly be called *Moroccan* Andalusian music (al-Fāsī 1962).

When it comes to the question of adding to the repertoire as it exists today, either new compositions or changes to existing songs, several prominent performers and teachers of the *ala* repertoire I interviewed denied this possibility. In Tétouan, when asked about the possibility of composing new materials in *al-ala*, Muhammad Amine al-Akrami, a respected performer, conservatory teacher, and ensemble leader, responded, "La yimkinsh al-talhin" (Composition is not possible). When I asked him why, he said that the repertoire was handed down as is and therefore must be preserved even where it is incomplete in order to prevent further loss; this echoes the trope of decline and decay. Moreover, al-Akrami claimed that, compared to the masters who created and carried on the tradition, today no one can do justice to the repertoire by adding new materials, either poetic or musical. They just are not up to the task. Hence they must work hard to preserve what did make it into their hands. At the same time, he acknowledged that some of the twentieth-century masters no doubt *did* compose songs, especially the instrumental preludes known as *bughya* and *tushiya*. However, they usually masked this through a number of claims. For example, he related a story I heard from several sources regarding the late master al-Temsamani (1920–2001), who was an innovator in many domains, not the least being his use of the piano in the *ala* ensemble. Many Moroccans find no difficulty in the use of other European instruments in the *jawq*, including clarinet, saxophone, and trumpet. Temsamani also collected a number of already existing instrumental overtures (al-Hajj) into one long performance piece called *al-Mshaliya al-Kabira* (The great prelude) as part of a competition in 1960.[28] This compositional intervention was understood as a revival of an earlier tradition of "The Great Prelude" and not as an innovation in the context of *al-ala* per se. In addition, Temsamani introduced instrumental preludes to suites that either lacked them or had only a few, such as the *tushia* for the suite *Rasd al-dhil*. However, he did not claim to have composed them but rather to have "learned" them from a *shaykh*, or master, in Tangier who had since died. Several artists who told me this anecdote mentioned that it was well known in the *ala* community that Temsamani had actually composed them. However, given the taboo on composition, he attributed them to a dead master as a way of deflecting controversy. In an example of what I call "the anxiety of musical influence" (Shannon 2007b), his additions to the core repertoire had to be authorized through reference to a (dead) precursor.[29]

The only contemporary innovations I noted in my stays in Fez and Tangier were limited to individual efforts to mix musical styles or, more commonly, to adapt the tradition. As an example of the former, in 2004 the young Fasi instrumentalist Driss Berrada, who performs in Muhammad Briouel's ensemble and directs the students' ensemble at the Fez conservatory, embarked on a series of musical experiments that combined aspects of *al-ala* with Gnawa music, a music having strong associations with spirit possession rituals and sub-Saharan African musical traditions.[30] Berrada hoped to find ways of hybridizing the Andalusian and sub-Saharan African musics, especially since the tonal system of *al-ala* evokes pentatonicity, a feature of many sub-Saharan African musics as well. The shared tonality opened up possibilities for musical fusion not dissimilar to how the perceived European nature of the modes (their diatonicity) allowed for collaborations with European musicians.

Not all Moroccans are eager to pursue such musical fusions. In fact, Omar Metioui, a leading performer and scholar in Tangier, asserted that *al-ala* is already a hybrid of various musics—Iberian, North African, Arab—that took place over the course of centuries. Hence there is no need to do more fusion, especially the easy ones of fusion of *al-ala* with flamenco or Gnawa or jazz. Metioui is well known for his collaborations with the Spanish artists Begoña Olavide and Carlos Paniagua, founders of the Ensemble Mudéjar. Yet, he doesn't see Olavide's role in his ensemble as fusion so much as an extension of elements already in the music. Her participation on period instruments is an extension of the authentic heart of the music. He even partly jokingly wondered why great Syrian artists like Sabah Fakhri don't wear traditional Arab clothing when they perform but instead wear Western clothes. He wears modern dress in everyday life, but when he performs he wears traditional Moroccan clothing, like almost all the other Andalusian performers in Morocco. It adds an air of authenticity to the proceedings.

DREAM VISIONS AND MUSICAL INTERVENTIONS

Ahmad al-Shiki, the Fasi *'ud* performer and instrument maker, also expressed anxieties of musical influence through recourse to dead precursors. In this case, he wanted to re-create the varieties of 'ud used in the early Andalusian ensembles and had amassed a collection of vintage instruments, including some such as the 'ud ramal (a long-necked, fretless, four-stringed lute) thought to predate the exodus of Andalusians from the Iberian Peninsula, based on similarities with medieval Iberian iconographic depictions of musical instruments. Al-Shiki was concerned, however, about the reaction of the descendants of the original luthier, Benhirbet, and of performers who use the standard lute. He confided to me that, while searching for a suitable luthier to re-create the older instruments, he had a series of visions (ru'ya-s) in which the ancestral luthier authorized him to remake the instruments; dream visions are a common motif in Sufi epistemologies (Mittermaier 2010). The artist seemed deeply and truly concerned about ensuring this "right" to himself, and the dream visions gave him what he felt was a seal of approval (khatim) to go ahead with his project of revival.[31] By 2004 he had commissioned three prototypes (of which I have one) and by 2008 had learned the fundamentals of lutherie and was fabricating the instruments himself. In a similar vein, during our weekly lessons Shiki also expressed the idea that contemporary artists could not add to the existing repertoire, though many changes had come to it as a result of outside influence. His goal was to return the music to as close a rendition as possible of its original, Andalusian character by eschewing not only European but also eastern Arabian influences (e.g., in the modal system). This he elaborated through his commitment to the ancient humoral theory of the musical modes and his understanding of their relationships to one another and to the eastern Arabian / Levantine modes and musical practices, which, while he admires, he does not perform.

There are other examples of interventions in the ala tradition that have been the subject of debate. One relates to the effort to compile and notate the repertoire as it exists today. The standard editions of the repertoire, which take their cue from the eighteenth-century Kunnash al-Ha'ik (Bennūna 1999; al-Rayyis [1982] 1998), organize the songs into eleven suites, each further organized by the four premodern rhythmic cycles (the fifth cycle, darj, was added in the late nineteenth century). This yields a total of forty-four performance units (one teacher called them "movements," as in European chamber music). Musical notation was not known at the time of al-Ha'ik's *kunnash,* so only the lyrics and the mode and meter are indicated in early texts and in most compilations published in the twentieth century. By this time the fifth meter (*darj*) had been extracted from the other four sections, so the repertoire consists of fifty-five discrete sections; some older texts still refer to the repertoire as "the fifty-five" for this reason.[32] Today Moroccan *al-ala* performers render the melodies as performed by the masters of the late nineteenth and early twentieth centuries as transmitted within the confines of particular ensembles (such as the ensemble al-Brihi, perhaps the most influential in contemporary performance practice; see Touma 1996). In addition to oral transmission, recording technology helped to preserve some of these early renditions, as performed, for example, at the Congress on Arab Music held in Cairo in 1932 (*Kitāb mu'tamar* 1933). Today most artists and scholars rely on the interpretations of the repertoire developed by masters from the 1950s through the 1990s, including Loukili, Tamsamani, al-Rayyis, Muhammad al-Taud, Ahmad al-Zaytuni, and Tazi Masanu. Their renditions were codified, indeed to some extent standardized, in the recordings that form the Anthology of Moroccan Andalusian Music. When asked, most older performers stated that they learned the tradition through listening; some even claimed not to know how to read musical notation, which has only played an important role in recent years. Given that standard musical notation was little known in Morocco until the colonial period (as elsewhere in the Arab world), older artists relied on oral tradition and recordings; even today, conservatory students are encouraged to memorize the repertoire as performed by certain masters and not to rely only on musical notation. As I found in Syria, there is a certain distrust of notation's ability to capture the nuances of the music.[33]

However, two contemporary Moroccan scholar-artists have published notations of several of the suites: Yunis al-Shami (1984a, 1984b, 1984c, 1996, 2011, 2013), former director of the conservatory in Rabat, and Muhammad Briouel (1985), current director of the conservatory in Fez and leader of the Ensemble al-Rayyis. While their texts are similar in organization—each begins with an historical overview and a review of the modes and rhythms of *al-ala*—the two authors take different approaches to notation. Al-Shami, in a series of interviews, claimed that the repertoire as performed today is riddled with inconsistencies and errors. Like Loukili, al-Shami aims not only to record the existing repertoire but to correct the obvious errors that have accrued over the years. Some of these include improper attribution of rhythmic cycle or even suite, poor scansion of texts in performance, and poor pronunciation, among others. For his part, Briouel asserted to me that he notates what he learned as a performer in the Ensemble al-Rayyis and from the late master's book (al-Rayyis [1982] 1998) and recordings, including what al-Shami might interpret as "errors" in the musical structure and poetic texts, and in performance practice. This was confirmed to me in my lessons with a sometime performer in Briouel's ensemble; he argued that certain pronunciations did not match the texts found in al-Ha'ik or deviated from standard Arabic grammar and should have been corrected, but out of deference to tradition he performs them as the masters did, with the "errors." A performer from Tangier even suggested to me that most of the older "masters" were in fact illiterate and uneducated, and therefore their interpretations are full of errors; like al-Shami, he aims to purge the "errors" in his own performances and recordings.

The debate about the recordings and notations of *al-ala* is in many ways a proxy for debates about Moroccan tradition itself. The taboo on composition and innovation in the *ala* community is curious given that Moroccan artists in other domains continually innovate and push the envelope of acceptability in literature, fine arts, architecture, and even other genres of music. What might account for the denial of innovation within the Andalusian tradition? Certainly the national conservatories play a larger role in the transmission of Andalusian music in Morocco than in Syria. The location of the *ala* repertoire in a state-sponsored conservatory system has had the combined effect of preserving it, raising it to the status of a national patrimony, and promoting it to a wider potential audience, but at the risk of fixing, even ossifying, the repertoire. Unlike Syrian understandings of tradition that invite innovation, Moroccan notions of national patrimony suggest that this heritage cannot—must not—change. This does not totally rule out innovation: *al-ala* performances often feature exemplary and moving instrumental and vocal improvisations, and some performers expressed their desire to play with the melodies, adding their own touches based on their mood and sensibility. Ensemble leaders choose from the many hundreds of songs in the *ala* repertoire when preparing a concert program so that any given concert program is itself an act of composition. Yet the aesthetic pulse of the music, from the specifics of pronunciation to the more general questions of structure and order, remains largely fixed.

GLOBALIZATION AND A NEOLIBERAL ALA

The conservatism of the *ala* tradition can also be understood as a reaction against the forces of globalization and cosmopolitanism, which have marginalized the music relative to more popular genres. This sentiment was expressed to me by 'Abd al-Fattah Benmusa, the well-known scholar of the music and leader of the Revival Ensemble (Jawq al-Ba'th) in Fez. Benmusa argued that he sees his work in the revival and preservation of Andalusian music, through both performance and scholarship, as a form of resistance to globalization (*awlama*). In a modern world awash with transnational popular musics and the temptation to imitate and adopt global forms, he hoped to preserve and extend a local tradition. Yet at the conclusion of our conversation about the dangers of globalization to local cultural authenticity, this same artist invited me to attend a concert his group was giving . . . at the opening of a new McDonald's restaurant in the *ville nouvelle* of Fez in a spot overlooking the ancient *medina*. When I pointed out to him the contradiction between his antiglobalization stance and the McDonald's concert, he merely raised his hands in mock submission and laughed. "What can I do? We need to perform!" Indeed, the event was quite a spectacle. When I arrived a few minutes before the show was to begin, I found a crowd of some two hundred Moroccans hanging around the restaurant, which was surrounded by a cordon of Moroccan gendarmes keeping the curious public at bay. The building takes inspiration from the traditional royal architecture of Morocco's imperial cities: green tiled roofs, whitewashed walls, almost as if it were a medieval building that just happened to have a McDonald's in it.

   I did not have an official invitation so could not enter, but from my spot on the sidewalk I could see the ensemble seated in the upper-level dining hall (if that is how one can describe a typical McDonald's seating area), which had been converted into a runway for a fashion show of traditional Moroccan caftan gowns. The contrast between the elegance of the models in their flowing gowns, the performers in their traditional white robes, red hats, and yellow slippers, and the curious throng outside the restaurant, as well as the absurdity of the location, was striking.

The McDonald's performance might strike readers as a singular occurrence—and as far as I know the ensemble did not perform at any other McDonald's elsewhere in Morocco, nor did this particular restaurant host other, similar events. However, this event must be read as an extension of the broader and deeper festivalization of Moroccan culture noted earlier. The contradiction lies *not* in the performance at a McDonald's but in the claim of being antiglobalization in the first place when, in fact, most aspects of the *ala* tradition today are marked by a deep immersion in the contradictions of global capital in a neoliberal era (see D. Harvey 2007). In other words, the very tradition itself is a product of the engagement of cultural agents with the forces of globalization. While performance of *al-ala* remains a staple of elite wedding celebrations, informants mentioned that it has declined in popularity in recent decades as a result of the rise in popularity of other genres of music, both local and transnational. The *ala* aficionado turned shoe salesman in Fez argued that the 1980s and early 1990s saw the end of an era when Andalusian music was integral in the ritual life of most Fasi families. Afterward, with greater access to mass media, the advent of satellite television, and the reconfigurations of the music market, fewer families hosted large wedding celebrations at home, and fewer still had live *ala* ensembles perform. The large groups continue to play at elite and state functions, but the performance economy has changed so that the festival concert, not the private social event, has become the primary performance practice/event of most ensembles today.

The transfer of the locus of performance from home to festival stage involves a wide range of changes in performance practice and aesthetics (see Davila 2013, 166–180). These include a number of features, including standardization, mediatization, and commoditization (see Auslander 1999; Erlmann 1996a; Feld 2000; Guilbault 1993; Shannon 2003b, 2011; Stokes 2004; Taylor 1997). The Andalusian repertoire has been standardized into "sets" that can more easily be tailored to fit the temporal demands of a festival performance, when usually more than one group will perform, and each has less time than at a traditional performance. A typical program of *al-ala* at a wedding might include several hours of songs performed over the course of an afternoon and evening, whereas at a festival an ensemble might have an hour or, at most, two hours, during which they would perform one or two rhythmic cycles and offer a range of styles and genres, from instrumental preludes and vocal improvisations to a complete suite or two of songs. As already mentioned, a number of Moroccan festivals feature Andalusian music either exclusively or as part of broader themes: the Andalusian festivals and concert series in Casablanca, Fez, Chefchaouen, Tétouan, and Tangier are well established and remained vibrant today. Others include the Fez Festival of World Sacred Music, which features a wide variety of musics (some only tangentially related to the sacred) and always includes several representatives of Moroccan Andalusian music, as well as international stars such as Patti Smith, under the motto "giving a soul to globalization." It might more properly be "giving globalization to the soul" (Shannon 2003b).

As David Guss (2001) has shown, festivals are primary means of performing—and of constructing and negotiating—national traditions. The Andalusian musical repertoire was in some ways preadapted to festivalization through the fraught processes of notation and recording of the tradition(s), which had the effect of standardizing performance practice and allowing an easier creation of "sets" to fit the more restricted temporal confines of a festival or programmatic concert. In addition, the recording and broadcast of the music via mass media has promoted what Philip Auslander (1999) calls the "mediatization" of the repertoire: shorter, more standardized, and more open to hybridization and coperformance with European musics. This allows for its commoditization and repackaging as a more global style: not quite a transnational music in the same ways that world music genres are (at least not yet), but nonetheless partaking of the aesthetic features of these musics as one music among many in the global cultural economy: the shoring up of tradition and indeed its reinvention are part of this process of transformation. For these reasons, *al-ala* is increasingly understood as an important, prestigious element of the Moroccan national soundscape, but one sharing this public space with other musical styles. Even at weddings, an

Andalusian ensemble might alternate with a *chaabi* group or even a DJ; at one wedding I attended in Fez, the ensemble of 'Abd al-Fattah Bennis performed *all* of these functions, an example of what I have elsewhere called "flexible musical specialization" (Shannon 2003b, 2011). Bennis has marketed his ensemble as having multiple repertoires, from *al-ala* to *al-sama'* (sacred), including *chaabi* and other popular musics. In this manner, a single ensemble can perform a wide variety of genres and styles, a stance at odds with some defenders of tradition such as Ahmad al-Shiki who claim to perform one and only one kind of music: *al-ala*.

AUTHENTICITY AND THE RHETORIC OF AL-ANDALUS

The rhetoric of al-Andalus in Morocco plays an important role in sustaining the Moroccan national imagery by connecting modern Morocco to a medieval Iberian past through a genealogical imagination linked to forms of nostalgic dwelling (on the whole, reflective). This is performed time and again on the festival stage as an integral part of a globalizing tradition. Nostalgic dwelling in Morocco is sounded musically so that it is "good to think"—for aficionados of the music and Andalusians themselves, as for the monarchy, devout Muslims, and elites and others wishing to stress their ties to Europe. Unlike in Syria, where the rhetoric of al-Andalus performs Pan-Arabism, in Morocco the ties to the prestigious past are more complex and nuanced, partly because of the very real presence of Morocco in al-Andalus and al-Andalus in Morocco both historically and today. In this environment, *al-ala* serves as a sonic marker of a prestige identity and complex cultural associations that transcend the Arab and even Middle Eastern and tie Moroccans to the larger Mediterranean field and to the global circulation of Islamic and other sacred songs; for this reason the pan-Arab elements are insignificant compared to the Islamic.[34] Crossing the Strait of Gibraltar to Spain, we shall see how the rhetoric of an Andalusian past irrupts into the present in the very site of its origins: Granada.

FOUR

The Rhetoric of al-Andalus in Spain

Nostalgic Dwelling among the Children of Ziryab

WE WILL GET YOU BACK, GOD WILLING!

At last I arrive in Granada! Having made the trans-Mediterranean crossing from Tangier the day before via the port of Algeciras, I eagerly toss my things in my hotel room and head up the hill for my long-awaited visit to the Alhambra, Qasr al-Hamra', as I would continue to call it, pedantically using the Arabic terms for things and places or attempting to find Arabic roots (*arabismos*) in almost every Spanish word I come across. The crowds are almost as intense as the heat that day, so after shuffling through the richly decorated rooms of the Nassirid Palace, I stand at a window and gaze out over the Patio de Lindaraja below, with its small fountain and orange and myrtle trees. Looking down, I notice that someone had recently engraved on the windowsill the Arabic phrase "sanastarji' iyaki in sha' allah"—"we will get you back" or "we will reconquer you, God willing." The Arabic verb *yastarji'* can mean "to reconquer" or "to forcefully return," a fitting response, I think, to the notion of the Christian reconquest (*reconquista*) of the Iberian Peninsula—fitting because many Arabs and Muslims consider al-Andalus to have been a golden age, *their* golden age. Exiting the palace an hour or so later, I walk over to the Generalife Gardens. While wandering amidst the lush vegetation and bountiful fountains, I overhear a man telling his young daughter in Levantine Arabic, "Kull had kan ilna!" (All of this was once ours!). Dreams die hard.

Later in the afternoon after a short siesta, I explore Granada's new mosque, La Mezquita Mayor de Granada, which only days before had opened on Plaza San Nicolas, on the hilltop opposite the Alhambra. "New mosque" is an understatement, for this is the first official mosque to be opened in Granada since 1492 after decades of negotiations between the governments of Spain, Morocco, and the United Arab Emirates.[1] I find the building to be elegant if modest in scale but nonetheless significant, especially given its prominent location on the hilltop overlooking the Alhambra (i.e., the Qasr al-Hamra'). Entering the flower-festooned courtyard, I am somewhat surprised to mostly hear European languages spoken: Spanish, to be sure, but a lot of English and French and also some German. No Arabic. On the way out I pick up a flyer by the main door announcing a forthcoming lecture, "Islam, pasado y futuro de Europa." The lecture will be given (in English, according to the flyer, with simultaneous translation into Spanish) by one Hajj Abdal-haqq Bewley, an imam from a mosque in Norwich, England.[2] I note that the title is not "Islam *and* Europe's Past and Future" but simply "Islam, Past and Future of Europe." It conveys a very self-confident moment: a new mosque serving a growing community of converts, immigrants, and "native" Muslims, and a growing sense of the rising importance of Islam in European society.[3] Walking around the back, I locate the Centro de Estudios Islámicos (Center for Islamic Studies), site of the forthcoming lecture. The Centro is closed at the time, but on a whitewashed wall near the main doorway I see scrawled another interesting graffito: "¡Moros Fuera!" (Out with the Moors!).[4] It seems clear that the future role of Islam in Europe, however hopeful the flyer or how promising the new mosque, is very much a matter of debate.

Feeling tired from all the walking in the hot sun, I wander down toward the Calle Calderería Nueva for a cup of tea. Located in the twisty lanes of the Albaicín, or so-called Moorish quarter, the Calle Calderería Nueva has scores of *teterías*—small tea shops and stores featuring handicrafts (*artesanía*), boutique hotels, greengrocers, and restaurants.[5] Ducking into a shop decorated with Moroccan-style tiles (*azulejos,* from the

Conferencia:
Islam, Pasado y Futuro de Europa

HAJJ ABDALHAQQ BEWLEY,
Imam de la mezquita Ihsan de Norwich, Inglaterra,
autor, profesor. traductor del Corán al inglesa.

"Islam, Europe's past and future" La conferencia será en inglés con traducción simultanea.

Viernes 8 de Agosto 2003
8,00 de la tarde
Sala de Conferencias del Centro de Estudios Islámicos
(Entrada por Horno de San Agustín)
MEZQUITA MAYOR DE GRANADA
Mirador de San Nicolás

El Centro de Estudios Islámicos de la Mezquita Mayor de Granada inicia un ciclo de
conferencias sobre temas relacionados con el Islam en el contexto actual que tendrán lugar
todos los viernes a las 8 de la tarde. Las conferencias son abiertas al público.

Al final se servirá un refresco.

Para más información pueden llamar al 687710920

وقف مسجد غرناطة
Fundación Mezquita de Granada

Flyer for the conference "Islam, the Past and Future of Europe," Granada, 2003.

Arabic *zellij*), I take a seat. Andalusian music wafts from small speakers in the corner above the kitchen. The waiter, dressed in a white tunic and skull cap and sporting a well-groomed beard, approaches, and I order a tea but in Arabic, figuring he must be an Arabic-speaking immigrant. However, he apologizes and tells me in Spanish that he doesn't speak Arabic, so I order in Spanish. He is a convert (*converso*), he explains, and is just beginning to learn Arabic. Afterward, stopping at a small kiosk on the way to the hotel, I order a falafel sandwich from a man dressed in a white chef's apron, and we speak in Spanish. Noticing a flyer on the restaurant door announcing a forthcoming concert of "Oriental" music, I ask him if he knows anything about the ensemble. He apologizes and tells me he doesn't speak Spanish very well since he has only just arrived in the last few weeks and is still learning, but if I could wait a few minutes, the owner will be returning and can help me. It turns out he is from Lebanon, so we end up speaking in Arabic.

From Arabic to Spanish graffiti, to *conversos* who don't speak much Arabic to Arabs who don't speak much Spanish, and to still others like myself who confuse them, Granada is a place of contradictions and ambivalences. Indeed, if there is any site in Spain "where memory crystallizes and secretes itself," as Pierre Nora (1989) describes *lieux de mémoire*, then it is Granada that is the ultimate site for the crystallization and secretion—and contestation—of memory. The Alhambra, along with the Albaicín neighborhood or Moorish quarter, forms a memory palace extraordinaire: a place where dreams die hard, where visions are kindled, where history itself seems to murmur and burble in the fountains of the Patio de los Leones. This is because so much has been invested in the Alhambra—in Granada—that it is oversaturated with significance. Arabs and Muslims worldwide see it as a representation of "their" golden age, tourists and others find in it inspiration for Orientalist fantasies or see it merely as the backdrop to drug- and alcohol-induced adventures in the hillside squares of the Albaicín.[6] A UNESCO World Heritage site since 1984 (extended in 1994 to include the Albaicín quarter), the Alhambra is for Spaniards a source of pride, of tourist euros, but it is also an enigma: a magnificent representation of a past civilization that, as the standard narrative would have it, they mainly denied for the five centuries after the fall of Granada (what Spaniards celebrate as the *toma,* or "capture"). In this way, Granada has become a battleground over the significance of the past and its use in the present and future, not only for the city of Granada itself but for Spain if not all "Fortress Europe" as well. In the context of a modern Spain coming to terms with its heterogeneous pasts and diverse populations (witnessed in the numerous autonomous movements, especially in Cataluña but also in Andalucía) and in the context of a European community coming to terms with the growing presence of Islam within its borders, let alone a more menacing economic downturn, Granada stands in many ways as a symbolic frontline in the struggle for the past and the negotiation of the future.

This chapter explores the rhetoric of al-Andalus in contemporary Spain with a focus on nostalgic dwelling in the city of Granada. As in the previous discussions of Syria and Morocco, I focus here on the way music engages with debates about the past and aspirations for the future. In recent decades, as Spain has come to grips with its heterogeneous past, at the same time it has confronted a multicultural present. Arab-Andalusian music reverberates with this process of negotiation, sounding forms of memory and nostalgia and the politics of inclusion and exclusion at the heart of the debate about immigration, Islam, and Spanish society.[7] Especially in Granada, the music of North Africa and the Middle East, sometimes performed and in many cases classified with folk and popular musics of Spain such as flamenco, serves as a musical bridge spanning the cultures, histories, and peoples of Spain. At the same time, it also sounds the many boundaries that separate them. It is the tensions of the bridge and boundary-making zones of contact that I explore through analysis of musical practices in Granada.

Indeed, the two examples of graffiti in Granada mentioned above bespeak a broader and deeper set of debates concerning not only the past and how (even if) it is to be remembered but also the future direction of Spain and, by extension, Europe, "the West" (in a way a euphemism for Christendom and secularism). As Mikaela Rogozen-Soltar notes (2012a), such graffiti encapsulate an ambivalence toward the "Moorish" past in Spain. By "Moorish" I refer of course to the culture of medieval al-Andalus, but whereas in Syria and Morocco the terms *Andalusian,* *Arab,* and *Andalusi* have more currency, the term *Moor* captures best,

I believe, the complex ways of imagining the Arab, Berber, Jewish, and even to a degree Christian peoples and cultures of medieval and early modern Iberia. In modern Spain *moro* (Moor) signifies a heterogeneous past and serves as a racialized marker of difference and as a politically charged label (Aidi 2006, 2014).[8] Moreover, following literary scholars and historians of early modern Spain (Fuchs 2009, among others), I analyze the ways contemporary Spanish ambivalence toward North African and Middle Eastern peoples and their cultures engages earlier tensions between "maurophilia" (*maurofilia*) and "maurophobia" (*maurofobia*). In Spain today, "Moors" embody (literally) both a desired object (e.g., for tourists) and a loathed contagion (as markers of cultural impurity). The major points of debate and ambiguity revolve around how to understand the history of al-Andalus in the broader Spanish context. Was al-Andalus integral to Spanish self-constitution or alien to it? Was the Moorish influence limited to architecture, agriculture, and possibly cuisine and music, or did it survive in other ways in the five centuries since the fall of Granada? These are the central nodes of debates that are much more about the present and future constitution of Spanish society than they are about the past per se.

In what follows, I trace the development of a "Moorish" discourse in modern Spanish historiography and outline the main points of debate and those who support them. From early Republican literary and musical evocations of al-Andalus to midcentury historiographic debates, I show how the Andalusian past came to play a large role in definitions of self and Other in the Spanish province of Andalucía but also in the Spanish nation as a whole. I then turn to an exploration of the role of al-Andalus in contemporary debates about Spanish history and national identity. I emphasize the ambivalence of al-Andalus in modern Spain, at once an attractive internal exotic Other and a lightning rod for controversy. Al-Andalus therefore serves multiple roles in contemporary Spanish society: as a marker of Spanish heterogeneity, past and present; as a beacon of hope for a restorative nostalgia among new-old Muslims and North African migrants; and as a marker of difference and disjuncture with the "true" Spain (especially among postrevisionist historians). Thus, the rhetoric of al-Andalus in Spain is complex and often ambiguous. As a site of memory making and refashioning, Granada is an important node for all three axes of my research: the Syrian, the Moroccan, and the Spanish. For it is here, in the hilly quarters of the Albaicín and the Alhambra, where the various tributaries of the story of al-Andalus meet in a cultural confluence laden with contradictions.

THE RHETORIC OF AL-ANDALUS IN SPAIN: ANXIETY, AMBIVALENCE

Much of the discussion to this point has been devoted to revising what I call the "standard narrative" of al-Andalus. For Syrians, the story or rhetoric of al-Andalus is essentially one of "There and Back Again," of a Syrian-Arab adventure in Iberia that had lasting effects both there and in its Levantine homeland. For Moroccans, the rhetoric of al-Andalus activates a genealogical imagination that links contemporary Moroccans with their medieval ancestors through a revived Andalusi culture. In Spain, the rhetoric of al-Andalus has a different valence, in part because it is more than just a narrative: it is a chronotope of a national past with strong contemporary rhetorical force, a time and place coterminous with a portion of the current nation-state. Rather than a longed-for distant realm or marker of a golden age, from the Spanish perspective al-Andalus *is* home. In Spain the rhetoric of al-Andalus centers on how the medieval past resonates in the modern era: as an echo (as in the works of Federico García Lorca), as a distant trace (as in the writings of Blas Infante), or as a faded dream, if not a myth or fantasy (in the works of critics such as Serafín Fanjul).

In the midst of these debates, another Andalusian narrative has arisen, namely, the narrative of what happened from the period after the expulsions to the present day. Like the standard narrative we have traced in Syria and Morocco, this one traces the rise of al-Andalus to the intervention of "Arabs" in 711, the Muslim conquest and rule over Iberia, and the eventual reconquest by Christian forces after the capitulation agreements in 1492. This narrative circulates in Spain as it does in Syria and Morocco. Where the Spanish version differs from the other versions, however, is in the narrative of post-1492 events. As commonly expressed in interviews, the popular press, and scholarly works, the post-*partida* narrative argues that Spain essentially forgot its Moorish past in the five centuries since the fall of Granada; indeed, more than forgetting this past, Spaniards actively sought to erase it and enforce cultural amnesia through such practices as forced conversions, waves of expulsion, repression of Muslim and Jewish cultures, the Inquisition, and the imposition of a hegemonic Castilian and Catholic culture. This hegemony, according to the standard narrative, was especially strong in the Franco period (1939–1975). With the death of the dictator, Spain began to grapple once more with its Moorish legacy, and the repressed Moorish (and Jewish) past returned. For some, this has taken the form of conversions (sometimes referred to as "reconversions") to Islam, for others, the nostalgic consumption of things "Moorish," even as a fashion. For still others, the return of the repressed Moorish past occasions a staunch defense of the Christian and "Spanish" elements.

However, like the earlier standard narrative and the story of Ziryab, this narrative of repression and return is overly simple; it obscures more than it illuminates. As Barbara Fuchs (2009) demonstrates, the ambivalence about the Andalusian ("Moorish") past in contemporary Spain is not a modern phenomenon but rather dates to the time of al-Andalus itself and continued in the centuries after the expulsions. The complex entanglement of what Fuchs and others call postexpulsion "maurophilia" and "maurophobia" dates at least to the sixteenth century and is evident in a wide array of cultural practices at the dawn of the Spanish nation. From the Spanish language itself, which has many words and phrases of Arabic origin (known in Spanish as *arabismos*), and popular literary genres such as the *romanceros moriscos,* to vernacular architecture and domestic material culture, from popular and elite clothing styles, including gowns, cloaks, and headdress, to such practices as horsemanship and equestrian games and even notions of chivalry (as evidenced, e.g., in *Don Quijote*), postexpulsion Spanish history bespeaks a complex entanglement with the Moorish past. According to Fuchs, the Andalusi or Moorish origin of these maurophilic practices often went unmarked not because they had been suppressed or forgotten but because they had been naturalized as "Spanish." Because of the embodied nature of so many of these habits, from costume to cuisine, they marked a long-term shared culture, a *convivencia* of the everyday (Fuchs 2009, 13; see also Smith 1992).[9] Their continuation past the time of the expulsions reveals not only the extent to which literary and architectural maurophilia animated cultural production in early modern Spain but how the categories of "Moorish" and "Spanish" became inextricably intertwined during this period; as Fuchs notes, this is especially the case for the position of Spain in Europe as a racialized and exoticized internal Other—Europe's Moor.

That maurophilic practices and consumption continued despite maurophobic violence against Moors—expulsion, forced conversion, and discrimination—bespeaks as well a deep ambivalence toward the Moors and their cultural habits. As Fuchs notes, "A culture profoundly marked by Andalusi forms survived in sixteenth-century Spain, long after the fall of Granada, and stood as an often unacknowledged challenge to the official narrative of supersession" (2009, 11). On the contrary, the standard narrative that Spain excised the Moorish culture from the national body with the expulsion of the Moors is little more than "a rhetorical fiction designed to consolidate an emerging sense of national identity" (11), as well as a "reductive alternative to a more sustained engagement with Moorish costume and culture" (61). Moreover, far from being a fad or a sort of nostalgia for the vanquished, as many contemporary commentators would have it (Corriente 2000; Fanjul García 2002, 2004; Quiñones Estevez 2012), the abiding interest in things Moorish in the centuries after the expulsions and today indicates a lasting fascination with the Moorish past, an attraction mixed with a certain revulsion that far exceeds a mere nostalgia for the vanquished (a sort of "victor's remorse"), or what Renato Rosaldo (1989) and others have called "imperialist nostalgia."

Contemporary Spanish maurophilia has its roots in these early modern practices and in the literature of Spain's golden age, as well as in Romantic era writings by foreign authors, including René de Chateaubriand and Washington Irving, who actually resided in the Alhambra while writing *Tales of the Alhambra* (1832).[10] The discourse of maurophilia (and, more precisely, of the Arab or Moorish roots of Spanish and especially Andalusian culture and society) developed intellectual, political, and artistic dimensions in early twentieth-century Andalucía. Among the leading figures of the movement to recover the Arab roots of Spanish culture were the Andalusian politician and writer Blas Infante (1885–1936), the composer Manuel de Falla (1876–1946), and the poet Federico García Lorca (1898–1936). All three in their way contributed to the establishment of the intellectual and political terrain for the growth of Andalusian nationalism and the later rise of maurophilic and maurophobic discourses in the late twentieth and early twenty-first centuries.

Among these three, it was Infante who offered the most intellectual and political leadership. Considered the "father of the Andalusian nation" (*padre de la patria Andaluza*), Infante argued for the distinction of the region of Andalucía from the rest of Spain due to its main sources: the Greek culture of Tartessos, a harbor town at the mouth of the Guadalquivir; Roman Hispania Baetica, nearly coterminous with modern Andalucía, with its capital at Córdoba; and Islamic al-Andalus. It was in his study of the history of al-Andalus that Infante would discovery the "genius of Andalucía," which he would link to the Wilsonian principle of national self-determination (Ruiz Romero 2000). Infante was the leading proponent of the *Estatuto de autonomía de Andalucía* (Self-governance statute of Andalucía), which was not formally adopted in Spain until 1981 (revised in 2006).[11] He organized the first Assembly of Andalusian Provinces (1913), designed the Andalusian flag and coat of arms, composed the lyrics to the Andalusian national anthem, opened the first Centro Andaluz (Andalusian Cultural Center), and in 1936 was elected president of the first Andalusian national assembly.[12] Some also claim that he converted to Islam and took the name Ahmad Infante, though there is little evidence to support this.[13] His activism on behalf of Andalusian nationalism led to his imprisonment and execution at the hands of the Fascist forces of General Franco on 11 August 1936. Nonetheless, his legacy remained a powerful force of inspiration for decades, not only in the adoption of the statute of autonomy in 1981 but in the creation of the conditions for the rise of new forms of maurophilia (and, in reaction, maurophobia) across the twentieth century.[14]

The composer Manuel de Falla, from the Andalusian city of Cádiz, cultivated an interest in Spanish folk song. Under the influence of his teacher Felipe Pedrell, Falla incorporated many local Andalusian themes in his compositions, including *La vida breve* (The brief life, 1913), *El amor brujo* (Enchanted love, 1915), *Noches en los jardines de España* (Nights in the gardens of Spain, 1916), *El sombrero de tres picos* (The three-cornered hat, 1919), and *Siete canciones populares españoles* (Seven popular Spanish songs, 1922), based on Spanish folk songs, some from Andalucía.[15] Mirroring anxieties over the state of popular song found around the Mediterranean, Falla believed that flamenco was being contaminated by urban popular song. He therefore co-organized with García Lorca the Concurso de Cante Jondo (Deep Song Competition), held in Granada in 1922. Falla saw the Concurso as a means for reviving the art of flamenco, which he lamented had fallen into a state of desuetude and neglect (see Álvarez Caballero 1981, 179–186; Harper 2005; Hess 2001, 174–175; Molina Fajardo [1962] 1998).[16] In collaboration with intellectuals and artists such as Miguel Cerón and García Lorca, the flamenco *cantaores* (singers) Manuel Torre and Antonio Chacón, the classical guitarist Andrés Segovia, and other leading figures, Falla aimed to revive flamenco and protect it from the influence of popular musics. The desire of Falla and the Concurso organizers "to hear the 'admirable sobriety' of classical *cantaores* shows the extent to which the contest was, in effect, a classicizing gesture" (Hess 2001, 175). This classicization would go far in promoting flamenco not only as a legitimate art form but as a national one—for the budding Andalusian nation (as an expression of *andalucismo*, Andalusian nationalism) and, in the Franco period, for the Spanish nation as a whole (as a new expression of *españolismo*; see Hess 2001; Serrera Contreras 2010).[17]

It was the poet García Lorca, however, who would do the most to bring Infante's ideas to a much wider audience. Born in Fuente Vaqueros, just outside Granada, García Lorca cultivated an interest in the Moorish roots of Andalusian culture and especially of *cante jondo*, Andalusian "deep song," or flamenco song, music, and dance. Like Falla, with whom he organized the Concurso, García Lorca believed that flamenco represented the heart of Andalusian culture but had fallen into a state of decay and decadence. Along with the Concurso, García Lorca's scholarly and poetic works devoted to flamenco, including his study *Teoría y juego del duende* (Play and theory of the *duende*, published in English as *In Search of Duende* [1998]), as well as his *Poema del cante jondo* (Poem of deep song, composed in 1921 and published in 1931), helped launch the early twentieth-century flamenco revival. Like his Romantic forebears, García Lorca pursued the idea of the Arab and Romani ("Gypsy") roots of flamenco and presented flamenco as if it were a sonic representative of the deep identity of the Andalusian nation. Not only do his works attempt to describe the emotional character and passional qualities of flamenco deep song (*duende* is a heightened, trance-like state in performers not dissimilar from the concept of *tarab* in Arab music), but they, along with the 1922 Concurso, mark the beginnings of modern "flamencology" (*flamencología;* see Serrera Contreras 2010, 371).[18]

In his poetry and other writings, including lectures that he gave around the world, García Lorca advanced the idea that much of Andalusian culture derived from the Arabs. For example, in an essay on the Albaicín, García Lorca writes: "Here and there, always the Moorish echoes of the prickly pear. . . . In these crossroads lives the fearful and fantastic Albaizín, that of barking dogs and mournful guitars, of dark nights in white-walled streets, the tragic Albaizín of superstition, of fortune telling and necromantic witches, of rare Gypsy rites, cabalistic signs and amulets, of troubled souls, of the pregnant, the Albaizín of old prostitutes who know the evil eye, of the seductrices, of bloody maledictions, the passionate" (1994, 145–146, my translation).[19] In this short example, one finds a wide range of exotic and fantastic imagery about the Albaicín and, by extension, Moorish culture in Andalucía: danger, sorcery, darkness, Gypsy and Judaic rituals, the expectant and anxious, and the sad, mournful, and passionate. These associations would find fruition in his *Diván del Tamarit* (Tamarit diwan, 1981), twenty-one poems written in the Arabic poetic forms of *ghazal* (*gacela*) and *qasida* (*casida*) and treating, like the Arabic genres, the themes of passionate love, loss, natural splendors, and the like.[20] The very act of composing in traditional Arabic genres (at least in their titles and themes, if not their structure) manifests García Lorca's strong sense of maurophilia and what we might also be called "*gitano*-philia," though García Lorca was careful to note that he was not claiming to be a *gitano* (Gypsy), let alone a *moro,* but that his poetry was inspired by the histories and contemporary presence of Arab and Romani culture in Andalucía (García Lorca [1928] 2008).[21] Like Infante, García Lorca fell afoul of the Fascists for his political beliefs and possibly also for his homosexuality, and he was executed on 19 August 1936 at the age of thirty-eight (Gibson 1983; Stainton 1999).

The work of Infante, Falla, and García Lorca sought to cultivate acknowledgment of the diverse roots of the Andalusian "nation," including the importance of Arab/Moorish culture, which in their minds had lasting echoes and traces in contemporary Andalucía. Their efforts were cut short by the assassinations of Infante and García Lorca, the exile of Falla, and the violence of the Civil War and onset of dictatorship, during which time many intellectuals, artists, and dissidents were killed or exiled. According to the standard narrative, the sort of "maurophilia" at the heart of the politics of the *andalucismo* advanced by them waned in the aftermath of the Spanish Civil War and the rise to power of Francisco Franco and his Fascist regime (1939–1975). Franco indeed cultivated ties with the Catholic Church as a means of strengthening his hold on power (Preston 1994) and on numerous occasions exhibited often violent maurophobia. The result of this was, as the standard narrative has it, to promote an erasure of the Moorish elements of Spain's past while accentuating the Castilian and Catholic roots of the nation. However, the generalissimo's relationship to North Africa and to Moors and Islam was ambivalent and contradictory. On the one hand, he showed great cruelty and even barbarity in his treatment of Moroccans during the Rif War of the early 1920s, when he was a commander in the Spanish Foreign Legion: he once presented the duquesa de la Victoria with a basket of roses surrounding two severed Moorish (Moroccan) heads during her visit to Morocco in 1922 (Pavlovic 2003, 25). Yet, Franco spent over a decade in Morocco, his base of power at the beginning of the Spanish Civil War being in fact the Spanish enclave of Melilla (a garrison on the Mediterranean coast of Morocco), and over 100,000 of his troops were in fact North African, most Moroccan mercenaries (Madariaga 2006; Sánchez Ruano 2004). Some one thousand Republican troops are also thought to have been Muslims (El Merroun 2003, 41–62). As leader of Spain, Franco also had a "Moorish Guard," no doubt a colonialist appurtenance but significant nonetheless. As for flamenco, in his later years Franco cultivated it for the tourism industry, in the process erasing its Andalusian roots in favor of a pan-Spanish (and hypermasculinized) *nacionalflamenquismo* movement (Chuse 2003, 91). Moreover, as a consequence of its co-optation into the national imaginary, "the low-class positioning of flamenco performers in marginalized settings, [engaging] in 'bodily' practices like drinking, dancing, and sex, was replaced by an aesthetically pure environment where the *cante* [song] and the *toque* [guitar playing] figured most prominently" (Hayes 2009, 95). Finally, the fight against Republican forces and, after the Civil War, against the Spanish Left was often cast as a new *reconquista,* drawing on the struggle against Islam to promote the conservative and Catholic struggle for Spain (Preston 2012).

It was the work of midcentury historians that would bring this debate from the earlier literary salons to a broader national stage, and none more so than the polemic between Américo Castro (1885–1972) and Claudio Sánchez-Albornoz (1893–1984) regarding Spanish history.[22] This is not the place to review Castro's oeuvre, which was extensive. However, Castro, writing from exile in the United States, developed the thesis that the very idea of the Spanish nation did not come into existence until after the Muslim conquest of Iberia and the creation of what he described as a hybrid culture based in three "castes"—Christian, Muslim, and Jewish (Castro [1948] 1984; 1977, 105, 198, passim).[23] According to Castro, these three religious-ethnic castes lived in a state of multicultural tolerance and coexistence, what Castro famously described as *convivencia.* This term, which Castro coined, has been perhaps his most enduring legacy, since more than any other it has come to characterize not only medieval Spain but also a hoped-for contemporary condition, especially in the post-9/11 world.[24] It is the basis for the idea of the "Three Cultures of the Mediterranean," rhetorically important today not only for the tourist industry but for political and scholarly projects in the region as well (they are mutually supportive).

In his masterpiece of revisionist history *España: Un enigma histórico* (1956), Sánchez-Albornoz, Castro's near contemporary and also writing from exile (from Argentina, not the United States), argued against Castro's idea of medieval multiculturalism. Instead, Sánchez-Albornoz emphasized what he discerned to be the continuities between Spain's pre-Muslim and post-*partida* histories. Against Castro's work, he asserted that the Muslim and Jewish contributions to Spanish national culture were minimal. Rather, the pre-Islamic legal, political, economic, and cultural institutions and structures were more influential in the development of the Spanish national character, which, for Sánchez-Albornoz, runs throughout Spanish history from Byzantine times to the present; the Moorish interlude was a mere bump in the longer unfolding of an essential Spanish national character.[25]

CONTEMPORARY SPANISH MAUROPHILIA AND THE LATE CHILDREN OF CASTRO

The scholarly debate between the multiculturalism of Castro and the essentialism of Sánchez-Albornoz can in a sense be read as an extension of earlier debates about contemporary Spanish society and as a presentiment for contemporary polemics regarding the role of Islam in modern Spain (see Subirats 2003). In the aftermath of the "cataclysm" of 1898, with Spain's embarrassing defeats in the Spanish-American War, the question of foreign influences and native national character (*la raza española*) were central to the way intellectuals of the "generation of '98" (the *noventayochistas*) approached Spain's historical legacy; indeed, eminent Spanish historian José Luis Gómez-Martínez considers Castro to be a "late son" (*hijo tardío*) of the *noventayochistas* with his theory of *hispanidad* and notions of intercommunal *convivencia* and tolerance (Gómez-Martínez 1975, 198, cited in López-Baralt 1985, 29). One can also read the works of Castro and Sánchez-Albornoz as contrasting responses to exilic nostalgia; it is no surprise that the multicultural vision would emanate from a subject position in the United States, where such debates have been important for many generations, while the essentialist argument would emanate from a different exilic location: like Falla, Sánchez-Albornoz lived and worked in Argentina. Distance can create a nostalgic revisiting and reassessment of the homeland.

The works of both historians have been superseded by more nuanced accounts of the medieval and early modern periods (Doubleday and Coleman 2008; Fuchs 2009; Harvey 2005; Nirenberg 1996; among others). Nonetheless, they continue to be deployed rhetorically in support of or to contest maurophilic practices today, especially as Spain more tightly integrates in the global economy, with tourism playing a large role. Indeed, Castro's *convivencia* thesis has become the dominant new paradigm for understanding Spanish historiography, even though recent scholarship (Fernández-Morera 2006; Filios 2008; Soifer 2009) has shown, for example, that *convivencia* was not perhaps as extensive as

Castro made it out to be and, moreover, that it was a product of economic and political necessity rather than any ideology of multiculturalism, or what Menocal (2002b) describes as a culture of tolerance.[26] Given the mutual economic and political interdependence of these ethnoreligious groups, Brian Catlos (2001, 2002) suggests the term *conveniencia* (mutual convenience) as an alternative to Castro's more optimistic *convivencia* or the seemingly more neutral *coexistènsia* (coexistence), which is analytically poor. Whether among tourists and spiritual pilgrims seeking Andalusian authenticity, artists and musicians in search of inspiration, government and international observers seeking a way toward a multicultural future, and scholars at the nexus of these various currents, the idea of *convivencia*—and the rhetoric of al-Andalus as a place characterized by a harmonious coexistence—has come to stand for the legacy of Moorish Spain. Those who espouse the contemporary rhetoric of maurophilia are in some ways "late children" of Castro.

The rhetoric of maurophilia and the key trope of *convivencia* are most prominent in the tourist sector. In Granada one notes, for example, numerous "Three Cultures" tours exploring mainly Muslim but also Jewish and Christian sites in and around the old quarter of the Albaicín, producing what Giles Tremlett (2008) calls "Moorishland," given its Disneyland feel. During a visit there in 2008 I saw advertised a "Four Cultures" tour that added "Gypsy" culture (*la cultura gitana*) to the mix, with a visit to the Sacromonte for a flamenco *tablao*. I even saw a flyer announcing a "Five Cultures" tour, though the fifth "culture" was not specified (Visogothic? Roman?). Local shops and stalls throughout the city trade in the currency of *convivencia* as well, selling trinkets—inlaid boxes, engraved brass plates, the occasional menorah and Star of David, "Moorish" clothing, and "Oriental" musical recordings—related to the notion of three cultures. Much of the tourist promotion of the three cultures model rests on a convenient elision between medieval al-Andalus and modern Andalucía, as if the modern autonomous region were coterminous and synonymous with the medieval entity. This rhetorical move, supported by the local government through such agencies as the Junta Andalucía and El Legado Andalusí foundation, collapses the complex historical engagement of North Africa and the Levant with shifting portions of the Iberian Peninsula into a reductionist narrative more suited to the promotion of tourism: the old Orientalist dream can be revisited in its origin–cum–vanishing point and experienced as the re-creation of an ersatz past.[27] Yet, there is a curious absence of the main peoples being celebrated, namely, Jews and Muslims; as journalist Tomás Navarro archly notes, the message seems to be "visit Andalusia and Granada, a beautiful Muslim and Jewish land, but without any of the Jews or Muslims in it" (1998, 21, cited in Tremlett 2008, xiii).[28]

Moreover, the rhetoric of the three cultures presents communitarian-religious groups as "cultures" not too distinct from Castro's notion of religious-ethnic castes and implies not only a unity within each community and harmonious culture of tolerance among them but also some sort of symmetry, as if the Muslim, Christian, and Judaic "cultures" were in a sense equivalent. Few scholars have gone as far as the late María Rosa Menocal in advancing the idea; her landmark *The Arabic Role in Medieval Literary History* (1987) and *The Ornament of the World* (2002) are the leading testaments to this vision of a medieval culture of tolerance that somehow might play a role in the contemporary world (see also Menocal 2002a). Menocal's work has helped spawn a veritable cottage industry of al-Andalus studies in America. However, as numerous critics have pointed out (Catlos 2002; Corriente 2000; Fanjul García 2002, 2004; Fernández-Morera 2006; Fletcher 2006; Harvey 2005; among others), this vision of medieval Iberian society, of a culture of tolerance and living together, while attractive to modern sensibilities, is historically inaccurate. It misidentifies the past social relations among the various communities, in which the Muslim was the dominant, and perpetuates a mythological understanding of how medieval Spanish society operated. Serafín Fanjul García (1984), a respected Arabist and recent archcritic of contemporary Spanish maurophilia, asserts that contemporary maurophilia is little more than a fad, one reaching back to García Lorca's imaginings in the early twentieth century. According to him, the assertion of continuity between medieval al-Andalus and modern Spain is erroneous, as modern Spaniards have no relation to the medieval (Fanjul García 1984, 2002; and as cited in the documentary *When the Moors Ruled in Europe* [Copestake (2005) 2008]). Thus, for Fanjul García (1984) the search for the Arab roots of Spanish culture is the result of a "current more emotional than factual" that sustains "the maurophilic rhetoric" (la retórica maurófila) and a recently invented nationality.[29]

In a similar vein, Federico Corriente, also an Arabist, attacks the idea of Andalusian convivencia. He singles out for particular criticism the idea of a Mozarabic culture in medieval Spain that incorporated Christians, Muslims, and Jews into a unified cultural framework.[30] According to Corriente (2000, 42–44), this Mozarabic culture did not really exist; rather, there was only one culture in al-Andalus—an Arab-Muslim civilization in which all communities were de facto participants, but not as equal partners. As an essential element of the modern rhetoric of al-Andalus and convivencia, the idea of a medieval Mozarabic culture (like the idea of a Sephardic culture, which for the same reasons Corriente rejects), is "good to think"; it implies a medieval multiculturalism that has little evidence in the historical record but that serves modern scholarly and political needs.[31] It is a maurophilic response to blatant maurophobia, argues Corriente, "but the historian's mission is to transmit faithfully the facts and give them a correct interpretation, and in no case to alter them for moral or ideological ends" (2000, 47).[32]

Indeed, following Corriente's line of thought, numerous scholars have traced the rise of maurophilic discourses in post-Franco Spain to new educational initiatives based in the notion of tolerance and solidarity, if not political correctness (Martín Corrales 2004, 48). Maurophilic discourses of al-Andalus have been especially prominent since the sesquicentennial commemoration of the fall of Granada in 1992 (see Duran 1992) and the rise of what we might term the nuevo romancero morisco (see Fuchs 2009 for more on the older genre). Several modern novels depict al-Andalus in nostalgic ways akin to the older romancero. For example, Tarik Ali's Shadows of the Pomegranate Tree (1993) and Radwa Ashour's Granada (2003), among others (see Granara 2005), promote the idea of al-Andalus as a place of convivencia interrupted by the Spanish conquest. This is also one of the central themes of the documentary When the Moors Ruled in Europe. Hence the maurophilia-maurophobia debate lives on. It is tempting to see Corriente and Fanjul García as advocating if not a maurophobic stance, then an antimaurophilic one. Their critiques, advanced at the level of scholarly debate, contribute to a broader and deeper rethinking of medieval Spanish history in the last two decades, especially since the fateful events of 11 March 2004, when terrorists exploded bombs on trains in Madrid, killing and wounding hundreds (Spain's 3/11, or 11-M, to America's 9/11). In this charged political context of the War on Terrorism, the rhetoric of *convivencia* and a culture of tolerance assume greater political weight and for that same reason invite equally heavy responses.

In a crisis-ridden Spain confronting such problems as high inflation and high unemployment and underemployment, the face of mauropho-bia returns in the guise of racism, intolerance, and exclusion (Suárez-Navaz 2004). Even within the Muslim communities of Granada, non-Spanish Muslims (whom we might call *neo-moros*) feel excluded or marginalized, often by those who one might expect might be the most maurophilic: Spanish and other European Muslim converts (*conversos*; see Lassalle 1997; Rogozen-Soltar 2012b). Spanish maurophilia was perhaps easier to maintain, as Navarro and Tremlett suggest above, in the absence of real "Moors" from "Moorishland." With recent immigration from North Africa, however, the equation has changed (Rogozen-Soltar 2012a). While the tourism industry and many official and quasi-official organizations have jumped on the bandwagon of *convivencia,* including the Junta Andalucía, the Fundación Tres Culturas, and El Legado Andalusí, the old tensions of maurophobia can be felt among *conversos,* Catholic and secular Spaniards, and European observers (even global), on the one hand, and various immigrant groups, on the other—including, paradoxically, second- and third-generation North African residents in cities like Granada and Córdoba. Hence the "¡Moros Fuera!" graffiti I observed is a symbolic marker of a deeper ambivalence not only toward these "new Moors" but toward the Moorish past and the growing Islamic presence in Spain (see Coleman 2008). Therefore, the ambivalence of the Andalusian heritage in contemporary Spain has a long and complex prehistory.

RHETORICS OF AL-ANDALUS IN SPANISH MUSIC: FROM THE CHILDREN OF CASTRO TO THE SONS OF ZIRYAB

A few days before my departure from Granada I stroll aimlessly through the alleys of the Calderería Nueva again. I used to go on such wanderings in Damascus and Aleppo, letting my feet direct me where they would. There are always tea shops, cafés, and restaurants where I can escape the heat (at least until evening *tapas* on the other side of town). Passing a small *artesanía* shop, I notice an *'ud* resting against some cushions. Intrigued, I go inside, and the young owner greets me in Spanish. I reply in Arabic that I'd seen the *'ud* and wondered if he plays it. He smiles and says in Arabic, "No, but wait here and let me get my friend," and ducks out of the shop. After about a minute he returns with a small retinue: Yussef, who runs the shop and whose *'ud* it is, and Uzman Almerabit, who not only plays *'ud* but actually made the one I'd seen and admired. They ask about my interest in the *'ud* and the music, and when I mention my research Uzman recalls having seen me at an *'ud* festival in Morocco (the Third International 'Ud Festival in Tétouan in 2001). They invite me to play a little on the instrument, and I oblige with a small *taqsim* (improvisation), and then we head over to the Dar Ziryab (Ziryab's House) tea shop around the corner so we can speak some more. Uzman is a luthier, performer, and director of the Dar Ziryab Cultural Center (Centro Cultural Dar Ziryab), which opened in Granada's Calle Calderería Nueva in January 2009.[33] He also leads the Al Tarab Ensemble, in which Yussef plays *qanun*. They all come from north of Morocco and have been in Spain off and on for many years. They are very active in the local and regional music scene.

Uzman ('Uthman in Arabic) tells me about his various projects. In addition to the tea shop, the cultural center hosts workshops (*talleres*) on lutherie and crafts such as woodworking, a gallery of musical instruments, art and dance exhibitions, conferences on al-Andalus and music, poetry recitals, and, of course, musical performances. He had recently expanded into the space above the tea shop to create the cultural center. He invites me to two performances they are presenting over the weekend, one on Middle Eastern music, the other on Sufi music. I ask them how they like Granada and being in Albaicín, the Calderería Nueva, and Yussef claims it to be "Zwîna [beautiful], like home!" (referring to Tétouan). They all concur: Granada is fine, everything is great. I then ask them how they get along with the Spaniards and if there are any recriminations or problems, mentioning the "¡Moros Fuera!" graffiti I'd seen earlier. The younger man who had been running the shop when I arrived says that there are no problems. In fact, he claims that the Spaniards seem to be more interested in their culture than are the Arabs and other North Africans. Yussef agrees, but Uzman, who is in many ways their *jefe,* their leader, shakes his head. "No! Maybe in Madrid they are, or Barcelona. But here in Granada, the [Spanish] people are more narrow-minded, conservative." "And the Moroccans here?" I ask. "How do they get along?" Uzman tells me that they are *jdud* (new) to the city so in a way still making their way and learning the ropes. With a play on words I jokingly suggest that they are also *ajdad* (grandparents), that is, the ancestors of the modern Spaniards. "Of course," replies Uzman. "We influenced Spain. You can see our heritage here," as he gestures with his hands to indicate the surroundings, and the young shop attendant I'd first met chimes in, "And flamenco comes from the Arabs. You know, the word comes from the Arabic *fellah mangu,* a wandering peasant." I'd heard that folk etymology before and laugh, thinking it improbable, but when I suggest, again half jokingly, that Granada is therefore "theirs" (*biladkum*), Uzman replies with a shrug of the shoulders. "Ya'ni," mean-ing both yes and no. "I don't know about that. There's a lot of fear here. The people are very conservative," referring to both the North African immigrants and the native Granadinos.

In the background I notice that they are playing the recording *An-dalousiyyat,* a collection of *muwashshahat* by the famous Lebanese diva Fairouz.[34] I remark on the Fairouz recording and ask him what music they perform at Dar Ziryab. I half expect him to defend the "pure tra-dition" of Arab-Andalusian music, the music of Ziryab, but instead he says, "Our audience is mostly Spaniards and tourists, so we have to mix our music. Arab, Andalusian, Turkish, flamenco, Sufi, and others. It's a mix [*mazj*] but we have to do it. It's not like we are living in the Middle Ages. The Moroccans and *conversos* usually don't come to hear us." They all agree. Their music is enjoyed mostly by those outside their own com-munity, even if there are a few diehard North African and Arab fans who come to their shows. Indeed, at the Middle Eastern music concert the following evening, where they present a program of what are now "standards" of the Arab-Ottoman repertoire, the audience at Dar Ziryab, from what I can see and hear, consists mainly of Europeans and only a handful of Arab / North Africans (who were more noticeable due to their interactions with the performers in Arabic). Tellingly, the concert is listed on their website under *música del mundo* (world music).

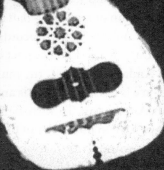

MÚSICA DE ORIENTE MEDIO

con

AL TARAB

Entrada 6 €
Aforo limitado

Viernes 20
febrero
21:00 h

Centro Cultural **DAR ZIRYAB**

c/Calderería Nueva 11,1º
(en la calle de las teterías)
altarabensemble.blogspot.com

tlf reserva:
660 868 183
958 228 344

Dar Ziryab Middle Eastern music concert, Granada, 2009.

Dar Ziryab Sufi music concert, Granada, 2009.

In the Granadino music shop, I encountered a panoply of diverse artists that were all "sons of Ziryab" (*hijos de Ziryab*). Now we find ourselves at "Ziryab's House" in the Moorish quarter of Albaicín. The Ziryab story—the legend, the myth—exercises a powerful hold over the musical imagination in Spain as it does in Syria and Morocco. In Granada and throughout Andalucía and even in much of Spain, the strongest musical associations with al-Andalus are not found in the small Arab and North African ensembles that ply their craft at restaurants and cultural centers and on festival stages or in the medieval or early music ensembles that aim to recover the lost sounds of earlier epochs. Rather, it is flamenco music that most evokes the Orient in the ears and eyes of many: from Spaniards to North African and Arab immigrants, to tourists and cultural programmers. The notion that musics as diverse as Arab-Andalusian *nuba,* modern Egyptian song, Syrian *muwashshahat,* and Spanish flamenco and the host of musical hybrids that have arisen between these and other "world musics" are all descendants of the music created by Ziryab in ninth-century Córdoba forms a sonic ideological backdrop to the rhetoric of al-Andalus in contemporary Spain. In symbolically oversaturated *lieux de mémoire* such as Granada, the various musical styles, in their complex interactions with each other and with forms of nostalgic dwelling, lend an ear to and reverberate with the maurophilia-maurophobia debate. Music offers a point of articulation for these debates, as it is a vehicle for sounding cultural differences and for finding a common group among diverse communities in Spain and the broader Mediterranean region. In particular, music is an important medium for negotiating Islam in Spain, as it allows people to relate to Muslims on an aesthetic, even a corporeal, level, not unlike the tea shops and bathhouses in the Albaicín, which serve as points of communion, of consumption, and of rhetorical elaboration. Often tied to Sufism, the diverse "Andalusian" musics performed in Granada are embodied practices that bring people into a Muslim-oriented community; musical performance provides Muslims a means for reaching out to others via what Deborah Kapchan (2008, 2009) terms the creation of a "literacy of listening." These musics can be vehicles for assimilation via fusion with flamenco, for example, or through their implication in Orientalist fantasies through the performance of a largely "Oriental" repertoire of Ottoman, Levantine Arab, and North African musics. Like the arts in general, from architecture and the visual arts to cuisine and poetry, music can be a path to connection and a bridge to understanding, but also a potential barrier.

In what follows, I outline the various musics performed in Granada and elsewhere in Andalucía that are presented as having a genealogical connection to al-Andalus. In addition to the main forms of Arab and Arab-Andalusian music, I focus on the rhetorical role of flamenco, which plays an important mediating role between the musics of East and West—as a sonic signifier of internal exoticism and difference, as a claimed "child of Ziryab," and as an integral part of the modern Spanish national imaginary. Audiences and performers alike utilize flamenco to construct, negotiate, and in some cases even challenge the Spanish rhetoric of al-Andalus. Moreover, via what I have elsewhere called "flexible musical specialization" (Shannon 2003c, 2011), Arab and North African musicians and audiences deftly negotiate their subordination to a racialized and Orientalized European cultural imaginary, to profit (literally) from the tourist gaze that is the primary public expression of the rhetoric of al-Andalus in contemporary Spain, and to carve a space for dwelling in what for many is an ersatz ancestral home. In this manner, they borrow the form and dynamics of neoliberal commodity capitalism to secure their nostalgic dwelling in Granada.

Because flamenco acts as one of the primary rhetorical means for (re)inserting Arab and North African musics into the Spanish context, I begin with a brief discussion of flamenco and what I will call the "flamenco discourse" in the study of Arab and Arab-Andalusian musics. While the associations of flamenco with Romani ("Gypsy" or *gitano*) culture are more common and more established in scholarly and popular circles than the Arab or Moorish (*moro*), I found that a common denominator in my interactions with performers and audiences of North Africa and Middle Eastern musics in Spain was the idea that flamenco was part of the mix—that it, too, was a child of Ziryab. I noted that Syrian commentators assert that all things Andalusian ultimately derive from Syria, including music. If Ziryab started the first music conservatory and inaugurated a golden age of poetic-musical developments in Córdoba, as the standard narrative has it, this was as a result of the

Levantine Arab musical heritage that he brought with him in his flight from Baghdad.[35] Fast-forward several centuries, and we find references to Ziryab aplenty in Granada, including the oft-mentioned notion that Spain's most famous music—flamenco—has its roots ultimately in the innovations of this earlier figure if not in the Arabic language itself (via the oft-mentioned folk etymology). The great Paco de Lucía (1947–2014), perhaps the best-known exemplar of flamenco guitar in the twentieth century, recorded the flamenco hit album *Zyryab* ([1990] 2006), evoking the earlier master and at the same time suggesting his virtual reincarnation in the body and spirit of the modern Spanish performer.[36] The associations between Ziryab, Arab music, and flamenco are as wide as they are deep. From the early twentieth-century interest in *cante jondo* among musicians, composers, and flamencologists, including Manuel de Falla and his teacher and mentor Felipe Pedrell, for example, to contemporary groups assuming his name, including the Spanish group Ziryab-Caló, the flamenco discourse is a powerful way for orienting relations between North African and Middle Eastern ("Oriental") musics, on the one hand, and flamenco, on the other.[37]

This is not the place to rehearse the debates about the origins and development of flamenco or to explore the contemporary performance and cultural dynamics of flamenco in the Andalusian and Spanish national contexts. There is now an extensive ethnographic and critical literature on flamenco history and performance (Álvarez Caballero 1981; Chuse 2003; Labajo 2003; Malefyt 1998; Manuel 1989; Mitchell 1994; Washabaugh 1996, 2012). A few scholars have also attempted to test the dominant flamenco discourse and investigate the "Moorish" influence on flamenco practice (Cruces-Roldán 2002, 2003b), or vice versa (Rossy 1966, cited in Cruces-Roldán 2003b, 11). The most important of these is the idea (ideology) that flamenco has Arab roots. Many Syrians and Moroccan argue for this connection both in the abstract and in musical recordings and performances, such as *Roots of Flamenco* and the various collaborations between performers of the *'ud* and flamenco guitar. Some of my musical and even scholarly interlocutors took for granted the folk etymology that the very word "flamenco" has Arabic roots—this despite other evidence showing that the word derives from "Flemish," invoking the long-standing historical ties between imperial Spain and the

Low Countries, where Spanish king and Holy Roman emperor Charles V (1500–1558) was born. Still others point to structural similarities between Arab and "Oriental" music and flamenco, including but not limited to shared features such as additive rhythms, modal tonality, ornamentation, and tense vocals, let alone a passionate and sad performance aesthetic (Cruces-Roldán 2003b).[38]

More important for the purposes of this text, over the course of the twentieth century flamenco has come to occupy such a prominent role in the Spanish national imaginary that not only is this once-denigrated music now performed and celebrated all over Spain, but Spain can now even be understood as a "flamenco nation" (Washabaugh 2012, 1). This is the result of a long history of adaptations and co-optations of flamenco into the national consciousness, from the work of Infante, Falla, and García Lorca to reinterpret flamenco as a part of Andalusian national culture, to the Franco-era promotion of flamenco on the Spanish national stage, along with other Andalusian practices such as bullfighting (see Mitchell 1991). These processes have only accelerated with the increasing incorporation since the 1960s of flamenco and flamenco-inspired musics into world music and more recently as a result of the global discourses of heritage and heritage preservation, since not only is flamenco now closely identified with the Spanish nation, but in November 2010 it was inscribed onto UNESCO's Representative List of the Intangible Cultural Heritage of Humanity.

Clearly, flamenco has transcended its "Gypsy" and "Moorish" origins to become world heritage, something for everyone. At the same time, the flamenco discourse rhetorically invokes both *gitanos* and *moros* to bolster exoticism and authenticity, the twin currencies of world music (Shannon 2003c; Taylor 1997). As a result it has become in important ways the primary medium for translating Arab and Andalusian musics into the Spanish and European popular consciousness, a sort of musical solvent that allows the fusion and mixing of various styles through its complex associations with internal Others (*gitano* and *moro*). It has done so primarily through its associations with heightened emotionality and passion, stereotypical features of both *gitano* and "Moorish" music and character. Indeed, it is the affective realm, expressed through the discourse of *tarab,* that grants music its authenticity in places like Syria and

Egypt (Shannon 2006).[39] In flamenco, it is the mysterious force of *du-ende*, a near equivalent to *tarab* (García Lorca 1981; Mitchell 1991; Racy 1991, 2004), that performs authenticity in both the flamenco discourse and the rhetoric of al-Andalus in the Spanish musical and racial imagination. Through a discourse of the emotions, flamenco thereby enacts a doubling of the exotic *and* the authentic, both important elements of the pan-Mediterranean rhetoric of al-Andalus.[40]

ANDALUSIAN MUSICS OF GRANADA: SOUNDING NOSTALGIC DWELLING

What of the nonflamenco ingredients in this Arab-Andalusian mix? In addition to background music in tea shops and restaurants around the Albaicín, one can hear concerts of Arab and Arab-Andalusian musics year-round in Granada. This is in addition to the rich musical offerings of the city of Granada and in Andalucía more generally, with a mixture of European classical music, flamenco, world music (including Arab and Arab-Andalusian), and so on. There are several musical ensembles based in Granada that specialize in the Arab and Arab-Andalusian genres. They mostly perform the standard Arab-Ottoman music that is similar to what one might hear in Egypt or Syria, sometimes in combination with North African Andalusian musics, and sometimes exclusively the latter music. Most performances take place in small concert halls, such as at the university, or in cultural centers, such as Dar Ziryab, and on festival stages in Granada and across Europe. In fact, the festival stage has become the primary locus of performance of Andalusian musics in Spain, as in Morocco and Syria.

A number of groups that perform Andalusian musics make their home in Granada. These include the Al Tarab Ensemble, directed by Uzman Almerabit and based at Dar Ziryab. According to its website, the ensemble was formed at the end of the 1980s by "Andalusis who lived between the two banks [*dos orillas*], al-Andalus and the Maghreb." It is interesting to note the deployment here of the idea of the "two banks" (the *'udwatan* of medieval Arabic letters), for it suggests that the music and the musicians themselves serve as bridges across the cultural span. Indeed, the text goes on to state that the group has performed "Arab-flamenco fusions, medieval Andalusian, Sufi, and medieval Oriental musics" and now focuses on the "synthesis of three cultures: Sephardic, Arab-Andalusian [*sic*] . . . always with an open spirit without forgetting its origins."[41] In this manner, the group plays on the two major sources of world music marketing: on the one hand, fusion and hybridity, and on the other, authenticity and roots (Shannon 2003c; Taylor 1997). The poly-valence of the group's repertoire suggests its incorporation into world music regimes of value, and the extensive nature of its performances and collaborations with major groups and artists, from the flamenco masters Tomatito and El Lebrijano to Oriental music masters Faruk Tekbilek, Haik Manoukian, and Said Chraibi, among others, suggests that the ensemble has been successful at translating its vision into artistic suc-cess. Al Tarab Ensemble now offers weekly concerts in its small gallery and performance space at Dar Ziryab, as well as performances at festivals in the major cities of Andalucía and across Spain. In recent years, for example, the group has performed in Seville, Córdoba, Jaén, Alcalá la Real, Cáceres, Málaga, Almeria, and Madrid, as well as internationally, including various cities in California (where Almerabit once studied), Estonia, Japan, and France.[42]

In a similar manner, other Granada-based groups perform mix-tures of Middle Eastern ("Oriental") and Arab-Andalusian repertoires. Of these, no fewer than three are directed by Abdel Karim, a Moroccan performer of the *nay* flute. His groups include the Abdel Karim Ensem-ble, which performs "classical Arab music" and incorporates musicians from Morocco, Syria, Egypt, and Spain.[43] Their repertoire includes "mu-sic from throughout the Middle East, from Turkey to Egypt, ranging from the sixteenth to the nineteenth centuries. Abdel Karim Ensemble also performs Andalusian Arabic music, a genre that originated in al-Andalus, Islamic medieval Spain."[44] The group performs not only in Granada but, like Al Tarab, at festivals and conferences around Spain. Karim also directs the Grupo Al-Baraka, which, like the first ensemble, performs music based in the "ethnic musics of diverse Arab, Turkish, and Mediterranean countries."[45] Moreover, he directs two other groups with similar, overlapping musical aims. The Ensemble Mil y Una Noches (Thousand and One Nights Ensemble) is inspired by the idea of the court music of Harun al-Rashid.[46] They offer "all the magic and exoti-cism of the music and dance of the Nights in a forceful and magnetic spectacle full of rhythm and beauty."[47] The Grupo Al Caravan, like the Ensemble Mil y Una Noches, specializes in "musics of the Orient, al-Andalus, and Morocco," often featuring the dancer and choreographer Samira Stella. Stella, for her part, directs the dance troupe Compañía al-Ghazalat, which performs to the music of the previous ensembles and independently.

In addition to these closely interrelated groups, there is the Granada-based Al Firdaus Ensemble, founded in 2012 by Ali Keeler, a British musician and convert to Islam who has extensive experience in Syria and Morocco.[48] Al Firdaus Ensemble includes musicians from England, Spain, and Morocco and specializes in Middle Eastern music but with a mixture of Sufi, Celtic, and flamenco influences; in this way, the group draws on some of the most common sources of inspiration for musical fusions in recent decades (Shannon 2011; Stokes and Bohlman 2003; Taylor 1997). According to the group's website,

> The unique sound of [the] music is due to a synthesis of different musical styles. These include original compositions of a more Western classical character with influences from both Celtic and flamenco traditions and arrangements of songs drawn from the rich heritage of traditional Sufi music from Arabic, Andalusi, and Turkish sources. The words of the songs are mainly in Arabic drawn from the poetry of great Sufis from al-Andalus and the Arab world such as Ibn Arabi and al-Shushtari. Also within their repertoire are musical adaptations of poems in *aljamiado*, the Spanish language written by the Moriscos using the Arabic script.[49]

Al Firdaus is active at festivals in Spain, including a concert during the "Ramadan Nights" programming of the Casa Árabe in Córdoba, and in Morocco, where they have performed at the Sufi Music Festival in Fez. Given their name, which in Arabic and Persian means "Paradise," their primary referent is Islam, and Sufi music is a speciality, even if they offer a broad gamut of aesthetic possibilities, including fusions of Sufi and Celtic musics.

Finally, among the main Granadino groups that play a role in promoting a musical rhetoric of al-Andalus in Spain is the ensemble Nassim al-Andalus. Unlike the above-mentioned groups that perform a mixture of "Oriental" and Arab-Andalusian music, Nassim al-Andalus performs only music of the traditional Moroccan *nuba*. Formed in the

1990s by *'ud* player Youssef al-Husaini and featuring the master *qanun* player Yussef Mezgildi and other Moroccan artists based in Spain, Nassim al-Andalus (Andalusian Breeze) gives performances in Granada, sometimes at Dar Ziryab, and at festivals across Andalucía.[50] Their nod to tradition is exemplified by their repertoire, which includes only works from the Moroccan tradition, and yet their performance aesthetic diverges from tradition: whereas in Moroccan *al-ala* performance, one song will flow into another, Nassim al-Andalus plays sets of discrete pieces, offering essentially mini-*nubas* that accommodate the restrictions of festival stage performance and European audience expectations.

There are other groups in Granada that perform similar musics (e.g., the Kamal al-Nawawi Trio and the Ensemble Al-Ruzafa), as well as regional and international ensembles and artists who perform in Granada.[51] The promotional materials for these ensembles, including blogs, websites, YouTube videos, and brochures distributed at concerts, focus on exoticism and on the pan-Mediterranean, pan-Arab, and pan-Islamic links among the performers and the musics. Not unlike the Franco-Swiss artist Julien Jalaladine Weiss (1953–2015), whose Ensemble al-Kindi performed a wide variety of genres, from the secular to the sacred, the Arab to the Turko-Persian, Abdel Karim's groups cover a wide range of musical geography. This fits with the neoliberal world music model of flexible musical specialization (Shannon 2003c, 2011). Nassim al-Andalus also submits to the cultural logic of world music through their performance of "authenticity" even if they do not mix musical styles.[52] A number of other groups pursue this latter orientation, eschewing musical fusions for a deeper engagement in the pursuit of authenticity and musical roots. Many of these groups arose in the late 1960s and 1970s from the early music movement and began experimenting with medieval Andalusian music, often finding inspiration in contemporary North African performance practice for their interpretation of medieval European musics, including the thirteenth-century *Cantigas de Santa Maria* and other works from Mediterranean European folk traditions. The aim of groups such as Mudéjar, Ibn Báya, Calamus, and Cinco Siglos, among many others, has been not only to find common ground between the medieval European and North African repertoires but to "claim or re-claim (depending on [one's] point of view) part of the mu-

sical heritage of Iberia and make a statement about the relationship between the cultures of Europe and the Middle East" (Reynolds 2009, 187).

In previous chapters we met Begoña Olavide at concerts she and her
group gave in Damascus and Morocco. Olavide plays the *salterio* (psaltery) and *qanun,* both varieties of zither, and sings in Spanish, French,
Arabic, Hebrew, Latin, and Ladino. In 1994 she founded the Ensemble
Mudéjar, borrowing the term for Muslims who were allowed to remain
under Christian rule, with the express aim of uncovering in sound the
traces of "Moorish" Spain that remain after centuries of erasure and
silencing. Like her husband and collaborator, the Madrileño artist and
luthier Carlos Paniagua (and his brothers Gregorio, Eduardo, and Luis),
Olavide was trained in the European early music movement and has a
strong interest not only in performing the medieval Arab-Andalusian
and Sephardic repertoires but in documenting and preserving them. The
ensemble's performance practice has a strong curatorial dimension to
it. For example, Paniagua, a skilled luthier, attempts to re-create instruments found in iconographic depictions as diverse as manuscript illustrations and architectural relief, and Olavide spent many years learning
Arabic in order better to understand the lyrics she was singing. Eduardo
Paniagua, a frequent collaborator, founded the record label Pneuma to
document the musical cultures of al-Andalus in all their diversity; his
list includes over 120 titles (produced in less than ten years!), including
over 25 in his al-Andalus collection and over a dozen and growing in the
Cantigas of Alfonso X the Wise and other collections (see Campbell
2011). Paniagua's recording project feeds the lutherie and performance
practices of his brother; both can be seen as part of the larger effort not
only to preserve but to explore the richness of Spain's musical patrimony
and to form rich connections among Spanish, Moroccan, and other artists. For example, the various configurations of these groups collaborate
with Sudanese singer and *'ud* player Wafir Sheikh el-Din (a former member of Radio Tarifa), Jordi Savall (the Spanish-Catalan master of the
viol and founder of the classical group Hespèrion XXI), Iraqi *'ud* master
Naseer Shamma, and Spanish lute and *'ud* player Luis Delgado, among
many others.

According to Carlos Paniagua, Mudéjar's aim is "to unearth and
understand the real history of these events. The deeper we look into it,

the more indebted we have come to feel to that Arab culture that left behind such evocative traces in our own."[53] With this in mind, the couple settled in Tangier from 2005 to 2012 and collaborated with Moroccan artist Omar Metioui in his Confluences musicales (Rawafid musiqiyya) association, giving concerts and running workshops on lutherie and the documentation and history of Andalusian music on both banks of the Strait of Gibraltar. Olavide performs regularly with Metioui's Tangier-based ensembles both in Morocco and internationally. Yet, they do not pretend to re-create the early Andalusian music in a straightforward manner. Recognizing that we cannot know what the medieval music actually sounded like, the members of Mudéjar claim instead to reconstitute the affective dimensions of the music. In the promotional material for a 2008 concert, they claimed that their goal is "to communicate the joy, sadness, or nostalgia that these songs evoke, as much today as they did then, connecting with modern sensibilities without forgetting the old ways and methods."[54] Nor do they search for musical purity. Over lunch with me in 2004, both Olavide and Metioui stressed that their work is not world music or fusion; recall Metioui's remark that the music is already a mixture of styles (North African, Arabian, European), so there is no need to further hybridize or fuse it with others. As with the flamenco discourse, the early music–inspired practices of Arab-Andalusian music focus on the affective realm: not *tarab* or *duende* but a transhistorical emotional authenticity in performance aided by careful study, cultural sensitivity, and not a small amount of marketing savvy (see also Shannon 2011).[55]

The quest for emotional authenticity can be heard in a variety of recordings by both Mudéjar and other ensembles and performers of Arab-Andalusian and flamenco-Arab fusions. Mudéjar's first major recording, *Cartas al rey moro* (Letters to the Moorish king, 1998), evokes the atmosphere of late fifteenth-century Spain at the time of the fall of Granada. *Cartas* contains a mixture of songs in Arabic and Spanish that are performed on Olavide's psaltery and the Arab instruments *'ud* and *qanun*, but also on such European instruments as guitar, *vihuela, vihuela bajo,* Middle Eastern drums (*darbukka, bendir, tar*), and even the *cajón,* a Peruvian box drum incorporated into flamenco by Paco de Lucía. The aesthetic is mournful, appropriate for songs that mainly speak of loss. The recording begins with the song "Apiadate de mi pequeño corazón" (Take pity on my little heart), sung in Arabic and adapted from the Moroccan *muwashshah* "Rifqan 'ala qulaybi" from the *nubat al-'ushshaq*. It departs dramatically from the Moroccan "original" with its somber, medieval air, very much reminiscent of other early music recordings (see Shannon 2007c). The other seven tracks draw on Spanish folk songs from the thirteenth through the sixteenth centuries and have the same general aesthetic. The liner notes to the recording describe the songs and provide semischolarly discussions of their provenance. For example, concerning "Apiádate de mi pequeño corazón," they write:

> Musical transcription with occidental annotation of the repertoire has, since 1930, allowed for a greater understanding of the mechanisms of the arábigo-andaluz musical legacy, but it has never been a substitute for oral transmission, as this music is filled with adornments and turns that are impossible to annotate. *"Apiádate de mi pequeño corazón"* is a *sana'* (song) that belongs to the *btaihi* rhythm (a cycle of 8 beats, subdivided in 3-3-2) of the *nuba,* the eleventh in the order of al-Ha'ik and based on a G major diatonic scale. It has been transcribed by Abdelkrim Rais and Mohamed Briouel. (Mudéjar 1998, original English)

The attention to curation and pedagogy, notable in all their recordings, serves to support the authenticity of their work.[56] Mudéjar's performance practice and recordings, along with Eduardo Paniagua's Pneuma record label, can be understood as an extension of the early music sensibility and what George Marcus and Fred Myers (1999) analyze as the traffic between art, culture, and scholarship. Similar processes can be traced in the recording projects of other artists involved in medieval and Andalusian music in Spain (see Reynolds 2009, 185–189).

I have already mentioned Paco de Lucía's *Zyryab*. It is noteworthy not only for the exquisite guitar playing of the late master but for the incorporation of Arab instruments and compositional elements that allow it to cross over from flamenco to world music. A number of other prominent Spanish flamenco artists have recorded Arab- and Andalusian-inspired musics, often in collaboration with North African and Middle Eastern artists. In his 1998 recording *Música Alhambra* (see figure 3), flamenco guitarist Juan Martín (b. 1948) offers what he describes in the CD liner notes as "an exploration into Moorish, Indian gypsy [*sic*] and

Flamenco musical styles, *aghani wa muwashshahat andalusiyya* [Songs and Andalusian Muwashshahat], five Sephardic songs and culminating in contemporary Flamenco" (Martín [1998] 2011). The tracks, organized under the heading "wasla min al-muwashshahat al-andalusiyya" (a suite of Andalusian *muwashshahat*), are listed in Spanish, English, and, for five of the tracks, Arabic (the Sephardic numbers are listed in Spanish). The liner notes include a brief review of "The Origins and influences leading up to flamenco" (in English) that recapitulates the standard narrative with the addition of information about "Indian Hindu" music and dance (especially Kathak; see Phillips 2013) and on Sephardic songs in Turkey and the Middle East. For Martín, there is an "unmistakable legacy of Arab rule in Spain" to be heard in "the sound of the flamenco voice with its melismatic style." Unlike Mudéjar's work, this is a purely instrumental recording, and there is little effort at scholarly treatment of the material. In fact, many of the songs have no connection to al-Andalus. Track 8, "Zourouni," is a popular song composed for the musical theater by the Egyptian artist Sayyid Darwish in the early twentieth century, as was track 9, "El Bint el Shalabiya." Track 2, "Lamma Bada Ytethena" (also listed in Arabic), is described as "pre-14th century Andalusí." This particular *muwashshah* is often described as Andalusian in performance and recordings, even though it commonly is attributed to the late nineteenth-century Egyptian composer al-Shaykh ʿAbd al-Rahim al-Maslub. While these historical shortcomings do not take away from Martín's artistry, they do indicate the extent to which the standard narrative expands in the Spanish rhetoric of al-Andalus to include just about anything that can be considered Arab, Jewish, and "Gypsy." The polyvalence of the model, like the flexible musical specialization explored earlier, in this case promotes exoticism and consumer-driven categorizations and forms bridges among peoples and their musical cultures.

El Lebrijano (Juan Peña Fernandez, b. 1941) is a *gitano* flamenco singer (*cantaor*) who rose to fame in the 1970s through his collaboration with Paco de Lucía and is known for his strong and intense voice, which led Gabriel García Márquez to note, "Cuando Lebrijano canta, se moja el agua" (When Lebrijano sings, the water gets wet).[57] Beginning in the 1980s, El Lebrijano began to expand his musical field to include collaborations with North African artists. His recording *Encuentros* (Encounters, 1985), made with the Andalusian Orchestra of Tangier, features, in addition to his unmistakable strong voice, the flamenco guitar of Paco Cepero and the traditional instruments of an *al-ala* ensemble. It inaugurated what was to be a series of collaborations with various North African artists and groups: *Casablanca* (with the Arab-Andalusian Orchestra of Casablanca, 1998) and *Puertas abiertas* (Open doors, 2005), with Moroccan violinist Faiçal Kourrich. These recordings have perhaps done more to promote the interests of his collaborators than his own (given the mixed critical reception to his work).[58] At the same time, like those of Mudéjar and Juan Martín, these recordings perform the standard narrative and give musical form to ideologies of a shared heritage. Even when the collaborations are not successful (several of the Moroccan musicians I spoke with in Tangier who had collaborated with El Lebrijano and other Spanish artists mentioned that they did it for the pleasure and prestige of recording with a European and for profit but that it was not always easy to translate the musical languages), El Lebrijano is deft at pulling together the two major strands of the rhetoric of al-Andalus in Spain: the Romani ("Gypsy") and the Arab ("Moorish").

The efforts to promote an idea of a shared heritage are legion in Granada: from Rafaela Carrasco and Cristina Hoyo's Ballet Flamenco de Andalucía program *Lorca y Granada,* held annually in the Alhambra's Generalife gardens, to concerts of Andalusian and Arab musics at the Granada International Festival of Music and Dance, there is no shortage of musical opportunities to sound the idea of Spain's multiple legacies. These Spanish artists are children of Castro and Ziryab, and they work to promote new forms of maurophilia via music to combat growing maurophobia. Their work is a means for bringing back al-Andalus into the national artistic fold without evoking the recolonization models that maurophobic critics fear (see Zapata-Barrero 2012).

NOSTALGIC DWELLING IN SPAIN AND THE CHILDREN OF CASTRO AND ZIRYAB

In contemporary Spain, al-Andalus serves multiple roles. First, it is a strong marker of Spanish heterogeneity, past and present. The presence of "Moorish" (North African and Arab) musicians in places like Granada resonates with commonly circulating ideologies of the Andalusian past. To some, they embody a past *convivencia* that progressives would like to re-create in Spain. To others, including postrevisionist Spanish historians, these same performers mark a disjuncture from the "true" Spain (the idealized Spain of Sánchez-Albornoz). In this view, their very presence marks an atavistic or even parasitic incursion into the Spanish mainstream, as they trade in the currency of exoticism and an ersatz nostalgia for profit, or worse: their intent is to create inroads into Spanish society so as to re-create not only a past time of coexistence but a present and future time of Muslim domination. For new Muslims and for some migrants, developments such as the opening of the Great Mosque of Granada encourage restorative nostalgias of a future past. Yet these nostalgic visions run against walls of intolerance and (politically motivated) aporias in the public management of diversity in Spain. For example, while Sephardic Jews who can demonstrate ancestry from expelled populations can apply for dual citizenship, this privilege has not been extended to Muslims. Likewise, after a well-publicized debate the Spanish village of Castrillo Matajudíos (Little Fort of Jew Killers) voted to officially change its name to Castrillo de Mota Judíos (Little Hill Fort of the Jews) to sever presumed links between the village and the anti-Semitic practices of the Inquisition. However, the village of Valle de Matamoros (Valley of Moor Killers) and other villages with similar names refuse to consider a change of name (Fotheringham 2014). Even though the population of Castrillo Matajudíos / Mota Judíos is small (Fotheringham places it at fifty-seven), the name change is significant given the broader context of historical revisionism and the management of internal difference in contemporary Spain. Hence the rhetoric of al-Andalus in Spain is contradictory, simultaneously opening and closing on possibilities of historical realignment and reconciliation.

Music is one point of articulation for these debates because it offers a public face to communities within Spain and their trans-Mediterranean counterparts. Music is a medium for negotiating Islam in Spain because it offers something that allows people to relate to Muslims on an aesthetic level, a corporeal level, in some ways like the tea shops and even bathhouses in the Albaicín and elsewhere. Tied to Sufism in many ways, music is an embodied practice that brings people in to a Muslim-oriented community (given the great diversity of views among Muslims) and also allows an avenue for Muslims to reach out. Music can be an assimilationist vehicle via fusion with flamenco, for example, or through its implication in Orientalist fantasies—through performing a largely "Oriental" repertoire of Ottoman, Levantine Arab, North African, and flamenco and flamenco-inspired musics, at least according to some, like Uzman Almerabet. The arts are in general a pathway to connection, a bridge to mutual understanding, such as in the association Confluences musicales, founded by a Moroccan and involving two Spanish artists. The other arts, including architecture, visual arts, cuisine, and poetry, may also serve as bridges to understanding, but they may also stand as potential barriers, depending on their forms. While bathhouses and tea shops are generally embraced, partly because they promote an embodied experience of difference, mosques, Islamic culture centers, and halal butchers, for example, might not be. As anthropologist Mikaela Rogozen-Soltar argues, the problems Muslims living in Granada face result from the fact that "Andalusia is experiencing a process of secularization, in which the presence of supposedly devout Muslims and 'the return of Islam' are seen as challenges. Rejection of immigrants, then, stems not from an embedded secular position, but rather from overt efforts of Andalusians to reconcile a predominantly Catholic worldview and secularism (equated today with authentic Europeanness). Muslims, interestingly, are cast in opposition to both the secular project and Catholicism" (Rogozen-Soltar 2007, 873).

To overcome these obstacles, North African and Arab musicians in Granada and many of their Spanish collaborators employ flexible musical specialization to adapt their practice to multiple situations and thereby deftly negotiate their subordination to a racialized and Orientalized European cultural imaginary. Such flexibility also allows tourists, Spanish audiences, and even Spanish and other European artists such as Olavide and the Paniaguas to serve as bridges between cultures. Flamenco plays an important mediating role between the musics of East and West as a sonic signifier of internal exoticism and difference, as a claimed "child of Ziryab," and as an integral part of the modern Spanish national imaginary. Audiences and performers alike utilize flamenco to construct and in some cases negotiate and challenge the Spanish rhetoric of al-Andalus. The musical practices at the same time mark a transition from a cultural amnesia of the "Moorish" past to a Spanish memory culture and reflective and restorative nostalgias that acknowledge, sometimes grudgingly, the Andalusian heritage, even if some, such as Fanjul, deny any relationship to the medieval Arab past. As sonic accompaniments to nostalgic dwelling, the musics variously labeled as Andalusian, Arab-Andalusian, medieval or early music, or even flamenco-Oriental fusions produce Granada as a site for symbolic contestation.

For whom is Granada home today? Gunther Dietz found that for some Muslims in Granada, the Albaicín "feels like home," as the young shop attendant in the Albaicín indicated. Yet, still others feel "instrumentalized by orientalist tourism policies" (Dietz 2003, 1011, cited in Rogozen-Soltar 2007, 872; see also Dietz and El-Shohoumi 2005). As we have seen, musical performance is very much tied into this double bind of feeling an attachment to an ancestral home, often via an ersatz nostalgia, and at the same time feeling objectified by tourists and others as somehow representative of that same past but via a different mode of nostalgic dwelling—the Orientalist, the exotic. The latter point was echoed by an Algerian friend who formerly lived and worked in Granada and claimed that the Albaicín was too "dirty" and even "sinister" for his tastes and that he now avoids it, even after having worked and lived there for several years. He said the tensions with new arrivals and growing conservatism among Muslims, both natives and *conversos,* made it difficult for him to live as he wished. He has since relocated to a small town in the west of Andalucía where he still plies his craft of *artesanía* production—and performance as a *moro* in local *moros y cristianos* festivals. There is seemingly no escaping the logic.[59]

Finalis

The Project of al-Andalus and Nostalgic Dwelling in the Twenty-First Century

Omar Metioui, whom we met in Morocco, is both a pharmacist and a skilled interpreter of Morocco's Andalusian musical heritage. Having grown up in multilingual Tangier and studied in Brussels, Metioui is comfortable in Arabic, French, and Spanish, as well as in the varied roles of pharmacist, ensemble director, cultural translator, researcher, and social entrepreneur, having founded in 2007 the association Confluences musicales (Rawafid musiqiyya) dedicated to preserving and performing the Andalusian musical legacy. While his pharmacy and the cultural center are in Tangier, he and his family reside in a spacious villa near Cape Malabata looking across the Strait of Gibraltar to Spain. A plaque near the front door reads "Las Dos Orillas" (the two banks), evoking the medieval concept of *al-'udwatan,* the two banks of al-Andalus—the African and the European. Metioui straddles these two banks as a performer and as a person.

On a fine spring day in Fez in 2004, I attended a concert that Metioui gave with Begoña Olavide, the Spanish artist who is also the founder of Ensemble Mudéjar. At the time, Olavide and her husband, Carlos Paniagua, were considering relocating to Tangier to work with Metioui on Confluences musicales. They in fact would later relocate there for

Omar Metioui and Begoña Olavide in concert, Fez, 2004.

some six years, performing regularly with Metioui's Tangier-based ensembles, both in Morocco and internationally, and conducting master classes on music and lutherie at Confluences musicales' headquarters in the Tangier *medina*.

The concert was held in a modern salon adorned in traditional Moroccan fashion—plenty of masterfully executed *zellij* tiles, elaborate carved and painted wooden ceilings, and portraits of the former and current monarchs overlooking the raised dais that served as a stage. The performance featured Metioui on *'ud* with a small traditional Moroccan ensemble (*jawq*), including the *rabab* fiddle, *tarr* drum, violin, and vocalist (Metioui has also mastered the violin). Olavide accompanied on *qanun* and sang in Arabic, Spanish, and Ladino. The audience included a wide cast of *mélomanes*, or local aficionados of the music, including many of my main interlocutors and teachers.

Metioui opened the concert with the remarks that the music they would be performing was meant to promote healing in the aftermath of 3/11, not 9/11, that is, in the aftermath of the March 11, 2004, train bombings in Madrid, as well as the terrorist bombings in Casablanca of May 16, 2003.[1] He asserted not only the value of music to help heal those wounds but suggested as well that having a Moroccan and Spanish artist performing songs from a common Muslim, Jewish, and Christian heritage might promote the type of understanding needed to combat the enemies of peace. It was a powerful reminder that Americans are not the only ones dealing with international terror and that the near-constant reification of 9/11 as the beginning of the Next Great Struggle is not universally shared. Metioui's remarks, like the music, were well received, and, standing with Paniagua at the back of the hall, I heard a number of local music lovers praise not only Metioui's musicianship—well known, given his extensive experience—but also Olavide's, who at the time was less well known in Morocco.

The next day we all met in the garden of my hotel for lunch to discuss the concert. Over couscous and mint tea I prodded Metioui on his comments concerning the role of music in promoting peace. Indicating with a sweep of his hands the presence of Olavide and Paniagua at the table, Metioui said that musical collaboration is one key in promoting understanding and bridging divides, especially between Europeans and North Africans (and, by extension, between Christians and Muslims). The concert was proof of this potential; if different peoples can perform music together, then they stand a better chance of getting along. Olavide and Paniagua agreed; there was hope.[2] That the concert and conversation were happening in Fez, Morocco's traditional spiritual and cultural capital, resonated with the similar message of hope promoted by the Fez Festival of World Sacred Music, what the organizers call "the message of Fez" and which is concerned with bringing about peaceful change and coexistence through the power of sacred sounds (see Kapchan 2008; Shannon 2003c). The discourse of healing through music also formed a key component of Metioui and Olavide's performance at the Festival of Andalusian Music, held in Fez in April 2009.

After lunch we strolled through the ancient alleys of Fez, and I spoke with Olavide about her participation in the ensemble. She reiterated her history with the music, the founding of her group, the work of Carlos to research and recreate the older instruments, and how her collaborations with Metioui and others have brought her to a deeper understanding of the music and its importance today. When I suggested that these performances might have a political edge to them, she agreed, stating that it was an important part of why they perform. In fact, she claimed, her group was invited to perform at a festival marking the five hundredth anniversary of the death of Queen Isabel of Castile, the conqueror of Granada. As an act of musical resistance, she prepared a program of songs entirely in Arabic, Hebrew, and Ladino—but not Spanish—commemorating the death of a Catholic queen with the musics of those whom she had expelled, the thousands of Jews and Moors who fled Granada after the abrogation of treaties that had ensured the continuation of a form of *convivencia*. By drawing on a heterogeneous musical and cultural past, Olavide aimed to combat a monocultural view of Spain and Spanish history, a view that still has many partisans despite changes in modern Spanish self-understanding.

Their concert in Fez was not the only one that year to draw on the Andalusian musical heritage and the model of making music together to promote a vision of peaceful coexistence. That fall, the Sephardic singer Françoise Atlan (born in France of a Spanish mother and an Algerian Berber father) performed at Carnegie Hall's Zankel Hall with the Moroccan Ensemble al-Rayyis, directed by Muhammad Briouel. Their program also performed musically the imagined *convivencia* and mutual influences among Jewish, Muslim, and Christian performers from the medieval and early modern eras. Atlan resides in Marrakech and told me in an interview that she found no problem with being a Jewish woman living in a Muslim country. And almost a year earlier, I had attended in Rabat a concert of the famous West-Eastern Divan Orchestra, led by the indefatigable Daniel Barenboim, cofounder of the initiative with the late Edward Said. The West-Eastern Divan Workshop brings together performers from the Arab lands, Europe, and Israel to perform European classical music together. Building on the idea that all peoples are "equal in music," the project, which their promotional materials describe as an ongoing "experiment in coexistence," hopes to allow participants to "[traverse] deep political and ideological divides" so that musicians who play music together might teach others to learn to live together.[3] The concert was by any standards a stunning success; an overflow audience packed Rabat's main concert venue (even the Moroccan queen was in attendance), and the musical program was as stimulating as it was challenging. I found similar reactions to another concert they gave in Madrid's Plaza Mayor that I attended in July 2012. Musical *convivencia* on the stage both drew upon and upheld the promise for a deeper *convivencia* in daily life among peoples.

Each of these musical events evoked rhetorically the power of music to transcend boundaries and borders: of the self, of nations and regions, even of history itself. Music's border-breaking power results from the fact that music requires listening and coperformance; you have to engage with an Other as a co-human being in order to truly connect and make music together. In Metioui's discourse, musical collaboration promises to heal historical and contemporary wounds by creating bridges between peoples, thereby spanning boundaries that are historical, cultural, and imaginative. For Olavide, Paniagua, and others on the other side of the Strait of Gibraltar, it is a means for reconnecting with one's own legacy while also forming deeper ties with neighboring civilizations. For audiences in Morocco, Spain, and abroad, the musics of al-Andalus and the notion of playing together hold the promise of translating experiences across or around barriers.[4]

The question then arises, What might these examples of musical outreach and coexistence teach us about tolerance, as well as its limitations? The rhetoric of Andalusian *convivencia* finds expression in musical projects that transcend national boundaries. These musical projects in turn rely on and also help promote ideological and political projects that are part of how Arab, North African, European, and global audiences understand and negotiate cultural difference—especially the difference posed by Islam and Muslims in places like Granada and other European cities. These negotiations have taken place in the context of a global war on terror, at once drawing on deep-rooted suspicions of Muslims as racialized and Orientalized subjects and also announcing new ideologies of belonging that are part of a cosmopolitan, postmulticultural world. In an era of neoliberal crises of confidence as much as of economy, the rhetoric of al-Andalus has become a powerful tool for managing cultural boundaries in the twenty-first century.

THE PROJECT OF AL-ANDALUS: NOSTALGIC
DWELLING IN THE MEDITERRANEAN AND BEYOND

If 1992 marked the sesquicentennial of the fall (*suqut*) or capture (*toma*) of Granada, it also marked the sesquicentennial of the first transatlantic voyages of Columbus.[5] While a number of works have investigated the social, cultural, and political dynamics of each event horizon, too few have pursued the idea that the closure of one horizon was also the opening of another.[6] In other words, the history of al-Andalus is inextricably linked not only to that past world but also to our modern world, including the rise of the global capitalist world economy, which is now in crisis. For this very reason, memorializing such historical events as the fall/capture of Granada through celebrations and festivals (as in the *fiesta de la toma de Granada* and the numerous *moros y cristianos* festivals all over Spain and in the New World), even if they have always been political events, has become especially politically charged in the contemporary moment.[7] Hisham Aidi (2006) notes that debates about the celebration—should the fall of Granada be cause for celebration or for mourning?—reveal competing understandings of al-Andalus. What Westerners tend to celebrate as a victory, many Arabs and Muslims understand as a defeat and reminder of their weakness.

The debate over how we understand the history of al-Andalus—as a lost paradise of *convivencia* or as a starting point for the rise of a hegemonic Europe and North America—has assumed new meanings in the twenty-first century in the aftermath of the events of 9/11 and 3/11. The symbolic struggle over the legacy of al-Andalus, and over the rhetorics and nostalgias that arise from it, tends to revolve around two primary debates. One, echoing the earlier debates of Castro and Sánchez-Albornoz, concerns the nature of medieval *convivencia* and how a modern postmulticultural form might serve as a model for structuring difference in contemporary society. The other debate focuses on the role of Islam in Europe and whether, as some claim, "Islam is the solution" to today's problems (including economic crisis, societal disintegration, and cultural decadence), or whether it is the problem.[8] These two sets of debates intersect in the competing rhetorics of al-Andalus as a once and future place of interfaith *convivencia,* as a tense border between West and East, and as a land of contemporary *jihad* to be reclaimed through force.

In what follows, I reflect on the global relevance of the Andalusian past—for the three cases of Syria, Morocco, and Spain, to be certain, but also for how we (in both "Occident" and "Orient") imagine building communities and resolving conflicts in the twenty-first century, one already marked by the kind of violence that we had hoped to leave behind in the twentieth.[9] What might the Andalusian musics of Syria, Morocco, and Spain and the various rhetorics of al-Andalus that feed and sustain them teach us about regional and global cultural politics around and beyond the Mediterranean shores? What sort of projects do the rhetorics of al-Andalus promote? Since 9/11 al-Andalus has become not only a privileged time-place or chronotope of authenticity, one infused with varieties of nostalgia both reflective and restorative, but also a project for dwelling in modernity, one haunted by the ghosts of past struggles, past rhetorics (see Flesler 2008). The old tensions of maurophilia and maurophobia, some dating to the medieval period itself, now find new expression in contemporary anxieties of modernity, especially given the dramatic increase in migration from North Africa and the Middle East to Europe, much of it irregular or clandestine, and a concomitant rise in Islamophobia in Europe.[10]

The use of the Andalusian past to evoke the traumas of the present has a long prehistory, as we have seen in the works of earlier poets and Arab nationalists in the Middle East, North Africa, and the wider Muslim world, as well as for Europeans for whom the Andalusian past served as a model for interpreting the present and crafting a future. The legacy of al-Andalus and its presumed *convivencia* have most frequently been used to criticize contemporary intolerances. For example, in his writings on the Bosnian War in the early 1990s, Spanish journalist and novelist Juan Goytisolo compares the devastation wreaked on the city of Sarajevo to the fall of Granada; for Goytisolo (2000, 25), the shelling of Sarajevo's library by Serbian forces echoes the burning of Arabic manuscripts in Granada under the orders of Cardinal Cisneros (see also Doubleday 2008, 14). In both cases, the victors enact what Goytisolo decries as "memoricide"—the killing and erasure of social memory—through the destruction of evidence of multicultural coexistence, of *convivencia.* In a similar manner, the Lebanese novelist Amin Maalouf draws explicitly on al-Andalus and the idea of the three cultures to comment on Lebanon during its long, sectarian civil war (1975–1991). In an interview in the inaugural issue of *El legado andalusí,* the magazine of the Granada-based public foundation of the same name, Maalouf asserts: "We know that [the idea of *convivencia*] is a myth, but in history there are symbols, and to be honest, we must recognize that such coexistence between the three religions was marked by tensions, conflicts, and even violence, but it has been an important foreshadowing of what we might expect for the future" (Tapia 1999, 18, cited in Viguera Molins 2006, 153–154; my translation).[11] Similarly, in the editorial to the same issue, Jerónimo Páez, director of the foundation, cites the Spanish author Antonio Gala: "Al-Andalus has the custom [of alternating] between adventure and mis-adventure, between the making, unmaking, and remaking of universality, and it has the historic mission of creating bridges, a bridge between Europe and the East, a bridge to America, a bridge between yesterday and today whose fruit is tomorrow" (Páez 1999, 2; my translation).[12] Note for all three authors the use of the rhetoric of *convivencia* for understanding the present and for imagining the future: for Goytisolo, as a reminder of the threats to cosmopolitanism of atavistic allegiances; for Maalouf, as a metaphor for a pluriconfessional Lebanon, whose diversity and long experience of coexistence did not prevent it from falling into internecine war; and for Gala, as a model for Spain in its Mediterranean context of growing aspirations for regional integration but also fears of cultural dissonance. For all three, the medieval past remains relevant for the Euro-Mediterranean present and future.

The growth in recent scholarship on medieval Spain—producing what is a veritable cottage industry—has furthered the metaphorical mining of Andalusian history to promote understandings of the present. Especially in the wake of the celebrations of the sesquicentennial of the fall of Granada, numerous studies have opened the way for a reassessment not only of the history of late fifteenth-century al-Andalus on the eve of the expulsions but also of its relevance for understanding multicultural relations in the (Euro-American) present.[13] In the period immediately following the attacks of 9/11, the resort to past analogies for making sense of the present intensified.[14] In the United States, the story of al-Andalus as a "first-rate place" that nurtured a "culture of tolerance" (Menocal 2002b) came to be more forcefully conscripted into narratives of multiculturalism and cosmopolitanism. At the same time, the Andalusian legacy fed narratives of the "clash of civilizations" between West and East, Christendom and Islam, civilization and barbarity.[15] Among American and European politicians, the most common trope used to frame the relationship between West and East was that of crusade, invoking the medieval Christian engagement with the Muslim Middle East to support a belligerent stance of Western nations toward the Arab and Muslim worlds and also with their own Muslim citizens (Doubleday 2008, 16–18).[16]

Few scholars went as far as María Rosa Menocal in advancing the project of mutual tolerance and understanding. Her landmark studies *The Arabic Role in Medieval Literary History* (1987) and *The Ornament of the World* (2002) promoted a vision of an Arabized medieval culture of tolerance that offered a model for how the contemporary world might envision relations among peoples of different creeds. In an op-ed essay published in the *New York Times* in 2002, Menocal advanced this theme by portraying al-Andalus as "a golden reign of tolerance." Arguing that "the lessons of history, like the lessons of religion, sometimes neglect examples of tolerance," Menocal outlined the history of the cultural achievements of al-Andalus—much like the standard narrative we have rehearsed throughout this text—and concluded with the observation, the plea, that "much of Europe far beyond the Andalusian world was shaped by the vision of complex and contradictory identities that was first made into an art form by the Andalusians. The enemies of this kind of cultural openness have always existed within each of our monotheistic religions, and often enough their visions of those faiths have triumphed. But at this time of year, and at this point in history, we should remember those moments when it was tolerance that won the day" (2002a).

In the end, sadly, the rhetorics of intolerant crusade, not tolerant understanding and coexistence, are winning the day—among American leaders and their allies, among militant Islamists, and among right-wing nationalists in Europe. The jihadist vision of al-Andalus as a lost paradise ripe for reconquest, while not very old, also assumed new force in this era.[17] Indeed, militant groups like al-Qaeda have been drawing on the narrative of al-Andalus for some years to support their cause. For example, after 9/11 Ayman al-Zawahiri, then Osama Bin Laden's deputy, asserted that his followers would not repeat "the tragedy of al-Andalus" (Doubleday 2008, 17), while Zacarias Moussaoui, the so-called twentieth hijacker of the 9/11 attacks, claimed in court that his principal demand was "the return of Spain to the Moors" (Aidi 2006, 81). His remarks recall the Arabic graffito I spotted at the Alhambra: "We will get you back, God willing!" Western commentators were not slow to pick up on this threat, denouncing the desire of militants to retake Spain, what Islamists referred to as "liberating" the West for Islam (see *El País* 2006; Socolovsky 2005). Charles Hirschkind (2014, 227) notes that after 9/11 then Spanish prime minister José María Aznar made use of a similar conflictual rhetoric of al-Andalus to argue that Spain has known Islamic terrorism since the eighth-century conquest (with the year 711 serving as a prefiguration of 9/11). Both the Spanish prime minster and Osama Bin Laden cynically drew on biased readings of the history of al-Andalus to promote projects: of Fortress Europe, on the one hand, and of an expanded and/or reconstituted Muslim community (*umma*), on the other. Responses in Spain intensified after the 3/11 train bombings in Madrid's Atocha station, and the history and rhetoric of al-Andalus came to serve as fodder both for apologists for a sort of *nueva convivencia* (Ferrín 2004; Herbert 2002) and for those who argued that Islam represents a threat to Spanish and Western civilization (Arístegui 2005; Fanjul García 2002, 2004; Fernández-Morera 2006; Vidal 2004; see also Aidi 2006, 81–82). Revisionist history cuts both ways, and in recent years we have seen yet more interpretations of al-Andalus, from those who argue against the notion that it was a culture of tolerance (Rothstein 2003) to those who claim it was, at best, a form of "apartheid in paradise" (Rodríguez Marcos 2009), if not a myth (Fanjul García 2002, 2004).

Thus the tensions of maurophilia and maurophobia resonate in these debates between the latter-day children of Castro and Sánchez-Albornoz, on the one hand, and between those who adopt reflective and more restorative stances toward history, on the other. Of these various accounts, Menocal's vision is the most remarkable not only for its eloquence and insights but also for how it presages not the coming of an era of multicultural tolerance (far from it) but rather how the rhetoric of al-

Andalus and the very idea of *convivencia* would come to play a central role in the political and cultural developments in the ensuing decade. For today, the idea of *convivencia* is more than just a subject for historiographical debate; it is a project. At once political, economic, and cultural, the project of al-Andalus draws on the rhetoric of Andalusian *convivencia* among the three cultures of the Mediterranean and is intimately tied to how Spain and the wider European community manage their relationships to their external Muslim neighbors and internal Muslim citizens. In more general terms, the project of al-Andalus aims to help the "secular" West come to terms with the challenge of Islam in and at its borders by building bridges of understanding between Europeans and these (usually racialized) Others, and also by erecting barriers to the free movement of peoples in the Mediterranean region.

THE PROJECT OF AL-ANDALUS: BRIDGES AND BARRIERS IN THE MEDITERRANEAN AND BEYOND

Both Metioui and Olavide advocated for the potential of music to erect bridges among peoples; their many concerts and recordings together are testament to this potential. This sentiment resonated as well with performances of the West-Eastern Divan Orchestra I attended in Rabat (2003) and Madrid (2012) and those many other musical groups working under the ideological flag of the three cultures of the Mediterranean. For his part, Eduardo Paniagua, founder of the Pneuma label, issued a recording called *Puentes sobre el Mediterraneo* (Bridges over the Mediterranean; Paniagua 2009) that echoes this idea: the Mediterranean as a space of bridges and cultural confluences. Indeed, as Christian Bromberger (2007) notes, the trope of the sea as a bridge between cultures constitutes one of the main gatekeeping concepts of the anthropology of the Mediterranean.[18] However, a closer examination of the bridges formed through music reveals that they usually offer only one-way access; that is, they offer a bridge for European artists and consumers to come to North Africa and the Middle East but almost never the reverse. Omar Metioui studied in Belgium, speaks three languages with ease, and is a successful pharmacist. As a result he has little difficulty securing a visa to Europe. However, his fellow Moroccan musicians, less cosmopolitan, would find it very difficult to leave. In the eyes of the European border patrol regimes, they are little better than the thousands of so-called *harragas*, who attempt to cross the strait every year, often in small boats.[19]

For their part, the North African and Middle Eastern musicians who perform in Granada tend to be recent immigrants who have settled there more or less permanently or are undocumented; only Arab star musicians, including the Iraqi *'ud* player Naseer Shamma, and those sponsored by their home governments, including the Syrian *'ud* players Sabsaby and Bouhassoun, are permitted to travel to give performances. Others must endure a tedious and costly application process with no guarantee of being granted a visa. On at least two recordings of Syrian *muwashshahat* (by the Al Turath Ensemble [2001, 2002]), Paniagua and Metioui found it more expedient to travel to Aleppo for the recording rather than bring the Syrian artists to Spain, which would have been difficult not only financially but logistically because European work and tourist visas are seldom forthcoming for Syrian artists. In the post-9/11 and 3/11 world, musical sounds may travel across barriers, thereby raising hopes for international understanding and peaceful coexistence, but more often than not the musicians who perform the music, especially if they come from outside the Schengen Area, may not.[20] In this way, the bridges erected and performed by these musical performances often also serve as barriers.

However, the idea of bridges, like that of the three (four? five?) cultures of the Mediterranean, serves an important political and rhetorical function: to manage the relations among European, North African, and other populations.[21] For European political leaders keen on defusing the tensions surrounding Islam and Islamophobia in "Fortress Europe," the rhetoric of al-Andalus has become a proxy for a project of managing difference. The notion of *convivencia* and the trope of the three cultures of the Mediterranean have increasingly been invoked to promote pluralism, mutual understanding, and tolerance in Europe, while at the same time European leaders have tightened immigration quotas and greatly securitized their borders. Faced with a refugee problem of unprecedented proportions, especially in the aftermath of the so-called Arab Spring, these contradictory processes—calls for opening and tolerance, and acts of closure and intolerance—have intensified. Anti-immigrant sentiment is on the rise in much of Europe and the United States, leading to Fortress Europe (and Fortress America) mentalities and programs.[22] Yet, Europe is a fortress only for those racialized subjects who reside in nonpreferential regions, typically those outside the Schengen Area though in effect including most of Africa and Asia. New technologies of surveillance and control, including the multibillion-euro Frontex and Eurosur initiatives, are merely the flip side to discourses of *convivencia* and the multicultural and tolerant projects of al-Andalus.[23] In other words, these projects of Andalusian multicultural tolerance are proxies for mostly European concerns with the management of internal Others.[24] In the context of the new Mediterranean, with its shifting and securitized borders (Andersson 2012; Suárez-Navaz 2004), European leaders hope that by containing and controlling the discourse, they might contain and control the populations.

One way to effect this contain-and-control policy is through projects devoted to promoting mutual tolerance and understanding; these should be understood as soft power counterparts to European hard power immigration and border enforcement. For example, in Spain there have been a number of initiatives aiming to build bridges between Europeans and the country's Muslim citizens that serve these projects of control and surveillance, but under the guise of a *nueva convivencia*. In 2006 the Spanish Ministry of Foreign Affairs and Cooperation inaugurated the Casa Árabe, a publicly funded cultural center with headquarters in Madrid and Córdoba. Casa Árabe was established to be "a strategic center for Spain's relations with the Arab world, a meeting point where different role-players and institutions, both private and public, from the worlds of business, education, academia, politics and culture can dialogue, interact, establish lines of cooperation and undertake joint projects." Far more than an art gallery, library, bookshop, and conference center, Casa Árabe is "an active platform and tool for Spain's public diplomacy, with activities which it has integrated into those of a strong network of similar Casas, including the Casa de América, Casa Asia, Casa África, Casa del Mediterráneo and Centro Sefarad-Israel." On the left margin of its informational page, the website states:

> Since it was founded in 2006, Casa Árabe has worked every day to achieve
> the goal of building bridges, strengthening bilateral and multilateral political
> relations, promoting and assisting with economic, cultural and educational

relations, and providing training and furthering understanding about the Arab and Muslim world.

In other words, Casa Árabe is a space for mutual knowledge and shared reflection: a meeting point between Spain and the world.[25]

In November of the same year, the Instituto Cervantes in conjunction with the Spanish Embassy in Jordan launched a conference called "Alandalus como proyecto / Al-Andalus ka-mashru'" (al-Andalus as a project). The brainchild of Spanish scholar Carlos Varona Narvión, former director of the Cervantes Institutes in Damascus and Amman, the project promoted "a critical vision of the historic al-Andalus, what it was, and what it contributed to Spain and Europe." Many of the conference papers dealt with the theme of Andalusian multiculturalism (*multiculturalismo*) and *convivencia,* offering medieval Spain as a model for the future. This is clear from the titles of two of the papers: "El modelo de Alandalus" (The model of al-Andalus), by the Egyptian thinker Hasan Hanafi, and "La presencia de Alandalus: Acercamiento a una cultura para el futuro" (The presence of al-Andalus: An approach to a culture for the future), by Syrian scholar Ganem Hanna.[26] Moreover, a key theme at the conference was how al-Andalus once served as a bridge between peoples and how it might do so again (see Ramón Guerrero 2007).

Both Casa Árabe and "al-Andalus as a project" share more than official sponsorship; they also share an underlying message that, in the post-9/11 and 3/11 world, al-Andalus can serve as a rhetorical bridge between West and East, as well as between the past, present, and future. Moreover, the rhetoric of an Andalusian *convivencia* serves as an important tool for managing internal populations and for international diplomacy. For Europeans (and for Spaniards in particular) the rhetoric of *convivencia* and the project of al-Andalus are means for rapprochement with the Islamic world and weapons against jihadist ideologies; they exist side by side with border patrol surveillance and enforcement programs such as the Spanish Integrated System for External Surveillance (Sistema de Vigilancia Exterior, SIVE).[27]

The effort to manage internal difference, especially of Muslim populations, is by no means limited to Spain. Recent ethnographic studies have analyzed European ambivalence toward Muslims and the management of difference in European contexts ranging from France (Bowen

2006; Fernando 2010; Silverstein 2004, 2005) and Germany (Özyürek 2009; Rosenow-Williams 2012), to Scandinavia (Bjørgo 1997; Nielsen 2012), the UK (Werbner 1996), and beyond (Göle 2011, 2014). Such controversies as headscarf bans, reactions to Islamophobic cartoons, and acts of violence committed by all parties to the conflict have led to a variety of calls for understanding, as well as for calls by a resurgent European right to place Muslims back on a one-way bridge to their "homelands" even when they are second- and third-generation Europeans or more (see, e.g., Ticktin 2011, 203). Those Europeans who embrace the medieval Andalusian past in order to promote a vision of future tolerance do so by drawing selectively on an ersatz nostalgia for an era that in fact others would like to forget. In the context of a contemporary world rife with radical restorative projects (from both militant Islamists and right-wing ideologues), they at the same time endeavor to advance a form of multicultural tolerance that secures the present hegemonic order by bringing Muslims into the national and regional polity—that is, by "taming" them, as it were, not unlike the old *mudéjar* population of Spain, those who were allowed to remain in a reconquered Spain.[28] Contemporary calls for a new *convivencia*, then, must be understood as part of a program of domesticating difference at home while at the same time enforcing border maintenance policies externally.[29]

MUSICAL PERFORMANCE, DEEP LISTENING, AND THE LIMITS OF TOLERANCE

What can we hope from music in this context of a fractured Europe, a fractured world? While the American appropriation of Moorish *convivencia* advocates for a renewed commitment to multicultural tolerance, using the past as a model for the present era, this model relies on the cooperation of the tolerated with a project of management and surveillance that secures the privilege of the majoritarian group. Tolerance and intolerance are, in fact, but two sides of the same coin. To tolerate someone (a cultural Other) is to mark that person as an outsider, as distinct, which is tantamount to denying that person's humanity. In their study of sexual difference in the American legal context, Janet Jakobsen and Ann Pellegrini argue that tolerance signifies "a grudging form of acceptance in which the boundary between 'us' and 'them' remains clear, sometimes dangerously so" (2003, 52). Moreover, according to these authors, to teach tolerance (in its multiple guises: religious, cultural, racial, ethnic) is "to teach precisely the type of us-them relationship upon which hate thrives. Teaching tolerance, then, can not be the answer to hate and excessive violence, nor can tolerance address other forms of social division" (52).

In a similar vein, the philosopher Slavoj Žižek asserts that the concept of tolerance, especially as espoused in American-style multiculturalism, bespeaks a shallow form of respect for otherness that does not actually engage with the deeper issues of cultural variation, ethics, and human dignity (Žižek and Daly 2004, 122–123). In fact, according to Žižek, this sort of superficial respect for cultural difference and tolerance of otherness is based in the treatment of others as abstractions and not as actual people—that is, as people occupying the position of Other in an abstract way, "as if they were already dead" (117). Tolerance, for Žižek as for Jakobsen and Pellegrini, is a mechanism for distancing from others, not engaging with them. Similar arguments are presented by Franco Cassano ([1996] 2012) regarding the relationships between northern and southern (i.e., Mediterranean) Europe. The European North has tended to view the European South through the optic of rationality and development, seeing the latter as inadequately modern on both counts. At the same time, a certain (no doubt ersatz) nostalgia for southern Europe as a sun-filled zone of cultural decay (if not decadence) has informed the North's preoccupations with its Mediterranean neighbors in ways that recall Orientalism (see, e.g., Dainotto 2007; Schneider 1998). To combat this reification of the North-South divide, Cassano calls for a "Mediterranean thinking" that would promote respect for the other and mutual understanding of differences and similarities. In Cassano's vision of Mediterranean thinking, the Self and Other are interconnected in important ways—historically, culturally, politically, and economically—but these connections do not erase differences; rather, they highlight complementarity and cooperation (see Bromberger 2006).

Given the inherent limits (legal, ethical, philosophical) of current notions of tolerance, how then can we best promote mutual understanding without falling into the trap of a facile multiculturalism that does little to change the status quo? Looking back to medieval Iberia may indeed offer us models of interfaith coexistence, but they hardly seem promising for a twenty-first century already rent by intolerances of every sort: the project of multiculturalism has seemingly failed. Indeed, critics of American multiculturalism have pointed to these contradictions and call instead for what some are calling a postmulticultural world (Vertovec 2010). Talal Asad, drawing on the work of William Connolly (1996, 61), argues that, rather than tolerating one another, we need to aim for a world where *"everyone* may live as a minority among minorities" (2003, 180). This model of "decentered pluralism" (Connolly 1996) requires that we deconstruct our cherished historical narratives—like the standard narrative of al-Andalus and its modern iterations—and rethink our identities and the boundaries we construct to defend them (Asad 2003, 177). This requires as well investigating what Iain Chambers calls the "tributary histories" of modernity, that is, the submerged and repressed histories and narratives that "suggest deeper and more dispersive currents which draw us back in time while simultaneously projecting a radically different understanding of the present and its potential futures. The map becomes an altogether more fluid and fluctuating composition" (2008, 2).

Toward this end we need more fluid and fluctuating models of culture and subjectivity, the sort of dwelling in complexities that marks, for example, Goytisolo's (2000, 27) Jewish interlocutor in Sarajevo, at once Bosnian, Jewish, and Spanish, or Olavide and Paniagua's collaborations with Metioui in Tangier, and countless other examples of intersubjective fluidities that challenge the terrestrial cartographies of our national imaginaries. If we are to transcend the monolithic discourses of identity and belonging in Europe and America that erect boundaries or one-way bridges to cultural Others, we need to embrace the sorts of plural subjectivities characteristic of the Mediterranean world throughout its history (Braudel [1972] 1995; Bromberger 2007; Cassano [1996] 2012). To do so requires not the superficial embrace and managed promotion of cultural difference, for example as promoted through world music consumption, tourism, and festivalization (see Guss 2001; Kapchan 2008; Shannon 2003c, 2011), but rather a different sort of narrative practice and understanding of Self and Other. Moreover, it requires a different sort of rhetoric, one based in a poetics of sound, body, and gesture that "exceeds the conclusive logic of a monument, a book, a map, an archive, a law" (Chambers 2008, 10). It is in the neglected spaces of embodied memories, so often evoked in musical performance, that we find the most powerful critiques of Western logos, akin to what Giles Deleuze and Felix Guattari ([1980] 1987) analyze as "rhizomatic" or nonlinear and nonteleological thinking about subjectivity.

Can music mend the world? The historian and "culture jammer" Mark LeVine (2005, 2008) argues that the West's deep-seated ideological opposition to Islam, Muslims, and Islamic culture is misplaced. "They" (referring to the populations of the so-called Axis of Evil) do not uniformly hate "us." "They" also create forms of music and culture that transgress our stereotypes of Islam and at the same time establish a common ground for understanding the contemporary world and for creatively engaging with and resisting it. Our interrelationships are complex and transcend the simplistic notion of a clash of civilizations. Yet the discourse of cultural tolerance sets up precisely this sort of situation—one of mutual distrust and hatred. Can we transcend this? The composer and performer Pauline Oliveros (2005) offers a way in her compositions and writings on the concept of "Deep Listening." In asking what power music or sound more generally has to effect change, Oliveros asserts that change must begin with the listener in the act of active, deep listening (as opposed to mere hearing): "The practice of Deep Listening provides a framework for artistic collaboration and musical improvisation and gives composers, performers, artists of other disciplines, and audiences new tools to explore and interact with environmental and instrumental sounds."[30] While Oliveros proposes deep listening as a creative tool for artistic endeavors, the concept has utility for reconsidering the ways in which understanding and community can be forged through the process of active, deep listening—to music, to one another. This requires nothing more than the simple act of "musicking"—that is, making and listening to music (Small 1998)—among cultural Others, who then become coconspirators in creating and re-creating our common humanity. This is what the West-Eastern Divan Orchestra attempts to do. This is what Metioui, Olavide, and their collaborators do. This is what musicians and everyday people on a quotidian level far from the front pages of our media do.

There are obvious limits to this model. I am not sure if all or any members of the Taliban or the recently declared Islamic State, for example, would agree with these sentiments, or even most radical activists in any community.[31] But even at the level of government, policy making without attention to close, deep, and compassionate listening can lead to major missteps. In our own communities, failure to take seriously the common humanity of our peers, students, and neighbors can lead to disaster. I also recognize that in the national contexts of Syria, Morocco, and Spain, this music can serve to divide even as it may unite. In Morocco, for example, Andalusian music (al-ala) is an object largely of elite consumption and marks clear class and status divisions within Moroccan society where other varieties of music such as Gnawa and chaabi are more popular (see Aidi 2014). For this reason, al-ala marks a rupture and a continuity. Andalusian-inspired musics of Syria often have the same effect, even as they may also offer forms of cultural continuity and comfort in times of crisis and displacement. No doubt in Spain the long-lived debates over regional cultural and political autonomy influence contemporary evaluations of the arts, music included, so we should hardly be surprised to learn that the performance of these and related musics in Spain may engender bitter reactions, even as some welcome them as harbingers of change. We all know from our own experiences of music that it has this power—perhaps emanating from its own condition of impermanence—to change our being in the world. Music may not necessarily heal the world, but it can help us to sound the boundaries that divide us and, by transcending them, find the common melodies that might bring us closer together. If we are to confront the anxieties of (post)modernity in an era of global economic insecurity, deep listening may be our only option.

FINALIS

It is time to take stock of our Andalusian journey. From the coast of Morocco looking to Spain, we voyaged to Damascus, land of Umayyad dreams, then back to Morocco to trace a genealogical imagination that invests al-Andalus with foundational status. Finally, we returned to the home (or at least one of the homes) of al-Andalus, southern Spain. In each of these sites I have endeavored to illuminate how the rhetoric of al-Andalus, especially as enacted in musical performance, engages not only with readings of the past but with contemporary cultural politics at the heart of national debates. These national debates in turn animate the regional circulation of ideologies and practices related not only the medieval past, but to the contemporary world and even the future.

In Syria the rhetoric of al-Andalus has served as a touchstone of pan-Arab ideologies, especially since the 1960s with the rise to power of the Ba'thist regime. At the same time, by mining a heterogeneous past, the rhetoric of al-Andalus offers a site of resistance by accessing claims to authenticity that counter what some Syrians perceive to be the vulgarity and inauthenticity of the secular regime and of contemporary culture in Syria and the Arab world in general. While some scholars and critics may read this concern with authenticity as a nostalgic escape from the realities of the present (see al-'Azm 2000), I prefer to read the interest in al-Andalus as an expression of a modern consciousness that is very much future oriented (see Shannon 2006, 198–199).

In the case of Morocco, the rhetoric of al-Andalus arises from a genealogical imagination that ties modern Moroccans to a prestigious Iberian past and at the same time supports the monarchical system of authority. Andalusian music plays an integral part in Moroccan nationalism and the construction of national culture by indexing a wide range of positive associations for middle-class and elite Moroccans: Muslim piety, aristocratic (read, "European, not Arab") ancestry, monarchical rule, and a quasi-ethnic identity and affiliation. In the hands and ears of some culture brokers, Andalusian music also reaches out toward a shared past in order to construct a regional trans-Mediterranean identity: this is especially the case for musicians in Tangier. As in Syria, Andalusian music in Tangier provides an antidote to the perceived decadence of contemporary culture (in an Adornian sense), but unlike in Syria, it is based in imaginings of direct ancestral ties to Europe, if not mnemonic and physical keys to the lost paradise of al-Andalus.

In Spain the rhetoric of al-Andalus allows immigrant North Africans, new Muslims (*conversos*), tourists, and government agencies to negotiate the place of Islam in modern Spain. As in Syria and Morocco, the idea of a shared Andalusian heritage in Spain has been linked to a variety of projects, from reflective—even ersatz—nostalgias that feed the tourist industry in "Moorishland" (Tremlett 2008), to restorative nostalgias that aim to reproduce an Andalusian-inspired sense of *conviven-*

cia or even a reconquered Islamic polity. Andalusian musics, from the Arab and Arab-Andalusian to flamenco and the sounds of the various children of Ziryab, resonate with the contradictions and ambivalences of the medieval past as it irrupts into the present. The tensions of medieval and early modern maurophobia and maurophilia remain relevant today as Spaniards, like many Europeans, attempt to understand—and manage—the participation of Muslims in their communities and their integration into the national consciousness.

In each of these sites, these *lieux de mémoire* that are also sites of trauma and sites of amnesia (see Huyssens 2003), musical performance contributes to practices of world making that draw selectively on readings of history, imaginings of the past, and fantasies of the future (see Stokes 2004, 51). They also help us to understand how various readings of the past and regimes of historicity might promote different modes of being in the world, and different means of reinvesting sites with meaning to create conditions of nostalgic dwelling. If, extending Susan Stewart's (1984) insights, we can say that nostalgia in musical performance serves as a metacommentary on contemporary issues, then the performance of Andalusian music in and around the Mediterranean (and well beyond) provides metacommentaries on the current context of crisis and strife. Especially as mediated by the circulation of ideologies and sounds on concert and festival stages, the rhetoric of a once and future Andalusian imaginative space produces forms of nostalgia even as it performs our (post)modern anxieties.

Returning to the coast of Tangier, the view across the strait to Europe now appears far more complex than before. One can trace, like an aquatic palimpsest, the routes of past migrations, past circulations of peoples and their dreams and aspirations, their memories and losses, among the *dos orillas,* the two banks. In the contemporary context, one can also trace the flows of migrants and their hopes floating (and too often drowning) in a sea of troubles, suspicions, and fears. Their circulations in and around the Mediterranean, like the circulations of the rhetorics of al-Andalus and such practices as musical performance, call into question our cherished notions of identity and culture, let alone the humanity of our current political cultures and the regimes of surveillance and punishment they foster. For these reasons, al-Andalus may

The Alhambra, Granada, 2009.

now more than ever be "good to think," for it engages with memory practices that offer, in their complexities and ambiguities, new forms of dwelling in nostalgia, and possibly new means for crafting a better future.

GLOSSARY

al-ala   Andalusian music of Morocco, also known as *al-musiqa al-andalusiyya* or *al-tarab al-andalusi*. Literally meaning "the instrument," it probably refers to song with instrumental accompaniment.

al-sama'   Islamic a cappella chant in Morocco. Literally meaning "audition," it refers to songs without instrumental accompaniment.

barwala   Poetic text in Moroccan colloquial Arabic sung as
(pl. *barawil*)   part of Moroccan Andalusian music (*al-ala*).

bilgha   Traditional yellow open-back slippers worn in Morocco.

bughya   Nonmetrical, free-form instrumental prelude in Moroccan Andalusian music (*al-ala*).

cantaor   Flamenco vocalist.

cante jondo   Flamenco "deep song."
(*hondo*)

chaabi   Genre of Moroccan popular urban music, also known as *sha'bi*.

converso   A convert to Christianity.

convivencia   Peaceful coexistence or living together, a social and cultural condition thought to characterize Muslims, Christians, and Jews in medieval al-Andalus.

darbukka   Goblet-shaped drum.

dhikr   Ritual invocation of God through prayer and chant in Islam.

duende	"Soul" or "spirit" evoked in flamenco music. García Lorca claims it derives from the Spanish *duen del casa* (spirit of the home).
gitano/roma/ romani	"Gypsy" peoples and their cultures.
hafla	A musical concert.
jalsa	An intimate musical listening session.
jawq	A traditional musical ensemble in Moroccan Andalusian music (*al-ala*).
jellaba (jalaba)	A traditional Moroccan robe.
judería	Former Jewish quarter in medieval Spain.
kunnash	A compilation of songs of Moroccan Andalusian music (*al-ala*).
maqam	A melodic mode in Levantine Arab music.
marrano	A Spanish Jew.
medina	A traditional walled city in Moroccan urban configurations.
mihrajan	A festival or fair.
mizan	A rhythmic movement or rhythm in Moroccan Andalusian music (*al-ala*).
morisco	Spanish Muslims.
moro	Moor. Spanish Muslim during medieval al-Andalus; also refers to an artistic style, "Moorish."
mozarabe	Arabized Christians in medieval al-Andalus; also an artistic style of this period.
mshaliya	A metrical instrumental prelude in Moroccan Andalusian music (*al-ala*).
mudéjar	Spanish Muslims in the postreconquest era. Possibly derives from the Arabic *mudajjin*, meaning "a tamed animal allowed to remain indoors."
mulu'	A music lover and aficionado of Moroccan Andalusian music (*al-ala*).

nuba (*nawba*)	A traditional suite form in Moroccan Andalusian music (*al-ala*).
palmas	The clapping of the hands in flamenco.
psaltery/salterio	A medieval zither similar to a *qanun* or dulcimer.
qanun	An Arabian plucked lap zither similar to the medieval psaltery and Turkish *kanun,* Greek *kanunaki.*
rabab	A traditional boat-back two-string fiddle used in Moroccan Andalusian music (*al-ala*).
tab'	A melodic mode in Moroccan Andalusian music (*al-ala*).
tarab	An emotional state of rapture or ecstasy produced in Arab music.
tarboush	A traditional conical red "Fez" hat with black tassel.
tarr	A small tambourine without jingles in Moroccan Andalusian music (*al-ala*).
tetería	A neighborhood of tea shops and small craft stores, such as in Granada.
toque	Flamenco guitar playing.
tushiya	A metrical instrumental prelude in Moroccan Andalusian music (*al-ala*).
'ud	An Arabian short-neck and fretless lute usually having five or six courses (also known as *oud*).
'ud raml	A Moroccan Andalusian fretless lute having four courses.
ville nouvelle	"New city," modern quarters in Moroccan urban configurations.
zawiya	A mosque or place for the practice of *dhikr.*

NOTES

1. The classical musical traditions of Syria are better understood as "classicized" as the result of the modernist practices of constructing a national heritage. The same can be said for other Middle Eastern (indeed, world) musics, since the periodization of European art music cannot be easily transferred to the musical cultures of non-European peoples. See Shannon (2006, 37).

2. The anthropological study of the Mediterranean had its origins in the so-called Oxford School of ethnography. See, among others, Peristiany (1966) and Pitt-Rivers (1971). For critical appraisals of the anthropology of the region, see, among others, Albera and Blok (2001), Boissevain (1979), Bromberger (2006, 2007), Gilmore (1982), Herzfeld (1984, 2005), and Pina-Cabral (1989).

3. Bohlman (1997) analyzes the musics of the Mediterranean with respect to seven tropes: Myth, Diaspora, Sacred Journey, Utopia, Promised Lands, Border Crossings, and Modernity. I am indebted to his formulation for my analysis of Andalusian musics.

4. We might also state, "Not so much the anthropology of performance, but performance as anthropology," given the "broad spectrum approach" to performance I adopt in this work.

5. See also Attali's famous pronouncement ([1977] 1985) on the prophetic nature of music.

6. For more on the contradictions of Europe's internal others, see, among others, Cassano ([1996] 2012), Dainotto (2007), and Schneider (1998).

7. For more on performance and performance studies, see Carlson (2007), Conquergood (2007), Geertz (2007), and Goffman (2007). For speech act theory, see Austin (1962), Butler (1997), and Felman (1983).

8. For Schechner, "restored behavior is living behavior as treated as a film director treats a strip of film" (2011, 35). The strips are independent and can be rearranged in unique patterns, so that the origin or source, even if known, is less important than the affect engendered in performance.

9. For more detailed analysis of the various musical cultures discussed in this book, readers are invited to consult specialists' texts. For example, on Syria, see Shannon (2003a, 2006); on Morocco, see Davila (2013); on Spanish flamenco, see Chuse (2003), Mitchell (1994), and Washabaugh (1996, 2012). On other Andalusian traditions, as well

as broadly integrative musicological and historical analyses, see Reynolds (2005) and Poché (1995).

10. For more on music and identity in Tanzania and Kenya, see Eisenberg (2010, 2012).

11. For more on the *jali* and drumming traditions of West Africa, see Charry (2000) and Chernoff (1981).

12. See also Meintjes (2003) and Turino (2008) on the social and political construction of South African musics.

13. For complementary treatments of the role of festivals in Latin American musical practices, see Bigenho (2002) and Romero (2001).

14. See, among many others, Askew (2003), Bigenho (2002), Dent (2009), Feld (1990), Kapchan (2007), and Romero (2001).

15. See Kapchan (2007), Scott (1990), and Taylor (2003).

16. Formed from the Greek roots *nostos* (home) and *algia* (pain, malady), nostalgia referred initially to a medical condition among displaced persons, such as Swiss soldiers removed from home, and was treated as a curable ailment. The treatment included opium, leeches, and a trip to the Swiss Alps. See Boym (2007, 7–8).

17. In a similar manner, Jan-Werner Müller, citing John Keane, notes that "'crisis periods . . . prompt awareness of the crucial importance of the past for the present. As a rule, crises are times during which the living do battle for the hearts, minds and souls of the dead.' But the dead also seem to be in battle for the hearts, minds and souls of the living, as the latter often resort during times of crisis to a kind of mythical re-enactment of the past" (2002, 4, cited in Lorenz 2010, 68).

18. On Aleppo, see Khirfan (2010), Vincent (2004); on Damascus, see Salamandra (2004), Totah (2014); on Fez, see Porter (2001, 2003); on Granada, see Murillo Viu et al. (2008).

19. Chronotopes ("time-spaces") in the work of literary theorist Mikhail Bakhtin are used to analyze the intrinsic connectedness of space and time in language and literature. For Bakhtin, literary genres can be identified by their different configurations of time and space. "Time, as it were, thickens, takes on flesh, becomes artistically visible; likewise, space becomes charged and responsive to the movements of time, plot and history. This intersection of axes and fusion of indicators characterizes the artistic chronotope" (1981, 84). In anthropology the term has been used to analyze discourse in its relationship to place and spatial awareness (see Basso 1996).

20. On memory and memory cultures in the modern and postmodern ages, see Huyssen (2000, 2003, 2006, 2012).

21. For a critical appraisal of the concept of flow as used in the work of Appadurai, among others, see Rockefeller (2011).

22. See Cohen (1999), Seroussi (1991, 2003), Shelemay (1998), and Shiloah (1995, 2001), among others.

1. IN THE SHADOWS OF ZIRYAB

1. For more on Paniagua and his Pneuma label, see Campbell (2011).

2. For more on Ziryab the man and the myth, see Davila (2009) and Reynolds (2008).

3. Etymologically, "al-Andalus" may derive from the *tamazight* (Berber) language term for "Land of the Vandals," though opinion varies on the matter. See Bossong (2002).

4. For overviews of the histories of al-Andalus, see Fletcher (2006) and Harvey (2005). On the notion of "imaginative geographies" of al-Andalus, see Said (1978, 1993).

5. I use the term *Berber* advisedly, as many so-called Berber peoples in North Africa prefer the term *Imazighen* (sing. *Amazigh*), among others.

6. This refers to the period of the Emirate (756–929) and Caliphate (929–1031) of Córdoba.

7. On al-Shaqundi, see Elinson (2008). The image of falling pearls evokes the common trope of the falling of the lover's tears in early Arabian *ghazal* poetry (Carl Davila, personal communication, August 2014).

8. As I will show in chapter 4, *convivencia* is a modern term, first coined in the 1940s. Moreover, the Arabic *al-ta'ayyush* is most likely a back translation from the Spanish.

9. Other objects of nostalgic remembrance include scientific advances, but these are less frequently cited than the architectural, literary, and sociopolitical legacies.

10. Christians commonly refer to this as the reconquest (*reconquista*), though this term implies an historical continuity with the populations of Iberia prior to the "Moorish invasion." In addition, in Spanish the fall of Granada is commonly celebrated as the *toma* (capture) *de Granada*.

11. *Mudéjar,* from Arabic *mudajjin,* means "tamed, allowed to remain behind." The latter term refers to "Moors" who were allowed to remain behind after the fall of al-Andalus in the capacity of craftsmen, farmers, and so on (Fletcher 2006). Recent genetic studies reveal that significant proportions of the male population of southern Spain carry haplogroups specific to northwestern African populations. See Capelli et al. (2009).

12. The struggle over Islam is the main theme of Youssef Chahine's film *al-Masir* (Destiny, 1997), in which the tolerance and cultural and scientific advances in the era of Ibn Rushd (Averroes, 1126–1198) are contrasted with a messianic and puritanical sect of Islam that gains sway over the caliph al-Mansour, leading to Ibn Rushd's exile and the burning of many of his works.

13. The theological associations of the concepts of paradise and fall are clear. See Aidi (2006) for more on the polarization of views concerning al-Andalus and its shifting meanings over the centuries.

14. The idea of al-Andalus as a religious frontier would become popular in the late twentieth century, as Spain was portrayed as a "shield" defending Europe from the perceived threat of Islam. See Aidi (2006, 75, 83).

15. On *ritha' al-mudun,* see Elinson (2008, 2009) and Muhammad (1983).

16. On gatekeeping concepts in anthropology, see Appadurai (1986b). On the medieval construction of an Islamic other, see Southern (1953). See Abu Lughod (1981) and Rabinow (1989) on the French colonization of Morocco.

17. Granara (2005) discusses the works of Jurji Zaydan, Radwa Ashour, and 'Ali Garim. One might add Tarik Ali (1992), among others. On al-Andalus in Arabic letters, see Elinson (2009, 2).

18. Various terms are used to describe the musical practices of medieval Iberia and its descendants: *al-musiqa al-andalusiyya, al-tarab al-andalusi, al-ala, al-ma'luf, al-san'a, la musique andalouse,* etc.

19. Although today Syrians tend not to mention al-Mansur al-Yahudi's role, he was an especially important interlocutor, and many Jews occupied high positions in Andalusian culture and in the Levant and North Africa into the twentieth century and, in the case of Morocco, the twenty-first (Menocal 2002b; Reynolds 2000b).

20. Whereas the term *converso* applied to all converts to Christianity (New Christians), the *moriscos* were Muslims forced to convert to Christianity or face expulsion or

death, whereas the *marranos* (which literally means "pigs") were Jewish converts. Their adherence to the Christian faith being suspect, as many were crypto-Muslims and crypto-Jews, it was the *moriscos* and *marranos* who bore the initial brunt of inquisitorial fervor. For an interesting case study of the inquisitorial trial of a seventeenth-century Portuguese *converso*, see Soyer (2011).

21. The term used for these refugees, *nazihun*, is the same one used in the Levant to refer to Palestinian refugees of the 1967 war and even Syrian refugees of the present conflict.

22. The earliest sources are those of Ibn 'Abd Rabbih (d. 940), Ibn al-Qutiyya (d. 977), Ibn Abi Tahir Tayfur (d. 893), Ibn Hayyan (d. 1076), al-Tifashi (d. 1253), Ibn Khaldun (d. 1402), and al-Maqqari (d. 1632).

23. Andalusian musical and poetic forms were well known in the Levant as early as the twelfth century. The *muwashshah* was most likely introduced to the Levant by itinerant scholars and pilgrims. Some Levantine scholars claim a parallel Levantine development from earlier Arabian sources of these musical structures, though little evidence supports this view. For an overview of the genre in Syria, see Raḥīm (1987), Qalaʿhjī (1988), Shannon (2003a), and al-Sharīf (1991).

24. Of the eleven major modes (*tubuʿ*) used in Morocco's *al-ala* repertoire, five are pentatonic or have a pentatonic flavor, indicating a close relationship to pentatonic modes in sub-Saharan African musics. None of the Levantine modes is pentatonic in form or character.

25. In modern Moroccan performance practice, *shughl* refers to the presence in the song text of *taratin*, filler words that align the poetic and musical meters. Some scholars relate the *muwashshah* to the earlier Arabian poetic form called *musammat*, which literally means "strung like a string of pearls" (see al-Faruqi 1975, 4–5). Sacred varieties of *muwashshah* are often called *tawshih*, and a composer of the *muwashshah* is generally called a *washshah*.

26. In modern performance practice, the opening section is called a *matlaʿ* or *dawr*; the middle section is variously called *ghusn, qufl, dawr,* or *khana*; and the final section is called *ghitaʾ, qafla,* or *kharja*, depending on the national context. On Syrian *muwashshah* performance, see Shannon (2003a).

27. These two patterns are the "bald" (*aslaʿ*), which begins with the main body, or *qufl* (A A), and the "complete" (*tamm*), which begins with the opening, or *matlaʿ* (A A A). For a more detailed discussion of the structure of the *muwashshah* in Moroccan performance practice, see Davila (2013, 13–18).

28. However, the medieval source for this claim is Ibn Hayyan. The terms for the rhythmic movements of the *nuba* vary according to the tradition and the era (Davila 2013, 13–14).

29. On the "mysterious" *urghun,* see Reynolds (2007).

30. Many of my teachers and interlocutors identified the performance practice of Tangier and Tétouan as constituting one "school" of *al-ala,* while others saw them as distinct. The cities are separated by about fifty kilometers.

2. THE RHETORIC OF AL-ANDALUS IN MODERN SYRIA, OR, THERE AND BACK AGAIN

1. Muhyi al-Din Ibn al-ʿArabi (1165–1240). Born in Murcia, Andalusia, Ibn al-ʿArabi made his way eventually to Damascus, where he died. His tomb in the Shaykh neighborhood (named after him) is a pilgrimage site (*mazar*) for Sufis and scholars alike.

2. The *salterio,* or psaltery, is, like the *qanun,* a type of zither, and in fact Olavide is a skilled performer on the *qanun* and an accomplished vocalist schooled in the performance of early music.

3. "Rifqan 'ala qulaybi ya man ablah" (Have pity on my heart O you who have afflicted it), a staple of the Moroccan Andalusian tradition from the *btayhi* section of the *Nubat al-'ushshaq* (al-Shāmī 1984c, 173).

4. Carlos Paniagua and Begoña Olavide, personal communication, Fez, Morocco, 2004.

5. For more about Syrian debates over the Arabness of Syrian music or the Syrianness of a pan-Arab music, see Shannon (2006).

6. These remarks are based on fieldwork and travel in Syria from 1994 through 2009 but do not include any information from the outset of the Syrian rebellion, which began in March 2011.

7. The Hijaz is the region of modern-day Saudi Arabia where the holy cities of Mecca and Medina are found. Claiming origins in the Hijaz is one way of shoring up one's Arab and Muslim credentials, and it was not the first or last time I would encounter popular genealogies tracing roots to the Arabian Peninsula.

8. The *batini,* a Sufi term, refers to hidden and even mystical meanings. The usual contrast is between *zahir* (manifest) and *batin* (latent). For more on the ideas of Sufism, see Schimmel (1975).

9. Fateh Moudarres (1922–99) was a Syrian painter and author considered a leader of the modernist movement in Syrian fine arts.

10. Bab Touma is a largely Christian neighborhood in the ancient walled city of Damascus and frequently depicted in Orientalist and touristic representations of the city.

11. Abu Bakr Muhammad ibn 'Abd al-Malik ibn Muhammad ibn Tufail al-Qaisi al-Andalusi (1105–1185), Andalusian philosopher, theologian, physician, and statesman. Wallada bint al-Mustakfi (1001–1091) was a daughter of the Umayyad caliph Muhammad II of Córdoba and a famous poet.

12. Muhammad ibn Zakariya Razi (854–925) was a Persian physician, scientist, and philosopher whose medical treatises were widely influential on medicine in the West. Abu 'Ali al-Hasan ibn al-Hasan ibn al-Haytham (965–1040) was an Arab scientist, mathematicians, and philosopher who contributed to the development of modern optics, among other scientific areas.

13. Abu Nuwas al-Hasan Ibn Hani al-Hakami (756–814), the great poet. Abu al-Tayyib Ahmad ibn al-Husayn al-Mutanabbi (915–965), among the foremost Arab poets of all time. Abu al-'Ala Ahmad ibn 'Abd Allah ibn Sulaiman al-Tanuhi al-Ma'arri (973–1058), a blind philosopher and poet. A well-known statue of al-Ma'arri in Aleppo was beheaded in February 2013.

14. Medina Azahara, the tenth-century palace built near Córdoba by the Umayyad Caliph 'Abd al-Rahman III. It was sacked and destroyed in 1010 in a civil war and left in ruins.

15. These include bilateral and regional trade agreements with Syria and other Arab nations, such as the 1977 agreement between the European Economic Community (EEC) and Syria (Bhagwati, Krishna, and Panagariya 1999, 84) and more recent agreements arising from the Barcelona Process, which began in 1995 (see Adamo and Garonna 2009; Del Sarto and Schumacher 2005; European Commission 2003).

16. Among the more noteworthy are the travelogues of the Syrian scholar Muhammad Kurd 'Ali (1923) and the Lebanese painter Moustafa Farroukh (1933), which are similar to the earlier memoir of Ahmad Zakī (1893). See also Noorani (1999) for an analysis of Zaki's, Shawki's, and Iqbal's memoirs and poetic works on al-Andalus.

17. For example, the newspaper *al-Thaqāfa* (Culture), published by Khalil Mardam Bey (brother of Jamil, the founder of the National Bloc and future prime minister), has little mention of al-Andalus and Andalusian literary figures despite being devoted to an Arab reawakening (*nahda*) and the necessity of studying the past in order to move into the future; the reformist publication *al-Shurūq* (The sunrise), founded in Damascus in 1931; *al-Tāj* (The crown), founded in Aleppo in 1928; and *al-Sha'la* (The spark), founded in 1920, a modernist publication promoting "literature, poetry, nationalism, and moderation." The only publications from this period to devote any space to al-Andalus is *A Nova Andaluza* (The new Andalusian) and *al-'Usba al-Andalusiyya* (The Andalusian league), published in São Paulo, Brazil, in the 1930s. This suggests that expatriate (*mahjar*) Arabs in the New World were more interested than Syrian-Arabs in the Andalusian heritage, and this in a part of Latin America that had under Spanish dominion been named Nueva Andalucía.

18. France's mandate over Syria and Lebanon officially began in 1922, but French control over Syria started in 1920. While France's effective control over Syria ended with the end of World War II, it officially ended in 1946.

19. The original Arabic title of *Why Did the Muslims Fall Behind and Others Progress* is *Limādhā ta'akhkhara al-muslimūn wa taqaddama ghayruhum*, translated and published as *Our Decline: Its Causes and Remedies* (see Arslān 2004).

20. Arslan's work can also be compared with that of the journalist and historian Muhammad Kurd 'Ali, founder of the Arabic Language Academy (Majma' al-Lugha al-'Arabiyya) in Damascus. He also wrote on al-Andalus from the perspective of a committed nationalist inspired, like Arslan, by the Islamic past in medieval Iberia (Kurd 'Alī 1923). See Zisser (2012, 126).

21. Drawing on a long literary tradition of lament dating back to the medieval city elegies (*ritha' al-mudun*) and early modern works such as the seventeenth-century al-Maqqari's *Nafh al-ṭīb* (1968), Arab and Muslim writers and thinkers in the first half of the century used the idea of al-Andalus as lost paradise as a spur toward national revival in the shadows of colonialism. Indeed, it was a confluence of the colonial environment and modern access to Andalusian sites through travel that provided the context for this renewed interest in the Andalusian past. As we shall see in the Moroccan case, it in many ways produced the very notion of "Andalusian" music in that national context.

22. Other Andalusian references in Syrian literature and popular culture include Sulaymān (2003), which describes a trip to al-Andalus, and television director Hātim 'Alī's Andalusian trilogy ('Alī 2002, 2003, 2005).

23. For example, see Darwish (2003) and Adonis et al. (2008).

24. For more on how the role of a rhetoric of Andalusian multiculturalism plays in contemporary European cultural politics regarding Palestine, see Beckles Willson (2013, 243–245).

25. The GCC (formally now known as the Cooperation Council for the Arab States of the Gulf) is a regional political and economic alliance that includes Bahrain, Kuwait, Oman, Qatar, Saudi Arabia, and the United Arab Emirates.

26. Abu Muhammad 'Ali ibn Ahmad ibn Sa'id ibn Hazm (994–1064) was an Andalusian jurist, theologian, and historian. Lisan al-Din ibn al-Khatib (Muhammad ibn 'Abd Allah ibn Sa'id ibn 'Ali ibn Ahmad al-Salmani, 1313–1374) was an Andalusian poet, historian, philosopher, and diplomat. Many of his poems are now sung as *muwashshahat* in the Arab and North African traditions.

27. Muhammad al-Qujjah, personal communication, Aleppo, 2004. Qujjah noted that there were Andalusian families who came to the Levant but that they were absorbed (*indamaju*) into Aleppine society and for the most part lost their Andalusian appellations. For that reason one does not find in Syria such names as al-Ishbili (The Sevillan) or al-Qurtubi (The Córdoban). Because the whole region of North Africa and al-Andalus was referred to as al-Maghrib al-Aqsa (The Farthest West), when Andalusians came to the Levant they were often referred to as Maghribi, and in fact one finds Aleppine families with the appellation Maghribi, Maghribiyya, or Maghariba. Other Andalusian family names found in Syria include al-'Abadi, al-Maliki (after the school of legal jurisprudence dominant in Morocco), and al-Kittani (a well-known Fassi name).

28. This program was launched by ISESCO (Islamic Educational, Scientific, and Cultural Organization). Modeled on UNESCO and founded in 1982, ISESCO is based in Rabat, Morocco.

29. Muhammad Qadri Dalal, personal communication, 2007.

30. "L'Andalousie n'est plus seulement en Andalousie.... Et si l'Andalousie contemporaine ne se sent pas particulièrement orpheline de ce monde arabe..., lui, en revanche, se sent bel et bien orphelin d'alAndalus. Pas seulement les intellectuals, les artists et les écrivains, toujours hantés par cette Atlantide sacralisée et irrémédiablement perdue, mais aussi le petit peuple du Caire, de Damas, de Marrakech ou de Bagdad. Car al-Andalus est toujours dans l'inconsicent collectif des peuples arabes. Pour eux, elle fut l'âge d'or, et elle le fut d'autant plus qu'ils s'en sentent dépossédés.... Dans les villes arabes, al-Andalus est partout" (my translation).

31. As I have argued elsewhere (2003a, 2007b), the *muwashshah* is a living compositional form in Syria. Some examples are thought to have been composed in medieval Iberia, while others are known compositions from the nineteenth and twentieth centuries. All are labeled "Andalusian" to indicate their generic form, not their provenance. For a history of the *muwashshah*, see al-Faruqi (1975); Monroe and Liu (1989).

32. Muhammad Qassas, personal communication, 5 March 2004.

33. See Frishkopf (2003) on the Spanish flavor or "tinge" in contemporary Arab popular music.

34. When I mentioned that for many Syrians al-Andalus represents a lost paradise, a well-known Aleppine composer laughed and said, "If that were true, then Syria would be a 'lost Roman paradise,' since they were in this region longer than the Arabs were in the Iberian Peninsula; the Greeks too!" (Nouri Iskandar, personal communication, 29 March 2004).

35. From the poem "Jadak al-Ghaythu" by the fourteenth-century Andalusian poet and vizier Lisan al-Din Ibn al-Khatib, as composed by the twentieth-century Syrian composer Majdi al-'Aqili. It is among the most popular of the *muwashshahat* performed in Syria, but it is not performed in the Moroccan *nuba*. In 1966 the Lebanese diva Fairouz recorded a different composition using much of the same poetic text. The previous line to the one I cite states, "Ya zaman al-wasl fil-andalusi" (O time of intimacy and pleasure in al-Andalus!).

36. "Al-Andalus, kalima natuq lil-tafawwah biha lama tash'arna bihi min fakhr wa kabriya' wa la nadri rubbama laysa min haqqina hatta hadha al-shu'ur. Al-Andalus wa al-baqiyya al-baqiya min athariha wa ma qad waththaqahu al-mu'arikhhun 'anha tadh-karuna bi-amjad kanat yawman sana'at ajdad 'uzama' li-sha'b yabhath l-yawm 'an makan bal 'an hamish fi kharita batat mu'aqqada" (Badr 2005).

37. For more on the *wasla*, see Racy (1983); Shannon (2003a, 2006).

38. For more on Levantine *muwashshahat*, see al-Afandī (1999).

39. These connections are also evident in the Iraqi *'ud* master Naseer Shamma's (2005) recording *Maqamat Ziryâb: Desde el Eufrátes al Guadalquivir* (Ziryab's modes/stations: From the Euphrates to the Guadalquivir).

40. The exhibit ran from 3 May through 30 September 2001 and was attended by Bashar al-Asad on what many deemed his first foreign trip as president of Syria.

41. Bashir also recorded *Raga Roots* (1997), which implies that the musical traditions from North India to Spain had roots in Arab musical cultures or at least strong associations with them.

42. The Arab Capital of Culture is an initiative of the Arab League organized under UNESCO's Cultural Capitals Program with the aim of promoting and celebrating Arab culture and encouraging cooperation in the Arab region. It was launched in 1996, and Arab capitals have included Cairo, Tunis, Sharjah, Beirut, Riyadh, Kuwait City, Amman, Rabat, Sana'a, Khartoum, Muscat, Algiers, Damascus, Jerusalem, Doha, and Baghdad (see Johnson 2012, 11). Damascus was chosen in 2008, and I was able to attend a number of events. Aleppo was selected as Capital of Islamic Culture in 2006 in a parallel effort.

43. *Dhikr* is the ritual invocation of God through prayer, chanting, and bodily movements. See Shannon 2004.

44. The *taqtuqa* and *ughniyya* are genres of light song usually in colloquial Arabic. The *qasida* is a genre of classical poetry set to music. The monologue, developed in the context of the musical theater, focuses on the virtuosity and emotional expression of a solo vocalist (see Danielson 1997, 203–204).

45. Agha al-Qalaa, personal communication, Damascus, 1997.

46. Muhammad Qadri Dalal, personal communication, 1997; Nawal al-'Aqili (Majdi al-'Aqili's daughter and executor), personal communication, 1998. Ottoman-era *muwash-shahat* compositions usually require filler words and phrases to match the melodies with the poetic meter, and this is thought to be a general and even desirable character of the *muwashshah* genre from its origin, since it allows the vocalist to elaborate and improvise (see, among others, Davila 2013; Monroe and Liu 1989; Shannon 2003a). Al-'Aqili's best-known compositions match the melodic and poetic meters. For example, in *Jadak al-ghaythu* (drawn from the poem by the fourteenth-century Andalusian poet Lisan al-Din Ibn al-Khatib), the musical meter is *dawr hindi* ($\frac{7}{8}$ or 3 + 4), which matches the poetic meter *al-ramal* (*fā'ilātun fā'ilātun fā'ilun*). Another example is the poem *Ayuha al-saqi*, by Ibn Zuhr (Seville, 1094–1162), also in *al-ramal*. It is important to note that neither of these poems was originally technically a *muwashshah* but rather a *qasida* that was used to create a *muwashshah*. The distinction is important, because in Syria the *muwashshah*, as I have argued elsewhere (Shannon 2003a), is a compositional form into which any poetic form can be fit and not a fixed genre of poetry.

47. This and the following undated newspaper clippings were provided to me by the festival organizers in 2004.

48. For a different announcement of the concert, see *al-Sharq al-awsat* (2000).

49. The translation into Arabic and the publication in Damascus of the Spanish Orientalist Juan Vernet's *Cultura hispanoárabe en Oriente y Occidente* (1978) as *Fadl al-Andalus 'alā thaqāfat al-gharb* (The contribution of al-Andalus to Western culture, 1997) reflects this interest in mining the past in order to assert glories that echo with nationalist pride. The editor of the text, none other than Fadil al-Siba'i, published the texts from his own publishing house, Dar Ishbilia.

50. Contemporary composers use the Andalusian forms. For example, from his exilic home in Alexandria, Egypt, my former Aleppine teacher recently composed a *muwashshah* based on a poem by the Andalusian poet Ibn 'Abd Rabbih.

51. I borrow this idea from Bahrami's (1995) discussion of "Andalus time" among Moroccan Andalusians.

52. I have in mind a combination of Foucault's ([1967] 1986) notion of "heterotopias of time" or "heterochronies" and Bakhtin's (1981) concept of "chronotope" to analyze how the Syrian rhetoric of al-Andalus is produced and sustained by heterogeneous temporal and spatial practices of memory making and performance.

3. THE RHETORIC OF AL-ANDALUS IN MOROCCO

1. There are various names for the robes, including *jalaba* (*djellaba, jilaba, jilbab*) and *fawqiyya* (a looser garment that goes over the *jalaba*), as well as traditional undergarments, *qamis* (shirt) and *shirwal* (pants).

2. Sefrioui now directs the Dar al-Ala museum and performance space in Casablanca.

3. On the links between nationalism and the genealogical imagination in Jordan, see Shyrock (1997).

4. Concerning festivals in Morocco, Deborah Kapchan argues, "In short, the nation has much to hope for in festival production, both materially and otherwise" (2008, 56). On festivalization and national culture, see Guss (2001), Noyes (2003).

5. The idea of the "two banks" dates to the ninth-century establishment in old Fez of an Andalusian neighborhood on the other side of the Wad Fas River from the neighborhood then known as the Qarawiyin. The notion of "two banks" was then metonymically expanded to include the two sides of the Strait of Gibraltar that formed the political entity of al-Andalus between the eleventh and thirteenth century. See Abun-Nasr (1987, 52, passim).

6. See al-Shāmī (1984a) for more on the relationship between social and musical developments in Morocco from the thirteenth to the seventeenth century. See Brown (1976) on the social history of the Andalusian city of Salé in the precolonial and early colonial periods.

7. See, among others, El Mansour (1994), Halstead (1967), al-Jābrī (1988), Laroui (1977), Stenner (2012), Zinsenwine (2010).

8. For example, Walter Cline (1947) argues that Morocco was too diverse to have any true sense of national belonging. In addition, Cline suggests that the Moroccan elites were too feckless to fight colonialism: "A second factor tending to retard the growth of a Moroccan nationalism may be seen in the timidity of the townsfolk, particularly those of Fez, Rabat, and Sale. They avoid physical violence at all costs, and tremble at the thought of bloodshed" (1947, 19). Paul Bowles depicts rather the opposite in his novel *In the Spider's House* (1955), which evokes a high degree of resistance to co-

lonialism. Clive also argues that French administration and policy of indirect rule were largely effective at preventing unrest or creating a viable alternative: "To follow this strategy is easy in a country where much of the social and political structure interlocks with a medieval religion. Most Moroccans certainly will not complain if the French fan the mystic frenzies of the brotherhoods, or leave the education of Moroccan boys to ignorant bigots, or refrain from any attempt to emancipate Moroccan women, or encourage the natives to preserve 'their beautiful old culture'" (1947, 19–20).

9. Davila (2013) uses "Andalusi" to refer to the peoples and cultures of medieval al-Andalus, as distinct from "Andalusian" in Morocco and "Andalusí" in Spain. For the sake of clarity I will use "Andalusian" for all contexts.

10. It is important to note the discrepancy between "Andaluz" (from the Spanish province of Andalucía) and "Andalusi" (having origins in al-Andalus). They are not coterminous, and much confusion arises in their conflation.

11. "Shaouen" refers to Chefchaouen, in the north of Morocco near Tétouan (formerly called Tetaouen).

12. In 2014 the Spanish government offered (some say cynically) dual citizenship to descendants of Sephardic Jews expelled from Spain in the *reconquista* but not to descendants of expelled Muslims. See Gladstone (2014).

13. See a more detailed description and analysis of *al-ala* and its history, major poetic-musical genres, institutional bases, and performance practice, see the comprehensive study by Davila (2013). For comparisons with the Syrian *wasla*, see Shannon (2007c).

14. This does not include, of course, the disputed territory of the western Sahara. The Spanish enclaves of Ceuta (Arabic Sabta) and Melilla (Arabic Maliliya), both coastal cities within the national boundaries of Morocco, remain under Spanish sovereignty, as do some islands, such as Isla Perejel (Layla).

15. For a detailed discussion of the Moroccan conservatory system, see Davila (2013).

16. *Zajal* is a type of oral strophic poetry in colloquial Arabic of Andalusian provenance.

17. Some commentators use the term *mizan* (pl. *mawazin*) to refer to meter. Due to the confusion from the use of the same word (*mizan*) for two concepts (rhythmic movement and meter), I will use the English terms when referring to the rhythmic movements and the individual meters.

18. The Moroccan master musician and scholar 'Abd al-Fattah Benmusa argued (personal communication, 2009) that in performance practice, some of the Moroccan modes may have brief instances of microtonality, depending on the mood of the performers and their sensitivity. Although commonly referred to as quarter-tone and three-quarter-tone intervals, in Levantine musical practice, which follows the classical Greek theory of commas and limas, the intervals are more complex. On tonality in Syrian music, see Shannon (2006). On fractional divisions of the whole tone in Greek music, see Herlinger (1981).

19. On Oujda, see Glasser (2008). Tellingly, there are few Andalusian associations outside these main cities.

20. See Moroccan Ministry of Culture (1989–1992).

21. The development of the earliest Arabian musical culture, including music theory and a conceptual architecture for musical performance, owed much to borrowings from Persian music. See Farmer ([1929] 1995).

22. Ahmad al-Shiki based this observation on the affinity between the melodic line and its performance on the four-course *'ud ramal* rather than on a five-course or modern six-course standard Arabian *'ud*. The relative facility of the four-course instrument implied that the melody might date to an era before the addition of the fifth course, a feat often attributed to Ziryab.

23. Muhammad Briouel is correct to the extent that musical collaborations between Levantine and European artists usually require the avoidance of the modes having microtonal intervals.

24. The idea that the musical modes are associated with certain times of day, seasons, and bodily humors and colors has a long history in Arab and ancient Greek music theory and remains popular among some musicians and scholars in Morocco today. I write about rhetorical uses of this association in early modern Syria in Shannon (2006). The humoral theory has been the basis of an ongoing recording and documentary project by Ahmad Shiki (2009).

25. Most major Moroccan cities were divided in the colonial period into the older walled city (*medina*) and the newer colonial quarter (*ville nouvelle*).

26. For more on the struggle between the state and Islamist parties, see Waterbury (1970).

27. Both Ibn Jallūn (1979, 5) and Guettat (2000, 258) claim that the change to the suite *Ramal al-maya* occurred sometime in the seventeenth or eighteenth century. Yet Davila (2013, 49) shows there is no evidence for this change and that in fact any transformation was incomplete, since many *ghazal* themes and images remain in the contemporary performance of the suite.

28. This is the only instance of an actual competition for musical composition in this repertoire as far as I can tell (Amin al-Akrami, personal communication, 2004; al-Shami, personal communication, 2006).

29. For the literary theory of the anxiety of influence, see Bloom ([1973] 1997).

30. Gnawa music is closely tied to West African spirit possession rituals. See Kapchan (2007).

31. In a sense, it is a matter of intellectual property rights.

32. Davila notes that two of the *nubat, al-Rasd* and *al-Hijaz al-mashriqi,* lack the second *mizan* (*al-qa'im wa-nisf*), yielding in effect fifty-three performance units. There are also two "orphan" movements of probable eighteenth-century origin that some scholars and performers include in the total. These are *Quddam bawakir al-maya* and *al-Quddam al-jadid* (Davila, personal communication, 2014).

33. On the mixed orality of the Moroccan Andalusian tradition, see Davila (2013).

34. As an index of the importance of the Islamic dimensions, the ISESCO (Islamic Educational, Scientific, and Cultural Organization) is based in Rabat.

4. THE RHETORIC OF AL-ANDALUS IN SPAIN

1. The mosque officially opened on 3 July 2003 after negotiations that began in 1981. For more on the controversies surrounding the opening of the mosque, see Coleman (2008).

2. Bewley is a follower of Shaykh Abdalqadir as-Sufi (né Ian Dallas), founder of the World Murabitun movement, an organization dedicated to proselytizing Islam. He is currently rector of the Muslim Faculty of Advanced Sciences, whose goals include "study, teaching and research with a view to identifying the roots of modern society's systemic

disorders and planning for the application of the knowledges and practices vital to the attainment of civic recovery and renewal" (http://themuslimfaculty.org/aboutus, accessed 3 March 2014).

3. As Rogozen-Soltar notes (2012b), there are tensions in Spain, as elsewhere in the West, between *conversos* and native-born Muslims from North Africa and the Levant over interpretations of Islamic piety and control over Islamic symbolic capital.

4. See Rogozen-Soltar (2007, 872) and Coleman (2008, 169) for similar accounts of anti-Muslim graffiti in Granada.

5. The neighborhood was not always a residential neighborhood for "Moors," and most of the buildings date from the postexpulsion era. Albaicín is sometimes written "Albaycín" and "Albayzín."

6. For images of the golden age, see, for example, the poetry of Ahmad Shawqi and Muhammad Iqbal, as discussed in Noorani (1999).

7. For more on the politics of immigration and border controls in contemporary Spain, see Suárez-Navaz (2004).

8. I use the terms *Moors* and *Moorish* to refer to populations that are described as *moros* in Spanish and that might be described as Andalusí or even Arab in other contexts. Because the label "Moor" marks a racialized subject, it could conceivably also include the Jewish populations of medieval Iberia, though I use "Jewish" for populations and practices specific to Jews. My use of the term *Moors* acknowledges the complex and contradictory meanings this term carries and is not meant to offend or to imply a historical continuity between the populations of al-Andalus and contemporary North Africans, Arabs, and others who are subsumed under the label in the European racial imagination, especially as targets of discrimination. See Aidi (2014), Flesler (2008, 118), and González Alcantud (2002).

9. For a similar treatment of the role of gesture and habit in the creation and preservation of memory in the Atlantic world, see Roach (1996).

10. For more on this so-called Alhambrist craze in European letters and its role in promoting an idea of Spanish difference, see Coleman (2008, 178–179).

11. The statute declares Infante the "father of the Andalusian nation" (*padre de la patria Andaluza*) and further sets out the bases for Andalucía's independent government institutions, including the Andalusian Autonomous Assembly (Junta de Andalucía), and a number of councils, including one dedicated to cultural affairs. See http://www .juntadeandalucia.es, accessed 8 July 2014.

12. The flag's white and green colors evoked flags dating to Moorish times, green being the color of Islam and of the Umayyad Dynasty in Córdoba.

13. See, among other sources, de Fina (2013).

14. See http://www.Andalucía.com/history/people/blasinfante.htm, accessed 17 February 2014.

15. In addition to Pedrell and Falla, Ruperto Chapí (1851–1909) was strongly inspired by the idea of Spain's Moorish past in his *Fantasía morisca*.

16. The *Concurso de cante jondo* was held that one time in June 1922 but inspired the creation of the Festival Internacional de Música y Danza de Granada (Granada International Festival of Music and Dance), including the Cursos Manuel de Falla (courses in musical pedagogy, composition, and other art forms), now in its forty-fifth season. See http:/www.cursosmanueldefalla.org, accessed 8 July 2014.

17. Falla differed with his mentor Felipe Pedrell, who traced flamenco, like other genres of Spanish music, to Byzantine roots (Hess 2001, 174).

18. See Racy (1991, 2004) on *tarab* and its comparison to *duende*. See also Mitchell (1990) on emotionality in Andalusian culture.

19. The original text reads: "Aquí y allá siempre los ecos moros de las chumberas. . . . Vive en estas encrucijadas el Albaizín miedoso y fantástico, el de los ladridos de perros y guitarras dolientes, el de las noches oscuras en estas calles de tapias blancas, el Albaizín trágico de la superstición, de las brujas echadoras de cartas y nigrománticas, el de los raros ritos de gitanos, el de los signos cabalísticos y amuletos, el de las almas en pena, el de las embarazadas, el Albaizín de las prostitutas viejas que saben del mal de ojo, el de las seductoras, el de las maldiciones sangrientas, el pasional."

20. Lorca composed the poems of the *Diván del Tamara* from 1931 to 1934, but they were published posthumously in a special edition of *Revista hispánica moderna* in 1940. See Lorca (1981).

21. Among his other works are *Suites*, written between 1920 and 1923 but published posthumously in 1983 (García Lorca 1983), and *Canciones* (Songs), written between 1921 and 1924 and first published in 1927 (García Lorca 1998).

22. For English translations of Castro's work, see Castro (1977, 1985). For an English translation of Sánchez-Albornoz's major work, see Sánchez-Albornoz (1975).

23. For a critical reading of Castro's notion of caste, see Beverley (1988).

24. *Convivencia* has been back-translated into Arabic as *al-ta'ayyush*. The term does not exist in earlier Arabic sources from or on al-Andalus.

25. For commentary on the polemic with Sánchez-Albornoz, see Gómez-Martínez (1975).

26. See Mullarkey (2010) for a Catholic response to the notion of medieval *convivencia* as portrayed in the exhibition *Uneasy Communion: Jews, Christians and the Altarpieces of Medieval Spain* at the Museum of Biblical Art (New York, 19 February–30 May 2010).

27. For information about El Legado Andalusí foundation, see http://www.legado andalusi.es, accessed 1 July 2014. Borrowing from Benjamin (1968), we might understand this process of re-creating the dream of al-Andalus as the result of a mechanical and virtual reproduction of the auratic dimensions of a culture that was itself more a rhetorical fiction than a reality.

28. Outside of Andalucía the mutual histories of Spanish Jews, Muslims, and Christians are less politicized and also less sensationalized. This can be seen, for example, in the exhibits at the Santa María Blanca Synagogue in Toledo or in tours of the *judería* (Jewish quarter) in Girona, which focus on history and are less enveloped in the three (or four) cultures ideology.

29. "Corriente más emocional que fundamentada, más fantasiosa que ceñida a los hechos, más expresiva de una negación que se precisa airear"; "la procura de elementos diferenciales, justificación y sostén de una nacionalidad recientemente inventada, aunque el tópico venga de las hermosas piedras de antaño."

30. "Mozarabic" comes from the Arabic *must'arib,* meaning "Arabized," and it usually refers to medieval Spanish Christians living under Arab-Muslim political and cultural dominance but not converting to Islam. It also refers to art, architecture, cuisine, and language and even to a Catholic Mozarabic rite and styles of chant. See Hitchcock (2008), Lapunzina (2005).

31. For an exploration of Spanish Jews, see Gerber (1992).

32. "Pero la misión del historiador es transmitir fielmente los hechos y darles su correcta interpretación, en ningún caso alterarlos con una finalidad moral o ideológica."

33. See http://darziryab.blogspot.com, accessed 2 July 2014, though it has not been updated in many years.

34. See Fairouz ([1966] 1997). This recording, first issued in 1966, remains widely popular today. Its release marked the ascendance of the rhetoric of al-Andalus in the Levant in an era during which Qabbani and al-Kuzbari were writing about Spain.

35. Tellingly, most commentators ignore the evidence that Ziryab may have been of African or Persian origin, since that does not fit well into the standard narrative.

36. It is important to note that de Lucia (né Franciso Gustavo Sánchez Gomes) was not of Roma origins.

37. Pedrell did not see the Arab influence as very large. See Cruces-Roldán (2003c, 11, 21–25), Falla (1922, [1950] 1988), and Molina Fajardo ([1962] 1998, 169–175). In notes to its 11 May 2013 Granada concert, "From al-Andalus to Andalucía," Ziryab-Caló is described as offering a "symbiosis between flamenco and Arab music. A musical encounter based in a search for a common heritage, a Hispano-Arab patrimony" (simbiosis entre el flamenco y la música árabe. Un encuentro musical basado en la búsqueda de un legado común, patrimonio musical hispano-árabe). See http://milenioreinodegranada .es/evento/ziryab-calo-de-al-andalus-a-andalucia-concierto-fusion-andalusi-flamenco/, accessed 30 June 2014.

38. Bernard Leblon (1995) offers an overview of flamenco, its origins, history, and styles, including the various proposed etymologies of the word itself. On the emotional and political dynamics of flamenco performance, especially how the emotional and corporeal dimensions helped to promote it as a national art form, see Washabaugh (1996, 2012) and Mitchell (1990, 1994).

39. See Stokes (2010) for an analysis of the role of sentiment in the creation of a Turkish affective public sphere.

40. The association of *duende* with Andalusian culture extends as well to horsemanship (*caballo andaluz*), as in this video: https://www.youtube.com/watch?v=FPxvm8q6Pyk, accessed 30 June 2014. For more on Andalusian horsemanship as a vestige of Arabian influence in Spain, see Fuchs (2009, 89–93).

41. "Se creó esta formación de músicos, a los finales de los 80 por músicos andalusíes que viven entre las dos orillas, Al-Andalus y el Magreb. Después de pasar por una etapa de fusión arábigo-flamenca, medievo-andalusí, sufí y oriental-medieval; se quedó en la síntesis de tres culturas: sefardí, arábigo-andalusí. Siempre con un espíritu abierto, sin olvidar sus orígenes. Al-Tarab, interpreta nubas, moaxachas adaptadas a nuestro tiempo con instrumentos tradicionales de la época andalusí." See http://darziryab.blogspot.com, accessed 27 June 2014.

42. See http://darziryab.blogspot.com, accessed 27 June 2014.

43. See their recording *Joyas de la música culta árabe* (Jewels of Arab classical music) (Abdel Karim Ensemble 2001).

44. See http://worldmusiccentral.org/artists/artist_page.php?id=8498, accessed 27 June 2014.

45. "Desde una perspectiva de fusión y en el ámbito de la World Music, en Al-Baraka se pretende exponer una música viva y original basada en un profundo conocimiento de las músicas étnicas de diversos países árabes, turcos y mediterráneos."

See http://worldmusiccentral.org/artists/artist_page.php?id=8498, accessed 27 June 2014.

46. The eighth- and ninth-century 'Abbasid caliph who features in many of the stories of the thousand and one nights.

47. "Toda la magia y el exotismo de la Música y la Danza de las Mil y una Noches en un espectáculo impactante, magnético, pleno de ritmo y hermosura." See http://www.jakarandamusic.com, accessed 27 June 2014.

48. See http://firdausensemblesufimusicgroup.blogspot.com.es, accessed 27 June 2014.

49. See http://sufisoulfestival.wordpress.com/al-firdaus-ensemble, accessed 26 June 2014.

50. Yussef Mezgildi's name is variously transliterated as Youssef El Mezghildi and Yussef Mezgildi. He is one of the musicians whom we met earlier at the *artesanía* shop in the Calle Calderería Nueva. For a description and videos of their performance in July 2013 at the fourteenth "Noches en los Jardines del Real Alcázar" in Seville, see http://www.actidea.es/nochesalcazar2013/grupos/nassim-al-andalus, accessed 27 June 2014.

51. For example, the Ibn Misjan Ensemble (based in France) was part of the 2012 "Three Cultures" music program in Córdoba. Ibn Misjan (named for a Persian musician during the Umayyad Caliphate of Córdoba) was founded by French flute player Vincent Molino, who also founded the now-defunct world music group Radio Tarifa. Like the various Grenadine ensembles formed by Abdel Karim, Ibn Misjan offers a range of styles: Sufi, Middle Eastern, and Arab-Andalusian. Molino studied with Moroccan artist Tarik Banzi, a cross-over flamenco-Andalusi artist and founder of the Al-Andalus Ensemble.

52. While these groups travel all over Europe and present concerts at festivals in Portugal, France, the UK, Germany, and elsewhere, I was unable to find any reference to these groups performing in North Africa or the Middle East, and none but Al Tarab had performed in the United States.

53. Ensemble Mudéjar website, http://www.musicamudejar.com, now defunct, accessed 14 May 2009.

54. The website http://www.musicamudejar.com is no longer functioning. See also a review of their 2008 Vienna concert, "Trovadores hispanos," at http://musictravellerstwo.blogspot.com/2008/08/; and their Tangier concerts: ensemble-mudejar-2008-01-27-vienna-fm.html and http://tanger.cervantes.es/FichasCultura/Ficha47563_35_1.htm, accessed 27 June 2014.

55. The Spanish ethnomusicologist Angel Berlanga commented that many of these musical interventions are little more than "invented traditions" (personal communication, 2005). Following Corriente (2000), we might state that "Arab-Andalusian music" per se does not exist; it is a category for consumption, an idea tied to a rhetoric.

56. See also *A las puertas de Granada* (2002) and *Al-son de musulmanes, judíos y cristianos en Al-Andalus* (2003).

57. Cited on El Lebrijano's website, http://www.deflamenco.com/revista/cante/el-lebrijano-3.html, accessed 1 July 2014. García Márquez and Lebrijano were friends.

58. See, for example, one reviewer of *Casablanca* who claimed, "It is unfortunate that an artist with so long and distinguished a career as El Lebrijano has succumbed to the recent trend of cheapening and denaturing flamenco—and North African music as well" (Keefner n.d.).

59. Dietz cites a Pakistani immigrant in Granada who says, "It still is funny anyways, the same people who don't like Muslims, who reject you in other places when they show up in this neighborhood they say 'How exotic, look at their headscarf, here they really fit into the picture!' It's a little bit like living inside a store front-window and being observed from the outside" (2003, 1101, cited in Rogozen-Soltar 2007, 872).

FINALIS

1. 9/11 of course refers to the attacks of 11 September 2001 on American targets, whereas 3/11 refers to the bombings in Madrid's commuter rail system on 11 March 2004, which killed 191 and injured 1,800. Moroccans also point to the 16 May 2003 suicide bombings in Casablanca as another example of the implication of its country in a global war on terror.

2. The conversation was conducted in Arabic, Spanish, and English so that all could express themselves, with Metioui and myself serving as interpreters.

3. See http://www.west-eastern-divan.org, accessed 7 July 2014.

4. On the concept of sonic translation of experience in the context of cultural difference, see Kapchan (2008).

5. 1992 also saw the signing of the Treaty on European Union (also known as the Treaty of Maastricht), marking Spain's final integration into the European fold and the siege of Sarajevo during the Bosnian War.

6. Mann, Glick, and Dodds (1992) and Jayyusi and Marín (1992) celebrate the Andalusian legacy in the sesquicentennial of the fall of Granada. For critical appraisals of this history, see Aidi (2003, 2006, 2014).

7. For an example of the changing political tenor of Andalusian carnival festivals, see Gilmore (1993).

8. "Al-Islam huwa al-hal" (Islam is the solution) is the most prominent slogan of the Muslim Brotherhood and has been adopted by *salafist* groups since the 1970s. See Kepel (2005, 2006), Rubin (2010).

9. As I conclude the writing of this book (in the summer of 2014), the United Nations High Commissioner for Refugees (UNHCR 2014) estimates that for the first time since World War II, the number of refugees and displaced persons worldwide exceeds 50 million people. Up to 200,000 Syrians have been killed in their ongoing conflict, the majority of them civilians, and over 10 million (of a population estimated at 23 million) have been directly affected by the violence.

10. Two examples of this are the anti-Muslim rallies organized by the German right-wing political movement PEGIDA (Patriotische Europäer gegen die Islamisierung des Abendlandes, or Patriotic Europeans Against the Islamization of the West) in Dresden from October 2014 through January 2015, and the French protests against the massacre by Islamist militants of twelve journalists and police officers at the offices of the Parisian satirical newspaper *Charlie Hebdo* on 7 January 2015. The anti-Muslim rallies in Germany have met with counterrallies expressing support for immigrants and calling for tolerance, whereas the French rallies have been marked more by support of freedom of expression and *laïcité* (secularism) than anti-Muslim sentiment.

11. "Sabemos que se trata de un mito, pero en la historia existen los símbolos, y para ser honrados hay que reconocer que esos convivencias entre las tres religiones estuvo marcada por tensions, conflictos e incluso por violence, pero . . . ha sido una prefiguración important de lo que podríamos esperar para el futuro."

12. "Al-Andalus tiene la costumbre, entre la aventura y la desventura, entre el hac-erse, el deshacerse y el rehacerse de la universalidad, y tiene la misión histórica de ser creadora de puentes, de puente entre Europa y Oriente, de puente hacia América, de puente entre ayer y hoy, cuyo fruto es el mañana."

13. See, for example, Dodds, Menocal, and Balbale (1992); Jayyusi and Marín (1992); and Menocal, Scheindlin, and Sells (2000); among others.

14. See also Bal, Crewer, and Spitzer (1999); Hartog (2003); Huyssen (2003, 2006); Müller (2002); and Zerubavel (2003) for theoretical discussions of the use of history in European memory cultures.

15. See Huntington (1993). See also Said (2001), among numerous critiques of the Huntington thesis.

16. See Carroll (2004) on the use of the crusade metaphor in the era of President George W. Bush.

17. Aidi (2006), drawing on Gilles Kepel's (2004) analysis of Muslim networks, sug-gests that the jihadist discourse of a reconquest of al-Andalus only took shape in the late 1980s, perhaps in response to developments in Afghanistan and later in Kashmir and Chechnya.

18. In a similar manner, the ethnomusicological study of the Mediterranean also shares this notion, whether through the concept of the region's musical cultures as con-stituting a mosaic (Plastino 2003) or as sharing musical DNA (Magrini 2003, 20).

19. The *harragas* ("those who burn," from the Arabic verb *ḥarraqa*, "to burn") refers to North and West African migrants who burn their identity papers so as not to be easily identified by the European border patrol for the purposes of repatriation (the act of migration itself is called "el Harga"). These migrants often attempt to traverse the Mediterranean on small boats such as the flat-bottomed boats known in Spanish as *pateras*, inflatable Zodiac rafts, or other small craft. See Suáraz-Navaz (2004, 51, 173). Since the Arab Uprisings, many hundreds of migrants from the Middle East and North Africa (frequently Syrians) and from even as far as China have attempted to cross to Europe on larger boats, many of which have sunk or been abandoned at sea by human traffickers; numerous migrants have drowned in the waters mere meters from shore because they could not swim. The phenomena of the *harragas* and clandestine immigration to Europe have been taken up by scholars (Lydie 2011), novelists (Ben Jelloun 2006; Gaudé 2006; Sansal 2005; Teriah 2002), journalists (Gatti 2008), and other artists (Gschery 2012; Séonnet 2010). Two recent films that treat the theme of *harragas* and clandestine immigration from Morocco are Allouache (2010) and Nadif (2011).

20. The Schengen Area refers to a zone of twenty-six European countries, twenty-two from the European Union (EU) and four non-EU countries (Iceland, Norway, Liech-tenstein, and Switzerland). Member states have a common visa policy that ensures open travel without internal border controls for certain passport holders. The area is named after the Schengen Agreement of 1985.

21. This includes, of course, other populations, for example, the Roma ("Gypsy") peoples of Europe, who continue to suffer from institutionalized discrimination well into the twenty-first century.

22. Fortress Europe policies are not limited to Europe's Mediterranean and Middle Eastern borders but also apply to the borders with Eastern Europe as well. See Follis (2012).

23. Frontex is the European Agency for the Management of Operational Cooperation at the External Borders of the Member States of the European Union and was established on 26 October 2004. While not responsible for border control, Frontex coordinates the border management technologies of member states. Eurosur (European Border Surveillance System) is "an information-exchange system designed to improve management of the EU external borders. Eurosur enables near real-time sharing of border-related data between members of the network, consisting of Schengen countries and Frontex." See http://frontex.europa.eu, accessed 6 January 2015.

24. On the role of NGOs in the management of Islam in Granada, see Rogozen-Soltar (2012a).

25. All quotations taken from the English version of the Casa Árabe website: http://www.casaarabe.es, accessed 7 July 2014.

26. See the conference website: http://hispanismos.cervantes.es/agenda.asp?DOCN =63844, accessed 5 July 2014.

27. For more on the operations of SIVE, see Carling (2007) and Andersson (2012).

28. Recall that *mudéjar* probably derives from the Arabic *mudajjin*, meaning "a tamed animal that is allowed to remain indoors."

29. It is important to note, following Suáraz-Navaz (2004), that Europe's border enforcement strategies extend well beyond the national frontiers into North and West African nations, as well as across the interior of the European mainland. This has had the effect of transforming much of Europe and the Mediterranean into a borderland.

30. Deep Listening Institute website: http://deeplistening.org, accessed 7 July 2014.

31. The Islamic State in Iraq and Syria, now simply the Islamic State, is often known by the acronyms ISIS, ISIL, and (today) IS. The Arabic acronym for the group is Da'ish, or DAESH (al-Dawla al-Islamiyya fi al-Iraq wa-l Sham).

References

Abbas, Ackbar. 2002. "Play It Again Shanghai: Urban Preservations in the Global Era." In *Shanghai Reflections: Architecture, Urbanism, and the Search for an Alternative Modernity*, 36–55. Princeton, N.J.: Princeton University Press.

Abrams, M. H. 1953. *The Mirror and the Lamp: Romantic Theory and the Critical Tradition*. New York: Oxford University Press.

Abulafia, David. 2011. *The Great Sea*. Oxford: Oxford University Press.

Abu Lughod, Janet. 1981. *Rabat: Urban Apartheid in Morocco*. Princeton, N.J.: Princeton University Press.

Abun-Nasr, Jamil M. 1987. *A History of the Maghreb in the Islamic Period*. Cambridge: Cambridge University Press.

Adamo, Katia, and Paolo Garonna. 2009. "Euro-Mediterranean Integration and Cooperation: Prospects and Challenges." UNECE *Annual Report, Economic Essays* 2009 9 UNECE. http://EconPapers.repec.org/RePEc:ece:annrep:2009_9.

Adonis ('Alī Aḥmad Sa'īd). (1985) 1992. *An Introduction to Arab Poetics*. Translated by Catherine Cobham. Cairo: American University in Cairo Press.

Adonis, Mahmud Darwish, Samih al-Qasim. 2008. *Victims of a Map: A Bilingual Anthology of Arabic Poetry*. London: Saqi Books.

Adorno, Theodor W. 1973. *The Jargon of Authenticity*. Evanston, Ill.: Northwestern University Press.

Afandī, Majd al-. 1999. *Al-muwashshaḥāt al-mashriqiyya wa athar al-andalus fīhā* [Levantine *muwashshahat* and their Andalusian influences]. Damascus: Dār al-fikr.

Aidi, Hishaam. 2003. "'Let Us Be Moors': Islam, Race and 'Connected Histories.'" *Middle East Report* 229. http://www.merip.org/mer/mer229/let-us-be-moors. Accessed 3 July 2014.

———. 2006. "The Interference of al-Andalus." *Social Text* 24(2): 67–88.

———. 2014. *Rebel Music: Race, Empire, and the New Muslim Youth Culture*. New York: Pantheon Books.

Albera, Dionigi, and Anton Blok. 2001. "Introduction: The Mediterranean as a Field of Ethnological Study: A Retrospective." In *L'anthropologie de la Méanthropolo / Anthropology of the Mediterranean*. Aix-en-Provence: Maisonneeuve & Larose / Maison Méaison MPrenne de sciences de l'homme.

Ali, Tarik. 1992. *Shadows of the Pomegranate Tree*. London: Verso.

Alkhalil, Muhamed. 2005. "Nizar Qabbani: From Romance to Exile." PhD diss., University of Arizona.

Álvarez Caballero, Angel. 1981. *Historia del conte flamenco*. Madrid: Alianza Ediorial.

Anderson, Benedict. (1983) 1991. *Imagined Communities: Reflections on the Origin and Spread of Nationalism*. Revised and extended edition. New York: Verso.

Andersson, Ruben. 2012. "A Game of Risk: Boat Migration and the Business of Bordering Europe." *Anthropology Today* 28(6): 7–11.

Anidjar, Gil. 2002. *"Our Place in al-Andalus": Kabbalah, Philosophy, Literature in Arab Jewish Letters*. Stanford, Calif.: Stanford University Press.

———. 2008. "Postscript: Futures of al-Andalus." In Doubleday and Coleman 2008, 189–208.

Appadurai, Arjun. 1986a. *The Social Life of Things*. Cambridge: Cambridge University Press.

———. 1986b. "Theory in Anthropology: Center and Periphery." *Comparative Studies in Society and History* 28(2): 356–361.

———. 1996. *Modernity at Large*. Minneapolis: University of Minnesota Press.

'Aqīlī, Majdī al-. 1979. *Al-samā' 'ind al-'arab* [Listening among the Arabs]. Damascus.

Arístegui, Gustavo de. 2005. *La yihad en España: La obsesión por reconquistar al-Andalus*. Madrid: La Esfera de los Libros.

Arslān, Amīr Shakīb. 1936. *Al-hulal al-sundusiyya fi al-akhbār wa al-athār al-andalusiyya* [The silk brocade garments in the annals and ruins of al-Andalus]. Fez: Muḥammad Mahdī al-Jābī.

———. 1975. *Limādhā ta'akhkhara al-muslimūn wa taqaddama ghayruhum* [Why did the Muslims fall behind and others progress]. Beirut: Al-hayāt.

———. 2004. *Our Decline: Its Causes and Remedies*. Translated by Ssekamanya Siraje Abdullah. Kuala Lumpur, Malaysia: Islamic Book Trust.

Asad, Talal. 2003. *Formations of Secularism*. Stanford, Calif.: Stanford University Press.

Ashour, Radwa. 2003. *Granada: A Novel*. Translated by William Granara. Syracuse, N.Y.: Syracuse University Press.

Askew, Kelly. 2003. *Performing the Nation: Swahili Music and Cultural Politics in Tanzania*. Chicago: University of Chicago Press.

Attali, Jacques. (1977) 1985. *Noise: The Political Economy of Music*. Translated by Brian Massoumi. Minneapolis: University of Minnesota Press.

Auslander, Philip. 1999. *Liveness: Performance in a Mediatized Culture*. London: Routledge.

Austin, J. L. 1962. *How to Do Things with Words*. Cambridge, Mass.: Harvard University Press.

'Azm, Ṣādiq Jalāl al-. (1968) 2011. *Self-Criticism after the Defeat*. Translated by George Sterglos. London: Saqi Books.

———. (1969) 1988. *Naqd al-fikr al-dīnī* [Critique of religious thought]. Beirut: Dār al-Talī'a.

———. 2000. "Owning the Future: Modern Arabs and Hamlet." *International Institute for the Study of Islam in the Modern World Newsletter* 5:11.

Badr, Qussay. 2005. "Nadwa fī rihāb al-andalus." *Al-Thawra* (newspaper), 4 April. Accessed 18 February 2013.

Bahrami, Beebe. 1995. "The Persistence of Andalusian Identity in Rabat, Morocco." PhD diss., University of Pennsylvania.

Bakhtin, M. M. 1981. *The Dialogic Imagination: Four Essays.* Edited by Michael Holquist, translated by Michael Holquist and Caryl Emerson. Austin: University of Texas Press.

Bal, Mieke, Jonathan Crewer, and Leo Spitzer, eds. 1999. *Acts of Memory: Cultural Recall in the Present.* Hanover, N.H.: Dartmouth University Press.

Barakat, Halim. 1993. *The Arab World: Society, Culture, and State.* Berkeley: University of California Press.

Basso, Keith. 1996. *Wisdom Sits in Places: Landscape and Language among the Western Apache.* Albuquerque: University of New Mexico Press.

Beckles Willson, Rachel. 2013. *Orientalism and Musical Mission: Palestine and the West.* Cambridge: Cambridge University Press.

Beckwith, Stacy N. 2000. *Charting Memory: Recalling Medieval Spain.* London: Taylor & Francis.

Benjamin, Walter. 1968. "The Work of Art in the Age of Mechanical Reproduction." In *Illuminations.* edited by Hannah Arendt, translated by Harry Zohn, 217–252. New York: Schocken.

Ben Jelloun, Tahar. 2006. *Partir.* Paris: Gallimard.

Bennūna, Mālik, ed. 1999. *Kunnāsh al-ḥā'ik.* Rabat: Moroccan Royal Academy.

Beverley, John. 1988. "Class or Caste? A Critique of the Castro Thesis." In *Américo Castro: The Impact of His Thought,* edited by Ronald Surtz, Jaime Ferrán, and Daniel P. Testa, 141–149. Madison, Wis.: Hispanic Seminary of Medieval Studies.

Bhabha, Homi. (1990) 2013. "Introduction: Narrating the Nation." In *Nation and Narration,* edited by Homi Bhabha, 1–7. London: Routledge.

Bhagwati, Jagdish N., Pravin Krishna, and Arvind Panagariya. 1999. *Trading Blocs: Alternative Approaches to Analyzing Preferential Trade Agreements.* Cambridge, Mass.: MIT Press.

Bigenho, Michelle. 2002. *Sounding Indigenous: Authenticity in Bolivian Music Performance.* New York: Palgrave.

Bin 'Abd al-Jalil, 'Abd al-'Aziz. 1983. *Madkhal ilā Ta'rīkh al-Mūsīqā al-Maghribiyya* [Introduction to the history of Moroccan music]. Kuwait: 'Alim al-ma'rifa.

———. 1988. *Al-Mūsīqā al-Andalusiyya al-Maghribiyya* [Moroccan Andalusian music]. Kuwait: 'Alim al-ma'rifa.

Bisharat, George. 1997. "Exile to Compatriot: Transformations in the Social Identity of Palestinian Refugees in the West Bank." In *Culture, Power, Place: Explorations in Critical Anthropology,* edited by Akhil Gupta and James Ferguson, 203–233. Durham, N.C.: Duke University Press.

Bjørgo, Tore. 1997. "'The Invadors,' 'the Traitors,' and 'the Resistance Movement': The Extreme Right's Conceptualization of Opponents and Self in Scandinavia." In *The Politics of Multiculturalism in the New Europe: Racism, Identity and Community,* edited by Tariq Modood and Pnina Werbner, 54–72. London: Zed.

Bloom, Harold. (1973) 1997. *The Anxiety of Influence: A Theory of Poetry.* 2nd edition. New York: Oxford University Press.

Bohlman, Philip. 1997. "Music, Myth, and History in the Mediterranean Diaspora and the Return to Modernity." *Ethnomusicology Online* 3. http://www.umbc.edu/eol/3 /bohlman/index.html. Accessed 1 July 2014.

Boissevain, Jeremy. 1979. "Towards a Social Anthropology of the Mediterranean." *Current Anthropology* 20(1): 81–93.

Bossong, Georg. 2002. "Der Name al-Andalus: Neue Überlegungen zu einem alten Problem." In *Sounds and Systems: Studies in Structure and Change: A Festschrift for Theo Vennemann,* edited by David Restle and Dietmar Zaefferer, 149–164. Berlin: Mouton de Gruyter.

Bowen, John. 2006. *Why the French Don't Like Headscarves: Islam, the State, and Public Space.* Princeton, N.J.: Princeton University Press.

Bowles, Paul. 1955. *In the Spider's House.* New York: Random House.

Boym, Svetlana. 2001. *The Future of Nostalgia.* New York: Basic Books.

———. 2007. "Nostalgia and Its Discontents." *Hedgehog Review* 9(2): 7–18.

Braudel, Fernand. (1972) 1995. *The Mediterranean and the Mediterranean World in the Age of Philip II.* Volume 1. Translated by Siân Reynolds. Berkeley: University of California Press.

Briouel [Abrīwil], Muḥammad. 1985. *La musique andalouse marocaine: Nawbat "Gribt al-hsin."* Fez: Matba'at al-najāḥ al-jadīda.

Bromberger, Christian. 2006. "Toward an Anthropology of the Mediterranean." *History and Anthropology* 17(2): 91–107.

———. 2007. "Bridge, Wall, Mirror: Coexistence and Confrontations in the Mediterranean World." *History and Anthropology* 18(3): 291–307.

Brown, Kenneth L. 1976. *People of Salé: Tradition and Change in a Moroccan City 1830–1930.* Manchester: Manchester University Press.

Bunten, Alexis. 2006. "Commodities of Authenticity: When Native People Consume Their Own 'Tourist Art.'" In *Exploring World Art,* edited by Eric Venbrux, Pamela Sheffield Rosi, and Robert L. Welsch, 317–335. Long Grove, Ill.: Waveland Press.

Burke, Kenneth. (1950) 1969. *A Rhetoric of Motives.* Berkeley: University of California Press.

Butler, Judith. 1990. *Gender Trouble: Feminism and the Subversion of Identity.* New York: Routledge.

———. 1997. *Excitable Speech: A Politics of the Performative.* New York: Routledge.

Campbell, Kay. 2011. "Listening for al-Andalus." *Saudi Aramco World* 62(4): 34–41.

Capelli, Cristian, et al. 2009. "Moors and Saracens in Europe: Estimating the Medieval North African Male Legacy in Southern Europe." *European Journal of Human Genetics* 17(6): 848–852.

Carling, Jørgen. 2007. "Unauthorized Migration from Africa to Spain." *International Migration* 45(4): 3–37.

Carlson, Marvin. 2007. "Performance." In *The Performance Studies Reader,* edited by Henry Bial, 68–73. New York: Routledge.

Carlyle, Thomas. 1888. *On Heroes, Hero-Worship and the Heroic in History.* New York: Fredrick A. Stokes & Brother.

Carroll, James. 2004. "The Bush Crusade." *Nation* 279(8): 14–20.

Cassano, Franco. (1996) 2012. *Southern Thought and Other Essays on the Mediterranean.* Edited and translated by Norma Bouchard and Valerio Ferme. New York: Fordham University Press.

Castro, Américo. (1948) 1984. *España en su historia: Cristianos, moros y judíos.* 3rd edition. Barcelona: Editorial Crítica.

———. 1977. *An Idea of History: Selected Essays of Américo Castro.* Translated and edited by Stephen Gilman and Edmund L. King. Columbus: Ohio State University Press.

———. 1985. *The Spaniards: An Introduction to Their History.* Translated by Willard F. King and Selma Margaretten. Berkeley: University of California Press.

Catlos, Brian. 2001. "Cristians, musulmans i jueus a la corona d'Aragó: Un cas de conveniència." *L'Avenç* 263:8–16.

———. 2002. "Contexto y conveniencia en la corona de Aragón: Propuesta de un modelo de interacción entre grupos etno-reliosos minoritarios y mayoritarios." *Revista d'història medieval* 12:259–268.

Chambers, Iain. 2008. *Mediterranean Crossings: The Politics of an Interrupted Modernity.* Durham, N.C.: Duke University Press.

Charry, Eric. 2000. *Mande Music: Traditional and Modern Music of the Maninka and Mandinka of Western Africa.* Chicago: University of Chicago Press.

Chatterjee, Partha. 1993. *The Nation and Its Fragments: Colonial and Postcolonial Histories.* Princeton, N.J.: Princeton University Press.

Chernoff, John. 1981. *African Rhythm and African Sensibility: Aesthetics and Social Action in African Musical Idioms.* Chicago: University of Chicago Press.

Chottin, Alexis. 1929. *La musique marocaine.* Paris.

———. 1931. *Corpus de musique marocaine: Fascicule I: Nouba de Ochchak.* Rabat: Librairie Livre Service.

———. 1939. *Tableau de la musique marocaine.* Paris: Geuthner.

Chraibi, Said. 2001. Liner notes. *La clef de Grenade* [The key to Granada]. Institut du Monde Arabe / Harmonia Mundi CD 321038. CD.

Chuse, Loren. 2003. *The Cantaoras: Music, Gender, and Identity in Flamenco Song.* New York: Routledge.

Ciantar, Phillip. 2012. *The Ma'luf in Contemporary Libya: An Arab Andalusian Musical Tradition.* Burlington: Ashgate.

Cleveland, William L. 2011. *Islam against the West: Shakib Arslan and the Campaign for Islamic Nationalism.* Austin: University of Texas Press.

Cline, Walter B. 1947. "Nationalism in Morocco." *Middle East Journal* 1(1): 18–28.

Cohen, Judith R. 1999. "Music and the Re-creation of Identity in Imagined Iberian Jewish Communities." *Revista de dialectología y tradiciones populares* 54(2): 125–144.

Cohen, Mark R. 1994. *Under Crescent and Cross: The Jews in the Middle Ages.* Princeton, N.J.: Princeton University Press.

Coleman, David. 2008. "The Persistence of the Past in the Albaicín: Granada's New Mosque and the Question of Historical Relevance." In Doubleday and Coleman 2008, 157–188.

Connolly, William E. 1996. "Pluralism, Multiculturalism and the Nation-State: Rethinking the Connections." *Journal of Political Ideologies* 1(1): 53–73.

Combs-Schilling, Elaine. 1989. *Sacred Performances: Islam, Sexuality, and Sacrifice.* New York: Columbia University Press.

Connerton, Paul. 1989. *How Societies Remember.* Cambridge: Cambridge University Press.

Conquergood, Dwight. 2007. "Performance Studies: Interventions and Radical Research." In *The Performance Studies Reader,* edited by Henry Bial, 311–322. New York: Routledge.

cooke, miriam. 1999. "Mediterranean Thinking: From Netizen to Medizen." *Geographical Review* 89(1): 290–300.

Cooper, David, and Kevin Dawe. 2005. *The Mediterranean in Music: Critical Perspectives, Common Concerns, Cultural Differences.* Lanham, Md.: Scarecrow Press.

Corriente, Federico. 2000. "Tres mitos contemporáneos frente a la realidad de Alandalús: Romanticismo filoárabe, 'cultura moarabe' y 'cultura Sefardí.'" In *Orientalismo, exoticismo y traducción,* edited by Gonzalo Fernández Parrilla and Manuel C. Feria García, 39–47. Cuenca: Ediciones de la Universidad de Castilla—La Mancha.

Crapanzano, Vincent. 2003. *Imaginative Horizons.* Chicago: University of Chicago Press.

———. 2011. *The Harkis: The Wound That Never Heals.* Chicago: University of Chicago Press.

Cruces-Roldán, Cristina. 2002. *Más allá de la música: Antropología y flamenco (I).* Sevilla: Signatura.

———. 2003a. *El flamenco y la música andalusí: Argumentos para un encuentro.* Barcelona: Ediciones Carena.

———. 2003b. *Más allá de la música: Antropología y flamenco (II).* Sevilla: Signatura.

Dainotto, Roberto. 2007. *Europe (in Theory).* Durham, N.C.: Duke University Press.

Davila, Carl. 2006. "Andalusian Strophic Poetry between the Spoken and the Written: The Case of the Moroccan Andalusian Music Tradition." In *Muwashshah: Proceedings of the Conference on Arabic and Hebrew Strophic Poetry and Its Romance Parallels.* Edited by Ed Emery. School of Oriental and African Studies (SOAS), London, 8–10 October 2004. London: RN Books.

———. 2009. "Fixing a Misbegotten Biography: Ziryab in the Mediterranean World." *Al-Masaq: Islam in the Medieval Mediterranean* 21(2): 121–136.

———. 2012. "*Yāman qātilī bi-l-tajannī:* Love, Contextualized Meaning and Praise of the Prophet in *Ramal al-Māya.*" *Quaderni di Studi Arabi,* special issue 7:47–68.

———. 2013. *The Andalusian Music of Morocco: History, Society and Text.* Wiesbaden: Reichert.

———. 2015. *Pen, Voice, Text: Nūbat Ramal al-Māya in Cultural Context.* Leiden: Brill.

Danielson, Virginia. 1997. *The Voice of Egypt: Umm Kulthum, Arabic Song and Egyptian Society in the Twentieth Century.* Chicago: University of Chicago Press.

Daoud, Hasna. 2004. "Las familias tetuaníes de origen andalusí." Andalucía, Comunidad Cultural. Accessed December 10, 2009. http://www.andalucia.cc/axarqiya/andalusies _tetuan.ht

Darwish, Mahmoud. 2003. *Unfortunately, It Was Paradise: Selected Poems.* Translated by Munir Akash and Carolyn Forché. Berkeley: University of California Press.

Davis, Ruth. 2004. *Ma'lūf: Reflections on the Arab Andalusian Tradition of Tunis.* Lanham, Md.: Scarecrow Press.

de Fina, Cristina. 2013. "La controvertida conversión al Islam de Blas Infante: El 15 de Septiembre 1924 es la Fecha de la Supuesta Conversión." *Diagonal Andalucas.* https:// www.diagonalperiodico.net/andalucia/19839-la-controvertida-conversion-al-islam -blas-infante.html. Accessed 1 July 2014.

Deleuze, Gilles, and Felix Guattari. (1980) 1987. *A Thousand Plateaus: Capitalism and Schizophrenia.* Minneapolis: University of Minnesota Press.

Del Sarto, Raffaela A., and Tobias Schumacher. 2005. "From EMP to ENP: What's at Stake with the European Neighbourhood Policy towards the Southern Mediterranean?" *European Foreign Affairs Review* 10:17–38.

Dent, Alexander. 2009. *River of Tears: Country Music, Memory, and Modernity in Brazil.* Durham, N.C.: Duke University Press.

Dietz, Gunther. 2003. "Frontier Hybridization or Culture Clash? Transnational Migrant Communities and Sub-national Identity Politics in Andalusia, Spain." *Journal of Ethnic and Migration Studies* 30(6): 1087–1112.

Dietz, Gunther, and Nadia El-Shohoumi. 2005. *Muslim Women in Southern Spain: Stepdaughters of al-Andalus*. La Jolla: Center for Comparative Immigration Studies, University of California San Diego.

Dodds, Jerrilynn, María Rosa Menocal, and Abigail Krasner Balbale. 2008. *The Arts of Intimacy: Christians, Jews and Muslims in the Making of Castilian Culture*. New Haven, Conn.: Yale University Press.

Doubleday, Simon R. 2008. "Introduction: 'Criminal Non-intervention': Hispanism, Medievalism, and the Pursuit of Neutrality." In Doubleday and Coleman 2008, 1–32.

Doubleday, Simon R., and David Coleman, eds. 2008. *In the Light of Medieval Spain: Islam, the West, and the Relevance of the Past*. New York: Palgrave Macmillan.

Duran, Khaled. 1992. "Andalusia's Nostalgia for Progress and Harmonious Heresy." *Middle East Report* 178:20–23.

Ebron, Paulla. 2003. *Performing Africa*. Princeton, N.J.: Princeton University Press.

Eisenberg, Andrew J. 2010. "Toward an Acoustemology of Muslim Citizenship in Kenya." *Anthropology News* 51(9): 6.

———. 2012. "Hip-Hop and Cultural Citizenship on Kenya's 'Swahili Coast.'" *Africa* 82(4): 556–578.

Eliade, Mircea. (1954) 1971. *The Myth of the Eternal Return: Or, Cosmos and History*. Princeton, N.J.: Princeton University Press.

Elinson, Alexander. 2008. "Loss Written in Stone: Ibn Shuhayd's Ritha' for Cordoba and Its Place in the Arabic Elegiac Tradition." In *Transforming Loss into Beauty: Essays on Arabic Literature and Culture in Honor of Magda al-Nowaihi*, edited by Marlé Hammond and Dana Sajdi, 79–114. Cairo: AUC Press.

———. 2009. *Looking Back at al-Andalus: The Poetics of Loss and Nostalgia in Medieval Arabic and Hebrew Literature*. Leiden: Brill.

El Merroun, Mustapha. 2003. *Las tropas marroquíes en la guerra civil español, 1936–1939*. Madrid: Almena Ediciones.

El país. 2006. "Al Qaeda dice en un nuevo vídeo que liberará la tierra del islam desde 'Al Andalus hasta Irak.'" *El país*, 27 July 2006, 27. http://internacional.elpais.com/internacional/2006/07/27/actualidad/1153951207_850215.html. Accessed 3 July 2014.

Ensemble Mudejar. 2009. http://www.musicamudejar.com. Accessed 1 November 2009.

Erlmann, Veit. 1996a. "The Aesthetics of the Global Imagination: Reflections on World Music in the 1990s." *Public Culture* 8:467–487.

———. 1996b. *Nightsong: Performance, Power, and Practice in South Africa*. Chicago: University of Chicago Press.

European Commission. 2003. *Europe and the Mediterranean: Toward a Closer Partnership: An Overview of the Barcelona Process in 2002*. Luxembourg: Office for Official Publications of the European Communities.

Falla, Manuel de. 1922. "La proposición del cante jondo." *El defensor de Granada*. 21 March.

Fanjul García, Serafín. 1984. "¿Andalucía árabe?" *El país*, 11 August 1994. http://elpais.com/diario/1984/08/11/espana/461023207_850215.html. Accessed 1 July 2014.

———. 2002. *Al-Andalus contra España: La forga del mito*. 2nd edition. Madrid: Siglo XXI de España.

————. 2004. *La quimera de al-Andalus*. Madrid: Siglo XXI de España.

Farmer, Henry George. (1929) 1995. *A History of Arabian Music to the XIIIth Century*. London: Luzac Oriental.

————. (1930) 1978. *Historical Facts for the Arabian Musical Influence*. New York: Arno Press.

Farroukh, Moustafa. 1933. *Riḥla ila bilād al-majd al-mafqūd* [Voyage to the lands of lost glory]. Beirut: Dār al-Kashaf.

Faruqi, Lois Ibsen al-. 1975. "Muwashshaḥ: A Vocal Form in Islamic Culture." *Ethnomusicology* 19(1): 1–29.

Fāsī, Muḥammad al-. 1962. "La musique marocaine dites andalouse." *Hespéris Tamuda* 3(1): 79–106.

Feld, Steven. 1988. "Aesthetics as Iconicity of Style, or 'Lift-up-over Sounding': Getting into the Kaluli Groove." *Yearbook for Traditional Music* 20:74–113.

————. 1990. *Sound and Sentiment: Birds, Weeping, Poetics, and Song in Kaluli Expression*. 2nd edition. Philadelphia: University of Pennsylvania Press.

————. 2000. "A Sweet Lullaby for World Music." *Public Culture* 12(1): 145–171.

Felman, Shoshana. (1980) 2002. *The Scandal of the Speaking Body*. Stanford, Calif.: Stanford University Press.

Fernández-Morera, Darío. 2006. "The Myth of the Andalusian Paradise." *Intercollegiate Review* 41(2): 23–31.

Fernando, Mayanthi. 2010. "Reconfiguring Freedom: Muslim Piety and the Limits of Secular Law and Public Discourse in France." *American Ethnologist* 37(1): 19–35.

Ferreira, Manuel Pedro. 2000. "Andalusian Music and the Cantigas de Santa Maria." In *Cobras e son: Papers on the Text, Music and Manuscripts of the "Cantigas de Santa Maria,"* edited by Stephen Parkinson, 7–19. Oxford: Legenda.

Ferrhn, Emilio Gonzá, E. 2004. *Las rutas del Islam en Andalucía*. Seville: Fundacile: el IManuel Lara.

Filios, Denise K. 2008. "Expulsion from Paradise: Exiled Intellectuals and Andalusian Tolerance." In Doubleday and Coleman 2008, 91–114.

Flesler, Daniela. 2008. "Contemporary Moroccan Immigration and Its Ghosts." In Doubleday and Coleman 2008, 115–132.

Fletcher, Richard. 1989. *The Quest for El Cid*. Oxford: Oxford University Press.

————. 2006. *Moorish Spain*. Berkeley: University of California Press.

Follis, Karolina S. 2012. *Building Fortress Europe: The Polish-Ukrainian Frontier*. Philadelphia: University of Pennsylvania Press.

Fotheringham, Alasdair. 2014. "Castrillo Matajudios: Name-Change Helps Village to Forget Its Links with Spanish Persecution." *Independent (UK)*, 26 May 2014. http://www.independent.co.uk/news/world/europe/castrillo-matajudios-namechange-helps-village-to-forget-its-links-with-spanish-persecution-9436193.html. Accessed 10 July 2014.

Foucault, Michel. (1967) 1986. "Of Other Spaces." Translated by Jay Miskowiec. *Diacritics* 16(1): 22–27.

————. (1972) 2010. *The Archaeology of Knowledge and the Discourse on Language*. New York: Vintage Books.

Frishkopf, Michael. 2003. "Some Meanings of the Spanish Tinge in Contemporary Egyptian Music." In *Mediterranean Mosaic: Popular Music and Global Sounds,* edited by Goffredo Plastino, 199–220. New York: Routledge.

Fuchs, Barbara. 2009. *Exotic Nation: Maurophilia and the Construction of Early Modern Spain*. Philadelphia: University of Pennsylvania Press.

García Barriuso, Patrocinio. 1940. *La música hispano-musulmana de Marruecos*. Larache: Artes Gráficas Bosca.

García Lorca, Federico. (1927) 1998. *Canciones, 1921–1924*. Edited by Mario Hernández. Madrid: Alianza.

———. (1928) 2008. *Romancero gitano* [Gypsy ballads]. Edited by Herbert Ramsden. Manchester: Manchester University Press.

———. 1981. *Diván del Tamarit (1931–1935); Llanto por Ignacio Sánchez Mejias (1934); Sonetos (1924–1936)*. Madrid: Alianza.

———. 1983. *Suites*. Barcelona: Editorial Ariel.

———. 1994. *Obras, VI, Prosa, 1*. Madrid: Ediciones Akal.

———. 1998a. *In Search of Duende*. Edited by Christopher Maurer. New York: New Directions.

———. 1998b. "Los puentes colgantes." In *Antología comentada (Poesía, teatro y prosa)*, edited by Eutimio Martín, 134. 2nd edition. Madrid: Ediciones de la Torre.

Gatti, Fabrizio. 2008. *Bilal sur la route des clandestins*. Translated by Jean-Luc Defromont. Paris: Éditions Liana Levi.

Gaudé, Laurent. 2006. *El Dorado*. Arles: Actes de Sud.

Geertz, Clifford. 1973. *The Interpretation of Cultures: Selected Essays*. New York: Basic Books.

———. 2007. "Blurred Genres." In *The Performance Studies Reader*, edited by Henry Bial, 64–67. New York: Routledge.

Gellner, Ernest. 1983. *Muslim Society*. Cambridge: Cambridge University Press.

Gerber, Jane S. 1992. *The Jews of Spain: A History of the Sephardic Experience*. New York: Free Press.

Gibson, Ian. 1989. *Federico García Lorca: A Life*. New York: Pantheon Books.

Gilmore, David. 1982. "Anthropology of the Mediterranean Area." *Annual Review of Anthropology* 11:175–205.

Gladstone, Rick. 2014. "Many Seek Spanish Citizenship Offered to Sephardic Jews." *New York Times*, 20 March 2014, A7.

Glasser, Jonathan. 2008. "Genealogies of al-Andalus: Music and Patrimony in the Modern Maghreb." PhD diss., University of Michigan, Ann Arbor.

———. 2010. "Andalusi Music as a Circulatory Practice." *Anthropology News* 51(9): 9–14.

———. 2012. "Edmond Yafil and Andalusi Musical Revival in Early 20th-Century Algeria." *International Journal of Middle East Studies* 44(4): 671–692.

Goffman, Erving. 2007. "Performances." In *The Performance Studies Reader*, edited by Henry Bial, 59–63. New York: Routledge.

Göle, Nilüfar. 2011. "The Public Visibility of Islam and European Politics of Resentment: The Minarets-Mosques Debate." *Philosophy & Social Criticism* 37(4): 383–392.

———, ed. 2014. *Islam and Public Controversy in Europe*. Burlington: Ashgate.

Gómez-Martínez, José Luis. 1975. *Américo Castro y el origen de los españoles: Historia de una polémica*. Madrid: Editorial Gredos.

González Alcantud, José Antonio. 2002. *Lo moro: Las lógicas de la derrota y la formación del estereotipo islámica*. Barcelona: Anthropos Editorial.

Goytisolo, Juan. 2000. *Landscapes of War: From Sarajevo to Chechnya*. Translated by Peter Bush. San Francisco: City Lights.

Granara, William. 2005. "Nostalgia, Arab Nationalism, and the Andalusian Chrono-tope in the Evolution of the Modern Arabic Novel." *Journal of Arabic Literature* 36(1): 57–73.

Gschery, Raul. 2012. "Tracing Borderlines: Shifting European Borders and Migratory Movement." In *Beyond Borders,* edited by John Hutnyk, 171–192. London: Pavement Books.

Guettat, Mahmoud. 2000. *La musique arabo-andalouse: L'empreinte du Maghreb.* Volume 1. Paris: Éditions El-Ouns.

Guilbault, Jocelyn. 1993. *Zouk: World Music in the West Indies.* Chicago: University of Chicago Press.

Guss, David. 2001. *The Festive State: Race, Ethnicity and Nationalism as Cultural Performance.* Berkeley: University of California Press.

Haddad, Mahmud. 2004. "The Ideas of Amir Shakib Arslan: Before and After the Collapse of the Ottoman Empire." In *Views from the Edge: Essays in Honor of Richard W. Bulliet,* edited by Neguin Yavari, Lawrence G. Potter, and Jean-Marc Ran Oppenheim, 101–115. New York: Columbia University Press.

Hakim, Mohammed Ibn Azzuz. 1988. "Apellidos tetuaníes de origen español." *Awraq: Estudios sobre el mundo árabe e islámico contemporáneo* 9:101–123.

Halbwachs, Maurice. 1992. *On Collective Memory.* Chicago: University of Chicago Press.

Halstead, John P. 1967. *Rebirth of a Nation: The Origins and Rise of Moroccan Nationalism, 1912–1944.* Cambridge, Mass.: Harvard University Press.

Hammoudi, Abdellah. 1997. *Master and Disciple: The Cultural Foundations of Moroccan Authoritarianism.* Chicago: University of Chicago Press.

Harper, Nancy Lee. 2005. *Manuel de Falla: His Life and Work.* Oxford: Scarecrow Press.

Hartog, François. 2003. *Régimes d'historicité: Présentisme et experience du temps.* Paris: Seuil.

———. 2005. "Time and Heritage." *Museum International* 57(3): 7–18.

Harvey, David. 2007. *A Brief History of Neoliberalism.* Oxford: Oxford University Press.

Harvey, Leonard P. 2005. *Muslims in Spain, 1500 to 1614.* Chicago: University of Chicago Press.

Hayes, Michelle Heffner. 2009. *Flamenco: Conflicting Histories of the Dance.* Jefferson, N.C.: McFarland.

Heijkoop, Henk, and Otto Zwartjes. 2004. *Muwashshah, Zajal, Kharja: Bibliography of Strophic Poetry and Music from al-Andalus and Their Influence East and West.* Leiden: Brill.

Herbert, Jean-Loup. 2002. "Place in the State for an Islamic Past and Present. Spain: Al-Andalus Revived." Translated by Luke Sandford. *Le monde diplomatique* (November). http://mondediplo.com/2002/11/08spain. Original French version, "Un statut pionnier pour l'islam espagnol: Le rvel." th-spanish-persecution-9436193.html. Accessed 3 July 2014.

Herlinger, Jan. 1981. "Fractional Divisions of the Whole Tone." *Music Theory Spectrum* 3:74–83.

Herzfeld, Michael. 1984. "The Horns of the Mediterraneanist Dilemma." *American Ethnologist* 11(3): 439–454.

———. 2005. "Practical Mediterraneanism: Excuses for Everything, from Epistemology to Eating." In *Rethinking the Mediterranean,* edited by W. V. Harris, 45–63. Oxford: Oxford University Press.

Hess, Carol A. 2001. *Manuel de Falla and Modernism in Spain, 1898–1936*. Chicago: University of Chicago Press.

Hinnebusch, Raymond. 2001. *Syria: Revolution from Above*. London: Routledge.

Hirschkind, Charles. 2014. "The Contemporary Afterlife of Moorish Spain." In *Islam and Public Controversy in Europe*, edited by Nilüfar Göle, 227–240. Burlington: Ashgate.

Hitchcock, Richard. 2008. *Mozarabs in Medieval and Early Modern Spain: Identities and Influences*. Burlington: Ashgate.

Hobsbawm, Eric, and Terence Ranger, eds. 1983. *The Invention of Tradition*. Cambridge: Cambridge University Press.

Hopwood, Derek. 1988. *Syria 1945–1986: Politics and Society*. London: Routledge.

Hordon, Peregrine, and Nicholas Purcell. 2000. *The Corrupting Sea: A Study of Mediterranean History*. Malden, Mass.: Blackwell.

Huntington, Samuel. 1993. "The Clash of Civilizations?" *Foreign Affairs* 72(3): 22–49.

Huyssen, Andreas. 2000. "Present Pasts: Media, Politics, Amnesia." *Public Culture* 12(1): 21–38.

———. 2003. *Present Pasts: Urban Palimpsests and the Politics of Memory*. Stanford, Calif.: Stanford University Press.

———. 2006. "The Cult of Ruins." *Grey Room* 23:6–21.

———. 2012. *Twilight Memories: Marking Time in a Culture of Amnesia*. New York: Routledge.

Ibn Jallūn Tumaymī, Hājj Idrīs. 1979. *Al-turāth al-ʻarabī al-maghribī fī l-mūsīqā: Mustaʻmalāt nawbat al-ṭarab al-andalusī al-maghribī: Shʻir, tawshīsh, azjāl, barāwil —dirāsa wa tansīq wa taṣḥīḥ Kunnāsh alḤāʼik*. Tunis.

Ibn Khaldūn, Abū Zayd ʻAbd al-Raḥmān b. Muḥammmad. 1969. *The Muqadimmah: An Introduction to History*. Translated by Franz Rosenthal. Princeton, N.J.: Princeton University Press.

Irving, Washington. 1832. *Tales of the Alhambra*. Paris: Baudry's European Library.

Jābrī, Muḥammad ʻÁbid al-. 1988. *Al-maghrib al-muʻāsir: Al-khusūsiyya wa-l-hawiyya, al-ḥadātha wa al-tanmiya*. Casablanca: Banchera.

Jakobsen, Janet, and Ann Pellegrini. 2003. *Love the Sin: Sexual Regulation and the Limits of Religious Tolerance*. New York: New York University Press.

Jameson, Fredric. 2002. *Singular Modernity: Essay on the Ontology of the Present*. New York: Verso.

Jayyusi, Salma Khadra, and Manuela Marín, eds. 1992. *The Legacy of Muslim Spain*. Leiden: Brill.

Jirat-Wasiutynski, Vojtech, ed. 2007. *Modern Art and the Idea of the Mediterranean*. Toronto: University of Toronto Press.

Johnson, Louise C. 2012. *Cultural Capitals: Revaluing the Arts, Remaking Urban Spaces*. Burlington: Ashgate.

Kapchan, Deborah. 2007. *Traveling Spirit Masters: Moroccan Gnawa Trance and Music in the Global Marketplace*. Middletown, Conn.: Wesleyan University Press.

———. 2008. "The Promise of Sonic Translation: Performing the Festive Sacred in Morocco." *American Anthropologist* 110:467–483.

———. 2009. "Singing Community / Remembering Common: Sufi Liturgy and North African Identity in Southern France." *International Journal of Community Music* 2(1): 9–23.

Kassab, Elizabeth Suzanne. 2010. *Contemporary Arab Thought: Cultural Critique in Comparative Perspective*. New York: Columbia University Press.

Kattānī, 'Abd al-Kabīr al-. 2002. *Zahr al-ās fī buyūtāt ahl fās*. 2 volumes. Casablanca: Dār al-Najāḥ al-Jadīdah.

Katz, Ruth. 1968. "The Singing of Baqqashot by Aleppo Jews: A Study in Musical Acculturation." *Acta Musicologica* 40:65–85.

Keefner, Kurt. n.d. Review of El Lebrijano. *Casablanca*. http://www.allmusic.com/album /casablanca-mw0000043515. Accessed 1 July 2014.

Kepel, Gilles. 2004. "La 'yijad' de Al Andalus." *El país*, 18 March. http://elpais.com/diario /2004/03/18/opinion/1079564408_850215.html. Accessed 3 July 2014.

———. 2005. *The Roots of Radical Islam*. London: Saqi Books.

———. 2006. *Jihad: On the Trail of Political Islam*. 4th edition. London: I. B. Tauris.

Khalidi, Rashid, Lisa Anderson, Muhammad Muslih, and Reeva S. Simon, eds. 1991. *The Origins of Arab Nationalism*. New York: Columbia University Press.

Khirfan, Luna. 2010. "From Documentation to Policy-Making: Management of Built Heritage in Old Aleppo and Old Acre." *Traditional Dwellings and Settlements Review* 21(2): 35–54.

Khoury, Philip S. 1983. *Urban Notables and Arab Nationalism: The Politics of Damascus 1860–1920*. Cambridge: Cambridge University Press.

———. 1987. *Syria and the French Mandate: The Politics of Arab Nationalism, 1920–1945*. Princeton, N.J.: Princeton University Press.

———. 1991. "Syrian Political Culture: A Historical Perspective." In *Syria: Society, Culture, and Politics*, edited by Richard T. Antoun and Donald Quataert, 13–28. Albany: State University of New York Press.

Kirshenblatt-Gimblett, Barbara. 2007. "Performance Studies." In *The Performance Studies Reader*, edited by Henry Bial, 43–56. New York: Routledge.

Kitāb mu'tamar al-mūsīqā al-'arabiyya [The book of the Congress on Arab Music]. 1933. Cairo: Al-Matba'a al-amīriyya.

Kligman, Mark L. 2009. *Maqam and Liturgy: Ritual, Music, and Aesthetics of Syrian Jews in Brooklyn*. Detroit, Mich.: Wayne State University Press.

Kurd 'Alī, Muḥammad. 1923. *Ghābir al-andalus wa ḥādiruhā* [The Andalusian past and present]. Egypt: Al-Maktaba al-Ahliya.

Labajo, Joaquina. 2003. "Body and Voice: The Construction of Gender in Flamenco." In *Music and Gender: Perspectives from the Mediterranean*, edited by Tullia Magrini, 67–86. Chicago: University of Chicago Press.

Lagerkvist, Amanda. 2013. *Media and Memory in New Shanghai: Western Performances of Futures Past*. Basingstoke: Palgrave Macmillan.

Lapunzina, Alejandro. 2005. *Architecture of Spain*. Westport, Conn.: Greenwood Press.

Laroui, Abdallah. 1977. *Les origines sociales et culturelles du nationalisme marocain*. Paris: Maspero.

Lassalle, Yvonne M. 2007. "The Limits of Memory and Modernity: The Cultural Politics and Political Cultures of Three Generations of Andalusians." PhD diss., City University of New York.

Lawrence, Bruce, ed. 2005. *Messages to the World: The Statements of Osama Bin Laden*. London: Verso.

Leblon, Bernard. 1995. *Flamenco*. Paris: Actes Sud.

LeVine, Mark. 2005. *Why They Don't Hate Us: Lifting the Veil on the Axis of Evil.* Oxford: Oneworld Publications.

———. 2008. *Heavy Metal Islam: Rock, Resistance, and the Struggle for the Soul of Islam.* New York: Three Rivers Press.

Lévi-Strauss, Claude. 1964. *Totemism.* Translated by Rodney Needham. London: Merlin Press.

———. 1966. *The Savage Mind.* Chicago: University of Chicago Press.

López-Baralt, Luce. 1985. *Huellas del Islam en la literatura española: De Juan Ruiz a Juan Goytisolo.* Madrid: Hiperión.

Lorenz, Chris. 2010. "Unstuck in Time. Or: The Sudden Presence of the Past." In *Performing the Past: Memory, History, and Identity in Modern Europe,* edited by Karin Tilmans, Frank van Vree, and Jay Winter, 67–102. Amsterdam: Amsterdam University Press.

Lowney, Chris. 2006. *A Vanished World: Muslims, Christians, and Jews in Medieval Spain.* Oxford: Oxford University Press.

Lydie, Virginie. 2011. *Traversée interdite: Les Harragas face à l'Europe forteresse.* Le Pré Saint-Gervais: Éditions Le Passager Clandestin.

Madani, Mohamed, Driss Maghraoui, and Saloua Zerhouni. 2012. *The 2011 Moroccan Constitution: A Critical Analysis.* Stockholm: International Institute for Democracy and Electoral Assistance.

Madariaga, María Rosa de. 2006. *Los moros que trajo Franco: La intervención de tropas coloniales en la guerra civil.* 2nd edition. Barcelona: Ediciones Martínez Roca.

Magrini, Tullia. 2003. *Music and Gender: Perspectives from the Mediterranean.* Chicago: University of Chicago Press.

Malefyt, Timothy Dewaal. 1998. "Inside and Outside Spanish Flamenco." *Anthropology Quarterly* 71(2): 63–73.

Mann, Vivan, Thomas Glick, and Jerrilynn Dodds, eds. 1992. *Convivencia: Jews, Muslims, and Christians in Medieval Spain.* New York: George Braziller / The Jewish Museum.

Mansour, Mohamed el-. 1994. "Salafis and Modernists in the Moroccan Nationalist Movement." In *Islamism and Secularism in North Africa,* edited by John Ruedy, 55–72. New York: St. Martin's Press.

Manuel, Peter. 1989. "Andalusian, Gypsy, and Class Identity in the Contemporary Flamenco Complex." *Ethnomusicology* 33(1): 47–65.

Manzano, Reynaldo Fernandez. 1985. *De las melodias del reino nazari de Granada a las estructuras musicales cristianas.* Granada: Diputación Provincial de Granada.

Maqqarī, Aḥmad ibn Muḥammad al-. 1968. *Nafḥ al-ṭib min ghuṣn al-andalus al-ṭīb.* 8 volumes. Edited by Iḥsān 'Abbās. Beirut: Dār Ṣādir.

Marcus, George E., and Fred R. Myers, eds. 1995. *The Traffic in Culture: Refiguring Art and Anthropology.* Berkeley: University of California Press.

Martín Corrales, Eloy. 2004. "Maruofobia/islamofobia y marofilia/islamofilia en la España del siglo XXI." *Revista CIDOB d'Afers Internacionals* 66–67:39–51.

Martínez Montávez, Pedro. 1992. *Al-Andalus, España, en la literatura árabe contemporánea: La casa del pasado.* Madrid: Editorial MAPFRE.

Matvejevic, Predrag. 1999. *Mediterranean: A Cultural Landscape.* Translated by Michael Henry Heim. Berkeley: University of California Press.

Meintjes, Louise. 2003. *Sound of Africa! Making Music Zulu in a South African Studio.* Durham, N.C.: Duke University Press.

Menocal, María Rosa. (1987) 2011. *The Arabic Role in Medieval Literary History: A Forgotten Heritage.* Philadelphia: University of Pennsylvania Press.

———. 2002a. "A Golden Reign of Tolerance." *New York Times,* 28 March. http://www .nytimes.com/2002/03/28/opinion/a-golden-reign-of-tolerance.html. Accessed 3 July 2014.

———. 2002b. *The Ornament of the World: How Muslims, Jews, and Christians Created a Culture of Tolerance in Medieval Spain.* Boston: Little, Brown.

Menocal, María Rosa, Raymond P. Scheindlin, and Michael Anthony Sells, eds. 2000. *The Literature of Al-Andalus.* Cambridge History of Arabic Literature. Cambridge: Cambridge University Press.

Mintz, Sidney. 1986. *Sweetness and Power: The Place of Sugar in Modern Society.* New York: Penguin Books.

Mitchell, Timothy. 1990. *Passional Culture: Emotion, Religion, and Society in Southern Spain.* Philadelphia: University of Pennsylvania Press.

———. 1991. *Blood Sport: A Social History of Spanish Bullfighting.* Philadelphia: University of Pennsylvania Press.

———. 1994. *Flamenco Deep Song.* New Haven, Conn.: Yale University Press.

Mittermaier, Amira. 2010. *Dreams That Matter: Egyptian Landscapes of the Imagination.* Berkeley: University of California Press.

Molina Fajardo, Eduardo. (1962) 1998. *Manuel de Falla y El "Cante Jondo."* Granada: Universidad de Granada.

Monroe, James, and Benjamin Liu. 1989. *Ten Hispano-Arabic Strophic Songs in the Modern Oral Tradition.* Berkeley: University of California Press.

Mufti, Malik. 1996. *Sovereign Creations: Pan-Arabism and Political Order in Syria and Iraq.* Ithaca, N.Y.: Cornell University Press.

Muḥammad, ʿAbd al-Raḥmān Ḥusayn. 1983. *Rithāʾ al-mudun wa-l-mamālīk al-zāʾila fī al-shiʿr al-ʿarabi ḥattā suqūt Gharnāṭa.* Cairo: Maṭbaʿat al-jabalāwī.

Mullarkey, Maureen. 2010. "The Popular Myth of *Convivencia.*" *First Things.* http:// www.firstthings.com/onthesquare/2010/06/the-popular-myth-of-convivencia. Accessed 1 July 2014.

Müller, Jan-Werner, ed. 2002. *Memory and Power in Post-war Europe: Studies in the Presence of the Past.* Cambridge: Cambridge University Press.

Murillo Viu, Joaquín, Javier Romaní Fernández, and Jordi Suriñach Caralt. 2008. "The Impact of Heritage Tourism on an Urban Economy: The Case of Granada and the Alhambra." *Tourism Economics: The Business and Finance of Tourism and Recreation* 14(2): 361–376.

Myers, Fred. 2002. Introduction to *The Empire of Things: Regimes of Value and Material Culture,* edited by Fred Myers, 3–64. Albuquerque: SAR Press.

Navarro, Tomás. 1998. *La mezquita de Babel: El nazismo sudista desde el Reino Unido a la Comunidad Autónomo de Andalucía.* Granada: Ediciones Virtual.

Nettl, Bruno. (1983) 2005. *The Study of Ethnomusicology: Thirty-One Issues and Concepts.* Urbana: University of Illinois Press.

Nielsen, Jorgen, ed. 2012. *Islam in Denmark: The Challenge of Diversity.* Lanham, Md.: Lexington Books.

Nirenberg, David. 1996. *Communities of Violence: Persecution of Minorities in the Middle Ages.* Princeton, N.J.: Princeton University Press.

Noakes, Greg. 1994. "Exploring Flamenco's Arab Roots." *Saudi Aramco World* 45(6): 32–35.

Noorani, Yaseen. 1999. "The Lost Garden of al-Andalus: Islamic Spain and the Po-etic Inversion of Colonialism." *International Journal of Middle East Studies* 31(2): 237–254.

Nora, Pierre. 1989. "Between Memory and History: Les Lieux de Mémoire." *Representations* 26:7–24.

Noyes, Dorothy. 2003. *Fire in the Plaça: Catalan Festival Politics after Franco.* Philadelphia: University of Pennsylvania Press.

Oliveiros, Pauline. 2005. *Deep Listening: A Composer's Sounds Practice.* Bloomington, Ind.: iUniverse.

Özyürek, Esra. 2009. "Convert Alert: German Muslims and Turkish Christians as Threats to Security in the New Europe." *Comparative Studies in Society and History* 51(1): 91–116.

Páez, Jerónimo. 1999. "El legado andalusí, realidades vivas." *El legado andalusí* 1:1–2. http://www.legadoandalusi.es/fundacion/presentacion/realidades-vivas. Accessed 3 July 2014.

Paniagua, Carlos. 2003. Liner notes. Mudéjar. *Cartas al Rey Moro.* Jubal JMPA 001. CD.

Pavlovic, Tatjana. 2003. *Despotic Bodies and Transgressive Bodies: Spanish Culture from Francisco Franco to Jesus Franco.* Albany: SUNY Press.

Peristiany, J. G. 1966. *Honor and Shame: The Values of Mediterranean Society.* Chicago: University of Chicago Press.

Perrin, Jean-Pierre. 2001. "L'Andalousie, mirage arabe" [Al-Andalus, an Arab mirage]. *LibAndalou,* 1 January. http://www.liberation.fr/culture/2001/01/01/l-andalousie-mirage-arabe_349784. Accessed 20 June 2014.

Phillips, Miriam. 2013. "Becoming the Floor / Breaking the Floor: Experiencing the Kathak-Flamenco Connection." *Ethnomusicology* 57(3): 396–427.

Pina-Cabral, João de. 1989. "The Mediterranean as a Category of Regional Comparison." *Current Anthropology* 30(3): 399–406.

Pitt-Rivers, Julian. 1971. *The People of the Sierra.* 2nd edition. Chicago: University of Chicago Press.

Plastino, Goffredo, ed. 2003. *Mediterranean Mosaic: Popular Music and Global Sounds.* New York: Routledge.

Poché, Christian. 1995. *La musique arabo-andalouse.* Paris: Cité de la musique / Actes de sud.

Porter, Geoffrey D. 2001. "From Madrasa to Maison d'hôte: Historic Preservation in Mohammed VI's Morocco." *Middle East Report* 218:34–37.

———. 2003. "Unwitting Actors: The Preservation of Fez's Cultural Heritage." *Radical History Review* 86:123–146.

Preston, Paul. 1994. *Franco: A Biography.* New York: Basic Books.

———. 2012. *The Spanish Holocaust: Inquisition and Extermination in Twentieth-Century Spain.* New York: W. W. Norton.

Qabbānī, Nizār. (1966) 1980. *Al-rasm bil-kalimāt* [Drawing with words]. Beirut: Manshūrāt Nizār Qabbānī.

———. (1967) 1973. "Hawāmish 'alā daftar al-naksa" [Margins of the notebook of the setback]. In *Al-a'māl al-siyāsiyya al-kāmila* [The complete political works], volume 3, 69–98. Beirut: Manshūrāt Nizār Qabbānī.

———. (1983) 2000. *Qissatī ma' al-shi'r* [My story with poetry]. Beirut: Manshūrāt Nizār Qabbānī.

Qala'hjī, 'Abd al-Fattāh Rawwās. 1988. *Min shi'r Amīn al-Jundī* [From the poetry of Amin al-Jundi]. Damascus: Syrian Ministry of Culture.

Quiñones Estevez, Diego. 2012. *Desmitificación de Blas Infante y al-Andalus*. Málaga: Editorial Canales Siete.

Rabinow, Paul. 1989. *French Modern: Norms and Forms of the Social Environment*. Cambridge, Mass.: MIT Press.

Racy, 'Ali Jihad. 1983. "The Waslah: A Compound-Form Principle in Egyptian Music." *Arab Studies Quarterly* 5(4): 396–403.

———. 1991. "Creativity and Ambience: An Ecstatic Feedback Model from Arab Music." *World of Music* 33(3): 7–28.

———. 2004. *Making Music in the Arab World: The Culture and Artistry of Tarab*. Cambridge: Cambridge University Press.

Rahīm, Miqdād. 1987. *Al-muwashshahāt fī bilād al-shām mundhu nash'atuhā hattā nihāyat al-qarn al-thānī 'ashr al-hijrī* [The muwashshahat in the Levant from their origins to the end of the twelfth century A.H.]. Beirut: 'Ālam al-kutub.

Rajā'ī, Fu'ād, and Nadīm al-Darwīsh. 1956. *Min kunūzinā* [From our treasures]. Aleppo.

Ramón Guerrero, Rafael. 2007. "Al-Andalus, vínculo de unión entre dos tiempos y espacios." *Cuadernos de pensamiento* 19:393–412.

Rasmussen, Anne K. 1996. "Theory and Practice at the 'Arabic org': Digital Technology in Contemporary Arab Music Performance." *Popular Music* 15(3): 345–365.

Rayyis, 'Abd al-Karīm al-. (1982) 1998. *Min wahy al-rabāb: Majmū'at ash'ār wa azjāl mūsīqā al-āla*. Fez: Matba'at al-Najāh al-Jadīda.

Reynolds, Dwight F. 2000a. "Music." In *The Literature of al-Andalus*, edited by María Rosa Menocal, Raymond P. Scheindlin, and Michael Sells, 60–82. Cambridge History of Arabic Literature. Cambridge: Cambridge University Press.

———. 2000b. "Musical <ap>Membrances of Medieval Muslim Spain." In *Charting Memory: Recalling Medieval Spain*, edited by Stacy N. Beckwith, 229–262. New York: Garland.

———. 2005. "La música andalusí como patrimonio cultural circum-mediterráneo." In *El patrimonio cultural, multiculturalidad y gestión de la diversidad* [Cultural patrimony, multiculturalism, and the management of diversity], edited by Gunther Dietz and Gema Carrera, 128–141. Seville: Instituto Andaluz del Patrimonio Histórico.

———. 2007. "Musical Aspects of Ibn Sanā' al-Mulk's Dār al-Tirāz." In *Muwashshah: Proceedings of the Conference on Arabic and Hebrew Strophic Poetry and Its Romance Parallels*, edited by Ed Emery, 211–227. School of Oriental and African Studies (SOAS), London, 8–10 October 2004. London: RN Books.

———. 2008. "Al-Maqqarī's Ziryāb: The Making of a Myth." *Middle Eastern Literatures* 11(2): 155–168.

———. 2009. "The Re-creation of Medieval Arabo-Andalusian Music in Modern Performance." *Al-Masāq: Islam and the Medieval Mediterranean* 21(2): 175–189.

Ribera, Julián. 1922. *La música de las cantigas: Estudio sobre su origen y naturaleza con reproducciones fotográficas del texto y transcripción moderna*. Madrid: Tipografia de la Revista de Archivos.

Ricard, Prosper. (1931) 1987. Preface to *Corpus de musique marocaine: Fascicule I: Nouba de Ochchk*, by Alexis Chottin, 3–7. Rabat: Librairie Livre Service.

Roach, Joseph. 1996. *Cities of the Dead: Circum-Atlantic Performance*. New York: Columbia University Press.

Rockefeller, Stuart. 2011. "Flow." *Current Anthropology* 52(4): 557–578.

Rodríguez Marcos, Javier. 2009. "The Poetry That Exposed Apartheid in Paradise." *El país* (English edition), 16 February, 8.

Rogozen-Soltar, Mikaela. 2007. "Al-Andalus in Andalusia: Negotiating Moorish History and Regional Identity in Southern Spain." *Anthropological Quarterly* 80(3): 863–886.

———. 2012a. "Ambivalent Inclusion: Anti-racism and Racist Gatekeeping in Andalusia's Immigrant NGOs." *Journal of the Royal Anthropological Institute*, n.s., 18:633–651.

———. 2012b. "Managing Muslim Visibility: Conversion, Immigration, and Spanish Imaginaries of Islam." *American Anthropologist* 114(4): 611–623.

Romero, Raúl. 2001. *Debating the Past: Music, Memory, and Identity in the Andes*. Oxford: Oxford University Press.

Rosaldo, Renato. 1989. "Imperialist Nostalgia." *Representations* 26:107–122.

Rosenow-Williams, Kerstin. 2012. *Organizing Muslims and Integrating Islam in Germany: New Development in the 21st Century*. Leiden: Brill.

Rossy, HipBrill. 1966. *Teoría del cante jondo*. Barcelona: Credsa.

Roth, Norman. 1994. *Jews, Visigoths, and Muslims in Medieval Spain: Cooperation and Conflict*. Leiden: Brill.

Rothstein, Edward. 2003. "Was the Islam of Old Spain Truly Tolerant?" *New York Times*, 27 September. http://www.nytimes.com/2003/09/27/arts/was-the-islam-of-old-spain-truly-tolerant.html. Accessed 3 July 2014.

Rubin, Barry, ed. 2010. *The Muslim Brotherhood: The Organization and Policies of a Global Islamist Movement*. New York: Palgrave Macmillan.

Ruiz Romero, Manolo. 2000. "Al-Andalus según Blas Infante, 'volver a ser lo que fuimos.'" *El Adarve: Revista de estudios andaluces*, 6 December. http://www.andalucia.cc/adarve/mruiz.htm. Accessed 17 February 2014.

Said, Edward. 1978. *Orientalism*. New York: Basic Books.

———. 1993. *Culture and Imperialism*. New York: Vintage Books.

———. 2001. "The Clash of Ignorance." *Nation*, October 22. http://www.thenation.com/article/clash-ignorance#. Accessed 3 July 2014.

Salamandra, Christa. 2004. *A New Old Damascus: Authenticity and Distinction in Urban Damascus*. Bloomington: Indiana University Press.

Sánchez-Albornoz, Claudio. 1956. *España: Un enigma histórico*. Barcelona: Editora y Distribuidora Hispanoamericana.

———. 1975. *Spain: A Historical Enigma*. Translated by Colette Joly Dees and David Sven Reher. 2 volumes. Madrid: Fundación Universitaria Española.

Sánchez Ruano, Francisco. 2004. *Islam y guerra civil española: Moros con Franco y con la República*. Madrid: La Esfera de los Libros.

Sansal, Boualem. 2005. *Harraga*. Paris: Gallimard.

Schechner, Richard. (1985) 2010. *Between Theater and Anthropology*. Philadelphia: University of Pennsylvania Press.

———. 2007. "Performance Studies: The Broad Spectrum Approach." In *The Performance Studies Reader*, edited by Henry Bial, 7–9. New York: Routledge.

Schimmel, Anne Marie. 1975. *The Mystical Dimensions of Islam*. Chapel Hill: University of North Carolina Press.

Schneider, Jane. 1998. *Italy's Southern Question: Orientalism in One Country*. Oxford: Berg Press.

Scott, James C. 1990. *Domination and the Arts of Resistance: Hidden Transcripts.* New Haven, Conn.: Yale University Press.

Seale, Patrick. 1987. *The Struggle for Syria: A Study in Post-war Arab Politics, 1945–1958.* New edition. New Haven, Conn.: Yale University Press.

Segal, Aaron. 1991. "Spain and the Middle East: A 15-Year Assessment." *Middle East Journal* 45(2): 250–264.

Séonnet, Michel. 2010. *Tanger, côté mer: Neuf photographies d'Olivier Pasquiers.* Paris: Créaphis Editions.

Seroussi, Edwin. 1986. "Politics, Ethnic Identity, and Music in Israel: The Case of the Moroccan Bakkashot." *Asian Music* 17(2): 32–45.

———. 1991. "Between the Eastern and Western Mediterranean: Sephardic Music after the Expulsion from Spain and Portugal." *Mediterranean Historical Review* 6(2): 198–206.

———. 2003. "Archivists of Memory: Written Folksong Collections of Twentieth-Century Sephardi Women." In *Music and Gender: Perspectives from the Mediterranean,* edited by Tullia Magrini, 195–214. Chicago: University of Chicago Press.

Serrera Contreras, Ramón María. 2010. "Falla, Lorca y Fernando de los Ríos: Tres personajes claves en el Concurso de Cante Jondo de Granada de 1922." *Boletín de la Real Academia Sevillana de Buenas Letras* 38:371–405.

Shāmī, Yūnis al-. 1984a. *Nawbat al-āla al-maghribiyya al-mudawwana bi-l kitāba al-mūsīqiyya.* Part 1, *Nawbat ramal al-māya.* Casablanca: Binmīd.

———. 1984b. *Nawbat al-āla al-maghribiyya al-mudawwana bi-l kitāba al-mūsīqiyya.* Part 2, *Nawbat raṣd al-dhīl.* Casablanca: Binmīd.

———. 1984c. *Nawbat al-āla al-maghribiyya al-mudawwana bi-l kitāba al-mūsīqiyya.* Part 3, *Nawbat al-ʿushshāq.* Casablanca: Binmīd.

———. 1996. *Nawbat al-āla al-maghribiyya al-mudawwana bi-l kitāba al-mūsīqiyya.* Part 4, *Nawbat al-ʿraṣd.* Casablanca: Binmīd.

———. 2011. *Nawbat al-āla al-maghribiyya al-mudawwana bi-l kitāba al-mūsīqiyya.* Part 5, *Nawbat al-māya.* Casablanca: Binmīd.

———. 2013. *Nawbat al-āla al-maghribiyya al-mudawwana bi-l kitāba al-mūsīqiyya.* Part 6, *Nawbat al-isbahān.* Casablanca: Binmīd.

Shannon, Jonathan H. 2003a. "Al-Muwashshahat and al-Qudud al-Halabiyya: Two Genres in the Aleppine Wasla." *MESA Bulletin* 37(1): 82–101.

———. 2003b. "Intersubjectivity, Temporal Change, and Emotional Experience in Arab Music: Reflections on *Tarab.*" *Cultural Anthropology* 18(1): 72–98.

———. 2003c. "Sultans of Spin: Syrian Sacred Music on the World Stage." *American Anthropologist* 105(2): 266–277.

———. 2004. "The Aesthetics of Spiritual Practice and the Creation of Moral and Musical Subjectivities in Aleppo, Syria." *Ethnology* 43(4): 381–391.

———. 2005. "Metonyms of Modernity in Contemporary Syrian Music and Painting." *Ethnos* 70(3): 361–386.

———. 2006. *Among the Jasmine Trees: Music and Modernity in Contemporary Syria.* Middletown, Conn.: Wesleyan University Press.

———. 2007a. "Andalusian Music." *Encyclopedia of Islam, THREE.* Edited by Kate Fleet, Gudrun Krämer, Denis Matringe, John Nawas, and Everett Rowson. Brill Online. http://referenceworks.brillonline.com/entries/encyclopaedia-of-islam-3/andalusian-music-COM_22873. Accessed 24 December 2014.

————. 2007b. "Composition, Tradition and the Anxiety of Musical Influence in Syrian and Moroccan Andalusian Musics." *Proceedings of the Congrès des Musiques dans le Monde de l'Islam / Conference on Musics in the World of Islam,* edited by Pierre Bois. Assilah, Morocco, 8–13 August 2007. Fondation du Forum d'Assilah. http://www .mcm.asso.fr/site02/music-w-islam/articles/Shannon-2007.pdf.

————. 2007c. "Performing al-Andalus, Remembering al-Andalus: Mediterranean Soundings from Mashriq to Maghrib." *Journal of American Folklore* 120(477): 308–334.

————. 2011. "Suficized Musics of Syria at the Intersection of Heritage and the War on Terror." In *Muslim Rap, Halal Soaps, and Revolutionary Theater: Critical Perspectives on Islam and Performing Arts,* edited by Karin Van Nieuwkerk, 257–274. Austin: University of Texas Press.

————. 2012a. "Andalusian Music, Cultures of Tolerance and the Negotiation of Collective Memories: Deep Listening in the Mediterranean." *Cuadernos de Etnomusicología* 2:101–116.

————. 2012b. Introduction to "Roundtable: Sounding North Africa and the Middle East." *International Journal of Middle East Studies* 44:775–778.

Sharīf, Ṣamīm al-. 1991. *Al-mūsīqā fī sūriya: a'lām wa ta'rīkh* [Music in Syria: Masters and history]. Damascus: Syrian Ministry of Culture.

Sharman, Russell Leigh. 2006. "Gauguin, Negrín, and the Art of Anthropology: Reflections on the Construction of Art Worlds in a Costa Rican Port City." In *Exploring World Art,* edited by Eric Venbrux, Pamela Sheffield Rosi, and Robert L. Welsch, 43–68. Long Grove, Ill.: Waveland Press.

Al-sharq al-awsat.. "Dimashq tastad.if al-mihrajān al-rābi' lil-mūsīqā al-andalusiyya" [Damascus hosts the Fourth International Festival of Andalusian Music]. November 12, 2000. http://www.aawsat.com/details.asp?article=13054&issueno=8020# .U6WHTRbFQts. Accessed 20 June 2014.

Shelemay, Kay Kaufman. 1998. *Let Jasmine Rain Down: Song and Remembrance among Syrian Jews.* Chicago: University of Chicago Press.

Shiloah, Amnon. 1995. *Jewish Musical Traditions.* Detroit, Mich.: Wayne State University Press.

————. 2001. *Music in the World of Islam: A Socio-cultural Study.* Detroit, Mich.: Wayne State University Press.

————. 2007. "Al-Manṣūr al-Yahūdī." In *Encyclopaedia Judaica,* edited by Michael Berenbaum and Fred Skolnik, 1:679. 2nd edition. Detroit, Mich.: Macmillan Reference.

Shryock, Andrew. 1997. *Nationalism and Genealogical Imagination: Oral History and Textual Authority in Tribal Jordan.* Berkeley: University of California Press.

Silverstein, Paul. 2004. *Algeria in France: Transpolitics, Race, and Nation.* Bloomington: Indiana University Press.

————. 2005. "Immigrant Racialization and the New Savage Slot: Race, Migration, and Immigration in the New Europe." *Annual Review of Anthropology* 34:363–384.

Slyomovics, Susan. 1998. *The Object of Memory: Arab and Jew Narrate the Palestinian Village.* Philadelphia: University of Pennsylvania Press.

Small, Christopher. 1998. *Musicking: The Meanings of Performing and Listening.* Middleton, Conn.: Wesleyan University Press.

Smith, Colin. 1992. "*Convivencia* in the *Estoria de España* of Alfonso X." In *Hispanic Medieval Studies in Honor of Samuel G. Armistead,* edited by Michael Gerli, 291–301. Madison, Wis.: Hispanic Seminary of Medieval Studies.

Socolovsky, Jerome. 2005. "Militants Invoke Spain's Andalusian Heritage." NPR *Weekend Edition*, 3 April. http://www.npr.org/templates/story/story.php?storyId=4573301. Accessed 3 July 2014.

Soifer, Maya. 2009. "Beyond Convivencia: Critical Reflections on the Historiography of Interfaith Relations in Christian Spain." *Journal of Medieval Iberian Studies* 1(1): 19–35.

Southern, Richard W. 1953. *The Making of the Middle Ages*. New Haven, Conn.: Yale University Press.

Soyer, François. 2011. "'It Is Not Possible to Be Both a Jew and a Christian': Converso Religious Identity and the Inquisitorial Trial of Custodio Nunes (1604–5)." *Mediterranean Historical Review* 26(10): 81–97.

Stainton, Leslie. 1999. *Lorca: A Dream of Life*. London: Farrar, Straus & Giroux.

Stearns, Justin. 2009. "Representing and Remembering al-Andalus: Some Historical Considerations Regarding the End of Time and the Making of Nostalgia." *Medieval Encounters* 15(2–4): 355–374.

Stenner, David. 2012. "Networking for Independence: The Moroccan Nationalist Movement and Its Global Campaign against French Colonialism." *Journal of North African Studies* 17(4): 573–594.

Stewart, Kathleen. 2007. *Ordinary Affects*. Durham, N.C.: Duke University Press.

Stewart, Susan. 1984. *On Longing: Narratives of the Miniature, the Gigantic, the Souvenir, the Collection*. Durham, N.C.: Duke University Press.

Stokes, Martin. 2004. "Music and the Global Order." *Annual Review of Anthropology* 33:47–72.

———. 2010. *Republic of Love: Cultural Intimacy in Turkish Popular Music*. Chicago: University of Chicago Press.

Stokes, Martin, and Philip Bohlman. 2003. *Celtic Modern: Music at the Global Fringe*. Lanham, Md.: Scarecrow Press.

Stoller, Paul. 2006. "Circuits of African Art / Paths of Wood: Exploring an Anthropological Trail." In *Exploring World Art*, edited by Eric Venbrux, Pamela Sheffield Rosi, and Robert L. Welsch, 87–110. Long Grove, Ill.: Waveland Press.

Suárez-Navaz, Liliana. 1997. "Political Economy of the New Mediterranean Rebordering: New Ethnicities, New Citizenships." *Stanford Electronic Humanities Review* 5(2). http://web.stanford.edu/group/SHR/5-2/navaz.html. Accessed 1 July 2014.

———. 2004. *Rebordering the Mediterranean: Boundaries and Citizenship in Southern Europe*. New York: Berghahn Books.

Subirats, Edouardo, ed. 2003. *Ambrico Castro y la revisión de la memoria: El Islam en España*. Madrid: Libertarias.

Sulaymān, Nabīl. 2003. *Fī ghiyābihā*. Damascus: Dār al-Ḥiwār.

Tabak, Faruk. 2008. *The Waning of the Mediterranean*. Baltimore, Md.: Johns Hopkins University Press.

Tapia, J. L. 1999. "Entrevista: Amin Maalouf." *El legado andalusí* 1:16–18.

Taylor, Diana. 2003. *The Archive and the Repertoire: Performing Cultural Memory in the Americas*. Durham, N.C.: Duke University Press.

Taylor, Timothy D. 1997. *Global Pop: World Music, World Markets*. New York: Routledge.

———. 2007. *Beyond Exoticism: Western Music and the World*. Durham, N.C.: Duke University Press.

Teriah, Mohamed. *Les "Harragas," ou, Les barques de la mort* [The Harragas, or, The boats of death]. Casablanca: Afrique Orient.

Ticktin, Miriam. 2011. *Casualties of Care: Immigration and the Politics of Humanitarianism in France*. Berkeley: University of California Press.

Totah, Faedah. 2014. *Preserving the Old City of Damascus*. Syracuse, N.Y.: Syracuse University Press.

Touma, Hassan Habib. 1996. *The Music of the Arabs*. Expanded edition. Translated by Laurie Schwartz. Portland, Ore.: Amadeus Press.

Tremlett, Giles. 2008. Foreword to Doubleday and Coleman 2008, xi–xx.

Turino, Thomas. 2008. *Nationalists, Cosmopolitans, and Popular Music in Zimbabwe*. Chicago: University of Chicago Press.

United Nations High Commissioner for Refugees (UNHCR). 2014. "World Refugee Day: Global Forced Displacement Tops 50 Million for First Time in Post–World War II Era." 20 June. http://www.unhcr.org/53a155bc6.html. Accessed 3 July 2014.

Vertovec, Steven. 2010. "Towards Post-multiculturalism? Changing Communities, Conditions and Contexts of Diversity." *International Social Science Journal* 61(199): 83–95.

Vidal, César. 2004. *España frente al Islam: De Mahoma a ben Laden*. Madrid: La Esfera de los Libros.

Viguera Molins, María Jesus. 2006. "Cristianos, Judíos y Musulmanes en al-Andalus." In *Espiritualidad y convivencia en al-Andalus,* edited by Fátima Roldán Castro, 151–167. Huelva: Universidad de Huelva.

Vincent, Lieza H. 2004. "When Home Becomes World Heritage: The Case of Aleppo, Syria." Thesis, Massachusetts Institute of Technology. http://hdl.handle.net/1721.1/17703. Accessed 20 June 2014.

Wallerstein, Immanuel. (1974) 2011. *The Modern World System I: Capitalist Agriculture and the Origins of the European World-Economy in the Sixteenth Century*. Berkeley: University of California Press.

Washabaugh, William. 1995. "The Politics of Passion: Flamenco, Power, and the Body." *Journal of Musicological Research* 15(1): 85–112.

———. 1996. *Flamenco: Passion, Politics, and Popular Culture*. Oxford: Berg.

———. 2012. *Flamenco Music and National Identity in Spain*. Burlington: Ashgate.

Wasserstein, David. 1985. *The Rise and Fall of the Party-Kings: Politics and Society in Islamic Spain 1002–1086*. Princeton, N.J.: Princeton University Press.

Waterbury, John. 1970. *Commander of the Faithful: The Moroccan Political Elite*. New York: Columbia University Press.

Werbner, Pnina. 1996. "Stamping the Earth with the Name of Allah: *Zikr* and the Sacralizing of Space among British Muslims." *Cultural Anthropology* 11(3): 309–338.

White, Hayden. 1978. *Tropics of Discourse*. Baltimore, Md.: Johns Hopkins University Press.

Wittgenstein, Ludwig. (1953) 2001. *Philosophical Investigations*. London: Blackwell Publishing.

Wolf, Eric. 1982. *Europe and the People without History*. Berkeley: University of California Press.

Wright, Owen. 1992. "Music in Muslim Spain." In *The Legacy of Muslim Spain,* edited by Salma Khadra Jayyusi, 555–579. Leiden: Brill.

Yafil, Edmond-Nathan, and Jules Rouanet. 1905. *Répertoire de musique arabe et maure.* Algiers: Gojosso.

Zakī, Aḥmad. 1990. *Riḥla ilā al-Andalus: 1893.* Edited by Muhammad Kāmil al-Khaṭīb. Damascus: Syrian Ministry of Culture.

Zapata-Barrero, Richard. 2012. "The Muslim Community and Spanish Tradition: Maurophobia as a Fact, and Impartiality as a Desideratum." In *Multiculturalism, Muslims and Citizenship: A European Approach,* edited by Tariq Modood, Anna Triandafyllidou, and Richard Zapata-Barrero, 143–161. New York: Routledge.

Zerubavel, Eviatar. 2003. *Time Maps: Collective Memory and the Social Shape of the Past.* Chicago: University of Chicago Press.

Zisenwine, Daniel. 2010. *The Emergence of Nationalist Politics in Morocco.* London: Tauris.

Zisser, Eyal. 2012. "Rashid Rida: On the Way to Syrian Nationalism in the Shade of Islam and Arabism." In *The Origins of Syrian Nationhood: Histories, Pioneers and Identity,* edited by Adel Beshara, 123–140. London: Routledge.

Žižek, Slavoj, and Glyn Daly. 2004. "Tolerance and the Intolerable: Enjoyment, Ethics and Event." In *Conversations with Žižek,* 110–123. Malden, Mass.: Blackwell.

DISCOGRAPHY AND VIDEOGRAPHY

Abdel Karim Ensemble. 2001. *Joyas de la música culta arabe.* Pneuma CDPN-300. CD.

'Alī, Ḥātim, director. 2002. *Ṣaqr Quraysh* [The hawk of Quraysh]. Sūriya al-Duwaliyya lil-Intāj al-Fannī. Television series.

———. 2003. *Rabī' Qurtuba.* [Córdoba spring]. Sūriya al-Duwaliyya lil-Intāj al-Fannī. Television series.

———. 2005. *Mulūk al-tawā'if.* [The Taifa kings]. Sūriya al-Duwaliyya lil-Intāj al-Fannī. Television series.

Allouache, Merzak, director. 2010. *Harragas.* Jour2fête. DVD.

Al Turath Ensemble. 2001. *Jardines de jasmin.* Pneuma PN310. CD.

———. 2002. *Hermana de la luna.* Pneuma PN330. CD.

Bashir, Munir. 1997. *Raga Roots.* Beirut: Byblos BLCD 1021. CD.

———. 1998. *Flamenco Roots.* Beirut: Byblos BLCD 1002. CD.

Chahine, Youssef, director. (1997) 1998. *Al-maṣīr* [Destiny]. Cinema Village. Film.

Copestake, Timothy, director. (2005) 2008. *When the Moors Ruled in Europe.* Narrated by Bethany Hughes. Acorn Media. DVD.

El Lebrijano [Fernández, Juan Peña]. 1985. *Encuentros.* Ariola 9J 257240. CD.

———. 1998. *Casablanca.* With the Arab-Andalusian Orchestra. Blue Note 4933422. CD.

———. 2005. *Puertas abiertas.* With Faiaal Kourrich. Ediciones Senador CD-02852. CD.

Fairouz. (1966) 1997. *Andalousiyyat.* Voix de l'Orient VDL CD 522. CD.

Lucia, Paco de. (1990) 2006. *Zyryab.* PolyGram Iberica / Verve World. 314 510 805–2. CD.

Martín, Juan. (1998) 2011. *Música Alhamra.* Flamenco Vision CD11. CD.

Moroccan Ministry of Culture. 1989–1992. *Al-ala / Moroccan Andalusian Music.* Maisons des Cultures du Monde. Seventy-three CDs.

Mudéjar. 1998. *Cartas al rey moro.* Jubal JMPA 001. CD.

———. 2002. *A las puertas de Granada.* Jubal JMPA 005. CD.

———. 2003. *Al-son de musulmaes, judíos y cristianos en al-Andalus.* Nuba KAR 707. CD.

Nadif, Mohamed, director. *Al-Andalus munamour / Andalousie, mon amour!* [Andalusia, my love!]. Awman Productions. DVD.

Paniagua, Eduardo. 2009. *Puentes sobre el Mediterraneo*. Karonte 800. CD.

Shamma, Naseer. 2005. *Maqamat Ziryeb: Desde el Eufrátes al Guadalquivir* [Ziryab's stations: From the Euphrates to the Guadalquivir]. Pneuma PN-480. CD.

Shiki, Ahmad. 2009. *Maroc: L'arbre des 24 modes*. BUDA 00050953. 2 CDs.

Turturro, John, director. 2010. *Passione*. FilmBuff Studios. DVD.

Zwick, Joel, director. 2002. *My Big Fat Greek Wedding*. IFC Films. DVD.

INDEX

Abbas, Ackbar, 15

'Abd al-Rahman al-Dakhil (Umayyad prince, founder of first al-Andalus kingdom), 26, 59, 60, 62

al-ala (Moroccan Andalusian music), 19, 43, 43n24, 47–48, 87; addition of *darj* movement, 109; in collaboration, 154; definition, 181; in Granada, 149; and grip of tradition, 110, 113–114; and innovation, 111, 176; as performed in Morocco, 93–94, 97–105, 96; relative popularity in Morocco, 116–118; rhythmic scheme, 97; and Sufism, 106. *Other musical terms appear under Music*

al-Andalus, 1–6, 8, 9, 14, 15, 19–20; etymology, 22n1; legacy, 178; legacy and mythology, 23, 25–28; in Morocco, 86–92, 102, 103, 108, 118, 177; and *muwashshah*, 44, 77–79; nostalgia, 29–39, 158, 162; post-Ziryab, 40–41; rhetoric and *convivencia*, 163–164, 168–171; in Spain, 123–128, 134–136, 138, 142–143, 146–150, 153–156, 177; in Syria, 52–83, 177; and Ziryab, 38–39, 75

Albéniz, Isaac, composer (1860–1909), 33

Algeria, 19, 22, 23, 31, 39, 43, 46, 94, 157, 168; centers of Andalusian music and repertoire, 48; historical reference, 94

Almohad dynasty, 30, 41, 88

Almoravid dynasty, 30, 41, 88

Andalusian music, 5, 6, 8, 15, 16, 18, 20, 160–161, 164, 176; and claimed affinity, 91; comparative structures, 4–56; conclusions, 176–178; confusion over definition of, 23; in contemporary Granada, 122, 139, 146; and flamenco, 143, 145–146, 148; historical ambiguity, 35–36; instruments, 60; legacy, 24; and the Mediterranean, 424; Moroccan patronage, 84–86, 88; and *muwashshah*, 74; recent Syrian patronage, 79–80; Suites: *nuba/nawba* (North Africa) 58; tempos, 59; *wasla* (Levant), 62, 74–75; and Ziryab and structure, 37–39, 76. See also *al-ala*; Ensemble Mudéjar; Metioui, Omar

Appadurai, Arjun, 7, 17, 18, 61, 87

Arslan, Shakib (1869–1946), Syrian writer, 65, 190n20

Asad, Hafez al-, former Syrian president, professed Pan-Arabism, 66, 71

Asad, Talal, 174

Atlan, Françoise, Sephardic singer, 161

authenticity, 17, 18, 25, 33; and emotion, 151; in Ensemble Mudéjar, 152; and flamenco, 145–147, 149; and Moroccan cultural heritage, 86, 91, 96, 100, 102, 104, 105, 108, 111; and rhetoric, 134, 164; and Sufism, 106; and Syrian self-identity, 46, 54, 67, 79, 80, 177

Bahrami, Beebe, 46, 90–93, 193n51

Barenboim, Daniel, 161

barwala (Moroccan colloquial Arabic poetry), 43, 47, 109, 181

Bashir, Munir (1930–1997), Iraqi *'ud* master, 76
Berber/Imazighen, 23n2, 26n5, 26, 37, 43, 49, 124; Almoravid/Almohad conservatism, 30; and Moroccan society, 89, 90, 91
Bowles, Paul, 89n8
Bouhassoun, Waed (Syrian *'ud* player and singer), 77
Boym, Svetlana, 12–16, 32, 67, 73, 81, 186n16
Briouel, Muhammad, 91, 113–114, 161
Burhan, Sami (Syrian artist), 77–79
Burke, Kenneth, 14

Cantigas de Santa Maria, 45, 51, 149
Castro, Américo, 132–135, 137, 154, 163, 167, 197n22
Chottin, Alexis, efforts to notate *al-ala* repertoire, 95
Chraibi, Said (Moroccan musician, *La clef de Granada*), 92, 147
Ciantar, Phillip. See also Libya, Andalusian music of
Cline, Walter, 193n8
collective memory. See memory, collective
Connerton, Paul, 11
convivencia (coexistence)/*al-ta'ayyush*, 20, 28, 28n8, 29, 126, 132–134, 136–137, 155, 161–165, 167–172, 181
Corriente, Federico, 127, 135–136, 199n55
Crapanzano, Vincent, 62, 67

Dalal, Muhammad Qadri, xiv, 71
Davila, Carl, 33, 36, 39, 43, 44, 95, 99, 107, 187n7, 188n27, 194n9, 194n13, 194n15, 195n27, 195n32
"Deep Listening," and Pauline Oliveros, 172, 172n30, 175
Deleuze, Gilles, and Felix Guattari, 24, 175
dos orillas, las (the two sides of the Strait of Gibraltar), 92, 146, 158, 178. See also *'udwatan*
duende, 130, 182. See also *tarab* (as emotional response to music)

Ensemble Ibn 'Arabi, 62
Ensemble Mudéjar, 53–54, 149, 150–152, 153, 158. See also Olavide, Begoña

Falla, Manuel de, 33, 96, 127–131, 133, 144, 145; and García Lorca, *Concurso de Cante Jondo*, 128–129, 196n16
Fanjul García, Serafín, 28, 125, 135, 136, 157, 167
fath (opening), 1, 25, 29, 56, 58
Fez Festival of Andalusian Music, 84, 86, 101, 160
flamenco, 23, 36; and the Al-Firdaus Ensemble, 148; and the Al-Tarab Ensemble, 146; context, 143–146, 156–157; and El Lebrijano, 153–154; and the Ensemble Mudéjar, 151; and de Falla, 129; under Franco, 131; and García Lorca, 129–130; and Juan Martín, 153; and musician Uzman Almerabit in Granada, 139; and "Orientalism," 142-143; and Syrian musicians, 76; terms defined, 180–182

Gala, Antonio, 224
García Lorca, Federico, 33, 96, 125, 128–131, 135, 145, 197n20; on *duende*, 129, 146, 182
Geertz, Clifford, 5
Gulf Cooperative Council (GCC) and funding of Great Mosque of Granada, 70, 71, 190n25

Halbwachs, Maurice, 18. See also memory
Hartog, François, 13. See also regimes of historicity
Hayik (or Ha'ik), Ibn al-Husayn al- (eighteenth-century Tétouan jurist), 42
Huyssen, Andreas, 13, 178, 186n20

Ibn al-'Arabi, Muhyi al-Din (1165–1240; scholar, Andalusia-Damascus), 41, 61, 188n1
Ibn Bajja, also Abu Bakr Ibn Yahya al-Sayigh (known in the West as Avempace; d. 1139, twelfth-century sage), 40
Ibn Hazm, Ibn Ahmad ibn Sa'id (994–1064; Andalusian jurist, theologian), 71, 191n26
Ibn al-Khatib, Lisan al-Din (1313–1374, Andalusian poet diplomat), 31, 71
Ibn Sana' al-Mulk (d. 1212) author of *Dar al-tiraz* (House of Brocade), 41

Ibn Ziyad, Tariq (Berber general, eighth century), 1, 2, 3, 26

Infante, Blas, 127–128

Iqbal, Muhammad, 34, 190n16, 196n6

Irving, Washington, *Tales from the Alhambra*, 33, 127

Islam: and al-Andalus, 1, 2, 20, 26, 30–37; as basis for new state, 16, 24, 55–56, 69, 71, 83, 178; and modern Morocco, 90, 91, 106–108; and modern Spain, 16, 120–128, 131–133, 137, 142, 147–149, 155–156, 162–172, 175, 177; and modern Syria, 55, 56, 61, 63, 64, 65; and song forms (*inshad*), 52, 53

Jabri, Muhammed 'Abid al-, 89, 107

jama'iyat (amateur associations), 47

Jews: in al-Andalus, 2, 28, 38, 124, 126, 182, 187n20, 196n8, 197n28; *baqqashot, piyyutim* forms, 44, 50–51; as performers of Arab, Arab-Andalusian music, 19, 38, 50, 51; and rhetoric of *convivencia*, 132–135, 153, 160, 161, 174

Khaligh, Ahmed El- (Moroccan musician, scholar), 68

Kunnash al-Ha'ik, and Andalusian musical tradition in Morocco, 36, 42, 47, 94, 112, 113

Kuzbari, Salma al-Haffar al-, 67–69, 198n34

Lagerkvist, Amanda, 8, 14, 15, 18

Laroui, Abdallah, 89, 193n7

Levantine and North African music structures compared, 36–37, 40, 42–45

Libya, Andalusian music of, 23, 46, 47, 49

Lost Paradise: al-Andalus as, 15, 28, 30–35, 37, 39, 40, 56, 57, 63, 65, 67, 70, 72, 74, 81, 92, 93, 163, 177, 190n21; and *convivencia*, 48; *firdawsuna al-mafqud* ("our lost paradise"), 57; and nostalgia, 15, 28, 32, 34, 35, 39, 56, 67, 70, 81, 93, 163; and Palestine, 70. See also *muwashshah;* Syria;

Loukili (al-Wakili), Ahmad (Moroccan musician), 98, 109, 113, 114

Lucía, Paco de, né Francisco Gustavo Sánchez Gomes (1947–2014), Flamenco guitarist and *Zyryab* album, 23, 144, 151, 152, 153

Maalouf, Amin (Lebanese writer), 165

malhun, Moroccan music, 48, 99

Maqqari, al- (seventeenth-century historian), 32, 65, 188n22, 190n21

Martín, Juan (Flamenco artist), 152–152

memory: collective, xi, 5, 8, 11, 14, 21, 72, 86; memory cultures, 14–18, 21, 42, 55, 157; and nostalgia, 11, 13, 16

Menocal, María Rosa, xiv, 5, 6, 27, 30, 56, 62, 83, 134–135, 166, 167, 187; and al-Andalus as "first-rate place," 25, 83, 166

Metioui, Omar (Moroccan performer, scholar), 111, 168, 158–161, 168–169, 175

Montávez, Martínez, 32

Morocco, 1, 3, 6, 19, 20, 36, 39, 52; and Al-Firdaus, 148; *fath,* 26; and Francisco Franco, 131; and Metioui, 158–160; its music as distinct from others, 42, 43, 46–49, 176; nostalgia, 15, 70; and Olivade and Paniagua, 150–151, 160; rhetoric of al-Andalus, 84–114, 118, 160, 177

Musical terms: *al-rast/al-rasd* (melodic mode), 103; *al-sama'* (Islamic chant), 40, 57, 106, 181; *chaabi* (Moroccan pop music), 100, 118; *hijaz* (differences in modes), 102; *jawq* (traditional ensemble in Moroccan Andalusian music), 47, 97, 110, 159, 182; *kamanja* (violin), 48, 50, 52, 75; *kunnash* (song book of Moroccan music), 42, 47, 182; *kwit(h)ra* (long-necked lute), 48; *ma'luf* (Andalusian music in Constantine, Algeria; Tunisia, and Libya), 48–49; *mizan* (rhythmic circle in North African music), 47, 48, 97, 109, 182; *munshid* (vocalist), 48, 49; *naqqarat* (small kettledrums) 49; *nawba/nuba* (musical suites), definition, 44, 183; Moroccan repertoire, 45, 47, 48; in Algeria and Tunisia, 48; in Libya, 49; nineteenth century reference, 94; and Alexis Chottin, 95; and modes, 97; in Granada, 148; and

Mudéjar ensemble, 152; *nay* (flute), 46, 48, 50, 52, 53, 75, 147; *qanun:* lap zither, 48, 50, 52, 53, 75, 78, 138, 149, 150, 151, 158, 183; *raddada* (small chorus), 49; *salterio* or psaltery (zither), 53, 150, 183; *tab'* (melodic mode in Moroccan music), 45, 47, 97, 183; *tarab* (emotional responses), 47, 48, 75, 79, 145; definition and differing perspectives, 104, 106, 183; likened to *duende*, 130, 145; *'ud 'arbi/ramal* (4-string lute), 48, 97; *zajal* (oral strophic poetry), 44, 47, 96; contrasted with *barwala*, 109

muwashshah, 31, 41; and Ibn Sana' al-Mulk's *Dar al-tiraz*, 41; defined and structure of, 43–45, 47; and *zajal*, 44, 47, 96, 109; in the Levant, 49–50, 74–75; in Syria, 54–55, 58, 71, 73, 75, 77–79; and Lebanese diva Fairouz, 139; influence on Ensemble Mudéjar, 152; and de Lucía's misinterpretation, 153; and Al Turath ensemble in Aleppo, 169

Myers, Fred, 18, 152

Naseem al-Andalus, Granada musical group, 148–149

Nora, Pierre, and *lieux de mémoire*, 13, 14, 18, 122, 142, 178

Olavide, Begoña: and Ensemble Mudéjar, 53, 111, 150, 156, 189n2; collaboration with Metioui, 151, 158–161, 162, 168, 174, 175

Oliveros, Pauline. *See* "Deep Listening," and Pauline Oliveros

Palestine: loss of and nostalgia, 35, 68–70, 92–93; and Syrian Pan-Arabism, 70; and European Classical music, 190n24

Paniagua, Carlos, luthier: Ensemble Mudéjar, 54, 158, 160, 162; and Metioui collaboration, 169

Paniagua, Eduardo, 150, 152; and Pneuma label, 23, 150, 152, 186n1; *Puentes sobre el Mediterraneo*, 168

Peña Fernandez, Juan, "El Lebrijano," flamenco singer, 153–154

Qabbani, Nizar: pan-Arabism, 68–69; poem "Gharnata," 67–69; and Andalusian music, 78, 198n34

Rashid, Harun al-, 'Abbasid Caliph, 38

Rayyis, 'Abd a-Karim al- (1912–1996), 98, 106, 113; and Ensemble al-Rayyis, 114, 161

regimes of historicity, 13, 15, 178. *See also* Hartog, François

Reynolds, Dwight, 36, 39, 44, 49

ritha' al-mudun (city elegies), 31, 187n15, 190n21

Sabsaby, Hussein, Syrian *'ud* player, xiv, 76–77, 169

Said, Edward, 161

Sánchez-Albornoz, Claudio, 132–133, 155, 167, 197n22

Schechner, Richard, 9, 16, 185n8

Sephardic Jews, and music, 19, 23, 36, 50–51, 93, 136, 147, 150, 153, 155, 161, 194n12. *See also* Atlan, Françoise, Sephardic singer; Jews

Shami, 'Abd al-Malik al-, 85, 102

Shami, Yunis al-, 113–114

Shaqundi, al- (thirteenth-century Andalusian poet), 27

Shawqi, Ahmad (Egyptian poet), "Siniyya" ode, 34, 67–68, 196n6

Shihab al-Din, Muhammed (1795/6–1857, collector of song texts), 49

Shiki, al-Hajj Ahmad al- (Moroccan musician), 102, 103–105, 111, 112, 118, 195n22, 195n24

Siba'i, Fadil al- (Syrian writer), 57, 58, 61, 63, 76, 82, 193n49

Spain, 3, 5, 6, 8, 9, 13–20, 23–25, 32–35, 38–39, 51, 52, 54, 57, 62, 68, 72, 176; Arab investment in, 70–71; and Syria, 77–78, 169; and Morocco, 87, 91, 93, 95, 118; and construction of La Mezquita Mayor in Granada, 120; and its heterogeneous past, 123; *maurofilia/maurofobia*, 124, 137, 166–167; and ambivalence over Muslim conquest, 126–128; and Franco, 131; and historians' debate, 132–137; and myth of Ziryab, 142–144; and flamenco,

145; and non-flamenco music, 146–154; and renaming communities debated, 155; official efforts to promote tolerance as well as control, 170–172, 177; Córdoba, 2, 16, 25, 30, 137, 142; and Umayyad Emirate, Caliphate, 27, 57, 80; its zenith, 27–28; fall of, 29; and Mohammed Iqbal, 34; and Ziryab, 38, 143; and Tlemcen and Tripoli, 46; and Syria, 62, 76–77; and Salma al-Haffar al-Kuzbari, 68; and Casa Árabe, 148, 170. Granada, 2, 5, 6, 15, 16, 18, 20; its golden age, 27–30, 41-; and nostalgia for al-Andalus, 34, 77, 122, 124–127, 136, 142–143, 163–165; and Morocco, 46, 90; and Syria, 58, 71; and Qabbani, 68–69; and Bouhassoun, 77; and the Albaicín neighborhood, 120, 122; and Dar Ziryab Cultural Center, 138–139; and references to Ziryab, 143; and music, 147–149, 151, 153, 155–157

Stewart, Susan, on nostalgia, 11–12

Sufism and Andalusian music, 106, 142, 155

suqut (fall) of Granada, 29, 56, 163

Syria, 2, 3, 3n1, 5, 6, 8, 13, 15, 17, 19–23, 34, 164; Umayyad Emirate in Córdoba, 26, 57; and introduction of *muwashshah*, 41; modal and rhythmic cycles of Syrian *mushwashshah*, 75; Syrian versus Moroccan poetic repertoire, 43, 50, 114; local reaction to the ensemble Mudéjar, 53–54; and al-Andalus, 54–64, 72–74, 76–77; Syrian nationalism, Pan-Arabism, and al-Andalus, 64–67, 78, 118, 143, 176–177; Syrian literary debt to al-Andalus, 67–69; and Instituto Cervantes, 71, 79; and authenticity debates, 79–80, 105, 106; and rhetoric of al-Andalus, 81–83, 92, 125

tai'fa kingdoms (city states) of Andalusia, 27–28

tarab (as emotional response to music), 75, 79, 104, 106, 130, 145; and authenticity, 145; and *duende*, 130, 146, 151, 183

tarab andalusi, see also Andalusian music

Temsamani, Mohamed Larbi (1909–1988), 98, 110

Tifashi, Ahmad, al- (thirteenth-century Tunisian writer), 40, 45, 188n22

'udwatan (notion of two banks of al-Andalus) 41, 88, 146, 158. See also *dos orillas*

Umayyad dynasty, 3, 56–57, 61, 62, 77, 82, 83; and caliphate of Cordoba, 26, 28; and Ziryab, 38; and Syrian imagination, 57, 62–63, 69, 80

West-Eastern Divan Orchestra, 161, 168, 175. *See also* Daniel Barenboim

Yahudi, al-Mansur al- (Jewish musician, Ziryab's reported companion), 38, 187n19

zajal (oral strophic poetry), 44, 47, 96, 109, 194n16

Zaki, Ahmad, Egyptian historian, 32, 190n16

Ziryab, nickname for Abu al-Hasan 'Ali bin Nafi', "dark nightingale", 23, 23n2; adopted home of Córdoba, 27, 37; background, legend and geographic influence, 38–40, 44; Aleppo and Syrian reference to, 76, 80, 103; legacy in Granada, 138–139, 142; and flamenco, 143, 144, 146, 147, 149, 178

Jonathan Holt Shannon is Professor of Anthropology at Hunter College, City University of New York. He is author of *Among the Jasmine Trees: Music and Modernity in Contemporary Syria* and *A Wintry Day in Damascus: Syrian Stories*.